LIVING THOUGHT

Cultural Memory

in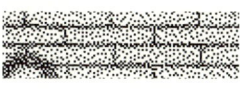

the

Present

Mieke Bal and Hent de Vries, Editors

LIVING THOUGHT

The Origins and Actuality of Italian Philosophy

Roberto Esposito

Translated by Zakiya Hanafi

STANFORD UNIVERSITY PRESS

STANFORD, CALIFORNIA

Stanford University Press
Stanford, California

Living Thought: The Origins and Actuality of Italian Philosophy was originally published in Italian under the title *Pensiero vivente: Origine e attualità della filosofia italiana* ©2010, Giulio Einaudi Editore S.p.A.

 The translation of this work has been funded by SEPS— SEGRETARIATO EUROPEO PER LE PUBBLICAZIONI SCIENTIFICHE. Via Val d'Aposa 7, 40123 Bologna, Italy. Email: seps@seps.it. Web site: http://seps.it/.

Printed in the United States of America on acid-free, archival-quality paper

Library of Congress Cataloging-in-Publication Data

Esposito, Roberto, 1950- author.
  [Pensiero vivente. English]
  Living thought : the origins and actuality of Italian philosophy / Roberto Esposito ; translated by Zakiya Hanafi.
      pages cm. -- (Cultural memory in the present)
  "Originally published in Italian under the title Pensiero vivente: Origine e attualità della filosofia italiana."
  Includes bibliographical references.
  ISBN 978-0-8047-8155-8 (cloth : alk. paper) --
ISBN 978-0-8047-8156-5 (pbk. : alk. paper)
  1. Philosophy, Italian. I. Hanafi, Zakiya, 1959- translator. II. Title. III. Series: Cultural memory in the present.
  B3551.E8713 2012
  195--dc23
                              2012032595

Typeset by Bruce Lundquist in 11/13.5 Adobe Garamond

Table of Contents

Illustrations

Note on the Book's Title

The Italian term *attualità* does not have a single equivalent in English. We have chosen to use the cognate *actuality* in the title due to the difficulty of finding another English term that contains the multiple meanings of the Italian word. *Attualità* not only refers to contemporariness and to matters of current relevance, but also to something that is "in atto," meaning "underway" or "in progress." It further calls to mind the notion of "action" (praxis) and the name of Giovanni Gentile's philosophy (Attualismo), which has been translated historically as "Actualism." What Esposito seeks to convey is the fundamental character of Italian philosophy as "un pensiero in atto": a thought in action that is also a philosophy of action and which is relevant to its time. This usage of *actuality* is also consonant with its standard meaning in the context of Scholastic philosophy: Italian thought is real, effectual, and effective rather than potential or virtual. In the text, these different nuances are rendered variously depending on the context.

The Italian Difference

Italian Theory

(1.) After a long period of retreat (or at least of stalling), the times appear to be favorable again for Italian philosophy. The signs heralding this shift, in a way that suggests something more than mere coincidence, are many. I am not just referring to the international success of certain living authors, among the most translated and discussed writers in the world, from the United States to Latin America and Japan to Australia, leading to a resurgence of interest in Europe as well. There have been other cases of this sort in the past, but they have involved individuals instead of a horizon: a group that in spite of its diversity of issues and intentions somehow remains recognizable by its common tone. This is precisely what has been taking shape in recent years, however, with an intensity that recalls the still recent landing of "French theory" on the coasts and campuses of North America.[1] Like what happened with other philosophical cultures—in the early decades of the twentieth century in Germany, between the 1960s and 1980s in France, and in the last two decades of the twentieth-century in the English-speaking world—Italian philosophy is now entering into an analytical and critical relationship with the dominant features of our time, to a greater degree than other traditions of thought. Of course, as often happens in the circuit of ideas, what appears to distinguish a given concep-

---

1. See François Cusset, *French Theory: Foucault, Derrida, Deleuze & Cie et les mutations de la vie intellectuelle aux États-Unis* (Paris: La Découverte, 2005).

tual horizon as independent also arises out of a process of contamination and elaboration of currents previously set in motion elsewhere, but which only in this new tonal register take on the thematic stability and conceptual force necessary to expand beyond their national confines onto a much wider scene.

However that may be, the perception of Italian philosophy outside Italian borders has changed in a matter of a few years. If we take as a point of comparison three anthologies of Italian contemporary thought appearing in English over the last twenty-five years, the perspective they point to appears to be on a continual rise. In the first, published in the late 1980s with the title *Recoding Metaphysics: The New Italian Philosophy*, the "Italian difference" that the editor rightly stresses in comparison with analytic philosophy as well as other strands of continental thought is attributed to two deficiencies, one linguistic and the other historical:[2] first, to the meager expansive capacity of the Italian language compared to English (and to French for a long time as well); and second, to the autarkic closure of Italian culture during fascism. Even after the Second World War, when an attempt was made to be less provincial by absorbing foreign-derived concepts and vocabulary, it was precisely due to this eclectic attitude that Italian thought is said to have demonstrated insufficient theoretical independence and originality. Its only distinguishing feature, dating back to the work of Giambattista Vico, later taken up and developed mainly by Benedetto Croce, would seem to be a kind of conservatively toned historicism, recognizable in its tired, weakened form in the post-Heideggerian hermeneutics of Gianni Vattimo. Even Vattimo's polemical confrontation with Emmanuele Severino, which the editor of the anthology sees as the most significant outcome of the Italian philosophical debate, somehow remains conditioned by this historicist cast, resolving itself in an opposing stance on the nature of becoming. In a nutshell, rather than opening up a new set of problems, Italian philosophy is judged to merely translate into its historicist vocabulary hermeneutic or metaphysical questions inherited from European thought.

Already in the second anthology, which appeared in the mid-1990s with the less neutral title *Radical Thought in Italy: A Potential Politics*, the change in interpretative framework is evident not only from the choice

2. Giovanna Borradori, ed., *Recoding Metaphysics: The New Italian Philosophy* (Evanston, IL: Northwestern University Press, 1988).

of predominantly political philosophy topics and writers—in itself symptomatic of a different perception of the specificity of Italian thought—but also by a different assessment of its role.[3] Directly influenced by the political and social struggles of the 1960s and 1970s, but also by the reflux that followed in the next decade, for the editors, "Italian theory" is a sort of privileged laboratory that other cultures lacking in these experiences, and therefore further behind in their development of political theory, can tap into for innovative paradigms. The implicit conclusion that follows from this view turns the previous assessment on its head: precisely because Italy has lagged behind in completing its process of modernization due to the cultural blockade erected by fascism, Italian thought is now better equipped than others to deal with the dynamics of the globalized world and of the immaterial production that characterizes the postmodern era.

The title of the third, most recent anthology reflects a focus that is increasingly honed on *The Italian Difference Between Nihilism and Biopolitics.* The line of difference is shifted still further forward, based not only on the often antagonistic relationship with the unique political landscape of contemporary Italy but also on specific topics.[4] Nihilism and biopolitics are presented by the editors as the two axes along which Italian philosophy tends to enter into critical confrontation with its time and, at least in some ways, to guide international debate. While it is true that they both originated elsewhere—nihilism in Germany and biopolitics in France—the fact remains that the work of Italian thinkers on these subjects is precisely what allowed, or caused, their growing diffusion. This is especially true for the category of biopolitics, now permanently installed at the heart of international philosophical, political, and juridical discussion.[5] Coined in the mid-1970s by Michel Foucault, only at the end of the late 1990s did it achieve the broad currency that has made it one of the world's major themes in the philosophy of the new century. Why? Why, after twenty years of latency, during which it remained largely inactive, did this paradigm have to go

3. Michael Hardt and Paolo Virno, eds., *Radical Thought in Italy: A Potential Politics* (Minneapolis: University of Minnesota Press, 1996).

4. Lorenzo Chiesa and Alberto Toscano, eds., *The Italian Difference: Between Nihilism and Biopolitics* (Melbourne: re-press, 2009).

5. The category of nihilism as developed by Italian thinkers also presents strongly original traits. See the genealogy of the concept traced out by a significant writer on the Italian philosophical scene, Sergio Givone, in *Storia del nulla* (Rome-Bari: Laterza, 1996).

through a number of Italian interpretations (albeit diverging or even at odds with each other) to find such transnational resonance? The editors of the anthology respond by referring to the particular capacity of Italian thought to situate itself at the point of tension between highly determined historical-political events and philosophical categories of great conceptual depth. The peculiarity of contemporary Italian thought resides precisely in this unprecedented double vision: a split gaze focused on the most pressing current events [*attualità*] and at the same time on the dispositifs that come with a long or even ancient history. Nihilism and biopolitics, in the unsettling, antinomic way they are articulated, are an exemplary distillation of this principle. While they stand on the shifting line of contemporariness, they overlook a metapolitical ridge that makes them adaptable to a wide variety of contexts. Although they come with a sophisticated theoretical apparatus, they have become part of such diverse disciplines as cultural studies and the domain of aesthetics, legal hermeneutics, and gender discourses. By projecting the archaic onto the heart of the present [*l'attuale*], or by exposing the present to the archaic, these categories diagonally connect knowledge and power, nature and history, technology and life. From this point of view, the Italian difference appears less as the recurring typology of a given tradition than a sort of semantic commutator that cuts across the entire panorama of contemporary thought, altering it in the process.[6]

2. But to get a feeling for the Italian difference and to understand the reasons behind its growing reception we need to start outside it—namely, from the general difficulty that contemporary philosophy is experiencing at this stage. It has been widely accepted that contemporary philosophy has been showing signs of uncertainty and even weariness for some time now. A radial look at its most traveled trend lines provides immediate confirmation of this impression. The analytic tradition, in its various branches and internal transformations, is engaged in a complex process of replacing its paradigms due to an obvious inability to expand its audience beyond a narrow circle of specialists. Critical theory, the dominant producer of German thought along with hermeneutics, does not appear to be in any better

---

6. As further testimony to the wave of interest that Italian philosophy has encountered in North America, see the recent overview by Brian P. Copenhaver and Rebecca Copenhaver, in *From Kant to Croce: Modern Philosophy in Italy, 1800–1950* (Toronto: University of Toronto Press, 2011).

condition, an impression that is also confirmed by a quick comparison between the earliest and latest productions of the glorious Frankfurt school. But even the health of French deconstruction in its poststructuralist and postmodern versions doesn't look any rosier. Still mourning the death of its most prestigious members, from Jean-François Lyotard to Jacques Derrida, although continuing to produce texts of some importance, it tends to shut itself up in a circuit of formulations that are often brilliant but ultimately repetitive and even self-referential. This is not to say, of course, that these schools are entirely devoid of vital elements or that one or both of them cannot reinvigorate their themes and conceptual lexicons. But it seems to me undeniable that something more than a setback is involved.

What is the underlying cause? I don't think it is just a question of communication difficulties or generational change; rather, it is something deeper, something that in a certain sense, despite the glaring differences, unifies these currents into the same transcendental horizon that, for reasons we will now examine, is foreign to much of Italian philosophy. I am referring to the dominant role the sphere of language plays—in different ways, of course—in all three of these traditions. While analytic philosophy was created explicitly for the critical analysis of philosophical language—of its improper deviations from ordinary language, or at least from given procedural rules that were definable from time to time—hermeneutics views the interpreting subject as always immersed in a pregiven linguistic situation which determines all its types of practices. Similarly, deconstruction, as it was intended by Derrida in particular, also starts from the assumption of the linguistic nature of all experience and seeks in writing the original key to dismantle the founding categories of Western knowledge by calling into question their hegemonic potential. At issue in each of these strands of thought is the problem of meaning in its relation to a possible and, to some extent, inevitable metaphysical closure: for analytic philosophy this is caused by logical-linguistic errors that threaten logical thought; for hermeneutics by the alleged transparency of a truth that by its very nature evades simple evidence; while for deconstruction it is ultimately coextensive with the entire history of thought. From this point of view, the three fundamental vectors of contemporary philosophy are all strongly marked, and possibly even constituted, by the linguistic turn that surreptitiously connects seemingly disparate or even contrastive conceptual chunks like those of Gottlob Frege and Martin Heidegger. For analytic philosophers, the original content, the raw material, is the set of linguistic statements; hermeneutics locates the possibility of interpretation at the heart of a given language; while deconstruction situates itself at the point of intersection and tension between speech and writing. Whether expressed more in an ontological sense, in an epistemological sense, or in a textual sense, the primacy of language is presumed in all these perspectives. Even the most recent shift toward cognitive psychology and the neurosciences that analytic philosophy has been making while going through its identity crisis remains essentially in the same field, extended now to the language of the brain, understood in its turn as a form of natural hardware. Regardless of which perspective you have on the philosophical quadrant of our time, from logic to phenomenology and pragmatics to structuralism, language appears to be the epicenter where all the trajectories of thought converge. In a perspective that pushes forward even beyond Heidegger's ontology to involve the spheres of action (in Karl-Otto Apel and Jürgen Habermas, but also in John Austin and John Searle), subjectivity (in Hans-Georg Gadamer and Paul Ricoeur), and the unconscious (in Jacques Lacan), language can even be considered the "dwelling of Being." Lacan is not the only thinker who believes that language is what speaks in human beings—and not the other way around—since the signifier precedes and determines the signified. Language is not our tool; rather, it is the only access through which we can connect ourselves to the occurrence of Being, the very place where we dwell, or to use different but equivalent wording, toward which we are always "on the way."

But as far as the incipient crisis of all these various linguistic or metalinguistic philosophies are concerned, even more important is the antiphilosophical (or at least postphilosophical) consequence they simultaneously presuppose and entail. The fact that the entirety of contemporary philosophy (in some respects from Hegel onward, certainly beginning with Wittgenstein and Heidegger, continuing along a bumpy track that arrives at Theodore Adorno, Richard Rorty, and Vattimo) places itself in the self-confuting framework of its own end,[7] yielding to that attraction for the "post-" that dominates the entire semantics of late modernity, is precisely connected with its subordination to the linguistic sphere. Once language, given its irremediable fragmentation into dialects or families of expres-

7. For more on this issue, but also for a comprehensive atlas of contemporary philosophy, see Franca D'Agostini, *Analitici e continentali: Guida alla filosofia degli ultimi trent'anni* (Milan: Cortina, 1996).

sions, declares its partial nature—namely, a structural inability to for-
mulate models of universal or universalizable rationality—the only room
left to philosophy is its own self-negation or weakening pursuit. Reading
in succession three influential texts that are largely symptomatic of this
skeptical attitude of contemporary philosophy—Lyotard's *The Postmodern
Condition*, Rorty's *Philosophy and the Mirror of Nature*, and *La crisi della
ragione* (The crisis of reason), a collection of essays published in Italy in
the wake of similar tendencies—provides a significant cross-section: the
present task of philosophy is apparently a self-critical refutation of its own
hegemonic claims to a Real that is located outside its reach.[8] Whence its
necessarily negative tones, in both a general sense and a technical sense:
contemporary philosophy affirms itself only by negating itself. Because
any hold on its object is elusive in principle, contemporary philosophy
can only grasp it through a reverse approach, through its unsaid or un-
thought. Which is why, according to a dialectical formula that has become
a commonplace, everything that is utterable presupposes silence, just as
every representation presupposes a point of invisibility lying behind it. Far
from creating its own concepts, a philosophy of this sort must confine itself to dismantling them or hunting them down without ever being able to
reach them, in a chase at the end of which looms its own dissolution.[9] For
this reason philosophical criticism regarding the outside world can only
be expressed in the form of its own internal crisis. Once the possibility of
thought, and therefore also of action, becomes dependent on the transcen-
dentality of language, it is as if the philosophical experience were continuously sucked into the same entropic vortex it seeks to escape.

3. If this is indeed the horizon in which contemporary thought experiences both its depth and its limit, then a large part of Italian philosophy
can be said to lie outside it. This is not to suggest that the sphere of lan-

---

8. Jean-François Lyotard, *La condition postmoderne: Rapport sur le savoir* (Paris: Éditions
de Minuit, 1979) (English trans.: *The Postmodern Condition*, trans. Geoff Bennington and
Brian Massumi [Minneapolis: University of Minnesota Press, 1984]); Richard Rorty, *Philosophy and the Mirror of Nature* (Princeton, NJ: Princeton University Press, 1979); Aldo
Gargani, ed., *La crisi della ragione* (Turin: Einaudi, 1979).

9. This is the thesis that Alain Badiou also arrives at, starting from a different set of
premises, in *Manifesto for Philosophy*, trans. and ed. Norman Madarasz (Albany: State University of New York Press, 1999).

guage doesn't constitute a terrain of philosophical investigation in Italy. On the contrary, starting from its origins with Dante and then throughout the period of Humanism up to Vico, language has been one of its privileged topics of reflection, contemplated from a unique angle that sometimes interweaves thought and poetic experience, as in the case of Giacomo Leopardi. Hermeneutics and semiotics have also found fertile ground in Italy, with authors like Luigi Pareyson, Umberto Eco, Carlo Sini, Enzo Melandri, and Diego Marconi. Moreover, the most recent Italian thought takes language as a given that is so constitutive of the human being that it can be identified as the point of suture between nature and mutation, invariance and difference, biology and history. In this last formulation, however, a movement can be discerned that shifts the terms of the discourse in a new direction: rather than being examined in its autonomous structure, language is situated within a broader horizon, described in terms of biology,[10] or of ontological realism.[11] The same shift that analytic philosophy has made toward the sciences of the brain expresses a need that in some respects is similar. Likewise, Italian feminism, initially engaged in a rediscovery of symbolic language, has begun to sense the inadequacy of the linguistic horizon with respect to something irreducibly corporeal that protrudes outside its confines, whether viewed as metaphorical or metonymic in nature.[12] It is as if at some point it began to occur to people, or it simply occurred, that there was a new "turn" coming after the linguistic one—in some ways encompassing it—that as a whole belonged to the paradigm of life. Already in the 1960s, after all, remarkably ahead of his times, Foucault had set out to problematize the transcendental primacy of language. He began by iden-

10. I am thinking of the views expressed by Paolo Virno in his seminal works. See for example his *Quando il verbo si fa carne: Linguaggio e natura umana* (Turin: Boringhieri, 2003).

11. I am referring to the philosophical work of Maurizio Ferraris, according to a particular meaning of the term *ontology* that he also discusses in his latest book *Documentalità: Perché è necessario lasciar tracce* (Rome-Bari: Laterza, 2009).

12. As Ida Dominijanni states in "L'ombra indecidibile," in *L'ombra della madre* (Naples: Diotima, 2007), p. 184. The same author provides a helpful overview of Italian feminist philosophy, starting from the position of Luisa Muraro, in the preface to the new edition of *Maglia o uncinetto: Racconto politico-linguistico sulla inimicizia tra metafora e metonimia* (Rome: Manifestolibri, 1998), pp. 7–46. The most relevant work by Muraro in this regard is *L'ordine simbolico della madre* (Rome: Riuniti, 1991). See Francesca Novello's dissertation, "A Critical English Translation of Luisa Muraro's *The Symbolic Order of the Mother*," University of Oklahoma, 1994.

tifying two other a priori notions making up the post-Classical episteme, namely, labor and life. But above all, he transformed them from simple transcendentals, in the Kantian sense of the term at least, into something slightly different because of their deep implication in the historical dimension. Of course life, labor, and language were the conditions of possibility for the formation of the nascent disciplines of biology, economics, and linguistics. And yet they were not located in the sphere of subjectivity; rather, they stood in a complex relationship with the world of history, one marked by inherence and tension. For example, with regard to life, it is obvious that Georges Cuvier was still far from formulating what with Jean-Baptiste Lamarck and then Charles Darwin would later become evolutionary theory. Yet, with Cuvier, for the first time, historicity penetrated deeply into the language of nature and into the constitution of the living being:

It is true that the Classical space, as we have seen, did not exclude the possibility of development, but that development did no more than provide a means of traversing the discreetly preordained table of possible variations. The breaking up of that space made it possible to reveal a historicity proper to life itself: that of its maintenance in its conditions of existence. Cuvier's 'fixism', as the analysis of such a maintenance, was the earliest mode of reflecting upon that historicity, when it first emerged in Western knowledge.[13]

Therefore, not only did history intervene in the definition of life—as its mode of expression—history was what, in its concreteness, made possible the new epistemic importance of life. History turned out to be a presupposition of what it presupposed: it was immanent to its own transcendental condition of experience. The result of this paradox (in semantic terms as well) that inscribed the a priori within its a posteriori was the "transcendental-historical," a notion used by Foucault as a genuine oxymoron.

Without pursuing the matter to the extent it deserves, and indeed, taking another tack altogether, it can be said that contemporary Italian philosophy pushes the dialectic of the "quasi-transcendentals," as Foucault himself called them,[14] to its densest point of synthesis. The act of questioning the transcendental primacy of language—assumed as such by the two strands of hermeneutics and analytic philosophy—is not meant to deny its impor-

13. Michel Foucault, *Les mots et les choses* (Paris: Gallimard, 1966); English version: *The Order of Things* (New York: Vintage, 1994), p. 274.

14. Ibid., p. 249.

tance, but rather to reconstruct the relationship that binds the primacy of language on the one hand to the biological substratum of life and on the other hand to the shifting order of history. To this end, however, another passage is required, situated precisely at the point of intersection between life and history that is constituted by politics. In this case, too, it is necessary to pass by way of Foucault, not only via the archeological route, but also via the genealogical one opened up before him by Nietzsche. From this point of view, not only are the conditions of possibility of the various disciplines of knowledge at stake, but also their performative effects. If human life, including the function of language that defines it as such, has become entirely historical, this means it is subject to political practices intended to transform it, and thus, inevitably, it is a matter for conflict. Coming from this angle, contemporary thought—still stuck in the postmodern celebration of its own end—may just find some leverage to resume functioning in an affirmative mode. Of course the opening referred to here is only one of the possible exits out of the long-standing impasse of contemporary thought. A number of thinkers who have already embarked on this path, in North America as well as in Europe, have achieved significant results. But Italian theory, as expressed by individuals and as a whole, seems more prepared to follow it to the end, if only because in some way the route is already familiar to them, imprinted as it is in their genetic heritage. The impact force of contemporary Italian philosophy also stems from its deep rootedness in a tradition constructed from its beginnings around the categories under discussion. Since its inception between the early sixteenth and the first half of the eighteenth centuries, life, politics, and history have been the axes of flow for a reflection that has largely remained extrinsic to the transcendental fold in which the most conspicuous, influential area of modern philosophy remains enveloped to this day. Unlike the tradition between Descartes and Kant, which was founded in the constitution of subjectivity or theory of knowledge, Italian thought came into the world turned upside down and inside out, as it were, into the world of historical and political life.

This movement toward the outside has long been identified by critics as the most consistent trait of the Italian philosophical tradition. Both the characteristics usually attributed to it, the epithet of "civil philosophy"[15]—

15. Without citing the extensive and well-known bibliography on Eugenio Garin, see also Giuseppe Cacciatore and Maurizio Martirano, *Momenti della filosofia civile italiana* (Naples: La Città del Sole, 2008).

elaborated upon primarily by Eugenio Garin and his school—and its artistic or literary style,[16] are premised on it. The point of tangency between them, it could be said, lies in the unique propensity of Italian philosophy for the nonphilosophical.[17] Both its civil commitment and its contamination from other styles of expression result in a rupture with the specialized, self-referential lexicon that characterizes the philosophical discourses of other traditions. While the privileged object of these traditions is philosophy itself—its internal forms and structurations—the content of Italian thought is what presses up against its exterior, somehow urging it to step outside itself to look onto the external space.[18] Remo Bodei has rightly talked about "impure reason," meaning thought that is not inward-looking but open to the influences of people and the force of circumstances.[19] In this tendency can be discerned the terms of a singular contradiction: by opting for engagement with the outside world instead of examination of consciousness or the interior dialogue, Italian philosophy has always appeared poised to cross over its own boundaries; but this overstepping is precisely what allows it to achieve a perspective that would otherwise be unattainable. The impression we get from the works of Vincenzo Cuoco, Giacomo Leopardi, and Francesco de Sanctis (and, in other respects, from the earlier ones of Machiavelli and Vico as well) is that in order to express an object that is unrepresentable in the professional jargon of philosophy,

16. See Ermanno Bencivenga, *Il pensiero come stile: Protagonisti della filosofia italiana* (Milan: Mondadori, 2009). On Italian style and language, from a different perspective, see also Emma Giammattei, *La lingua laica: Una tradizione italiana* (Venice: Marsilio, 2008).

17. On Italian philosophy in general, see Giuseppe Cantarano, *Immagini del nulla: La filosofia italiana in discussione* (Milan: Mondadori, 1998); as well as the different perspectives offered by Fulvio Tessitore, ed., *La cultura filosofica italiana dal 1945 al 1980* (Naples: Guida, 1982); A. Bausola et al., *La filosofia italiana dal dopoguerra a oggi* (Rome-Bari: Laterza, 1985); Francesco Paolo Firrao, ed., *La filosofia italiana in discussione* (Milan: Mondadori, 2001); Carlo Augusto Viano, *La filosofia italiana del Novecento* (Bologna: Il Mulino, 2006).

18. This is in no way meant to diminish a prestigious school of historical and etymological research that has gained worldwide prominence like the Institute for the European Intellectual Lexicon and History of Ideas led by Tullio Gregory.

19. The paper by Remo Bodei, *Langue italienne: Une philosophie, aussi, pour les non-philosophes*, which is the best summary on the subject, is included in Barbara Cassin, ed., *Vocabulaire européen des philosophies: Dictionnaire des intraduisibles* (Paris: Éditions du Seuil, 2004), pp. 625–43. Bodei had already published a book on the topic entitled *Il noi diviso: Ethos e idee dell'Italia repubblicana* (Turin: Einaudi, 1998).

Italian thinkers employ a lexicon culled variously at different times from politics, history, and poetry, which is then reconstituted in each of these disciplines but in an inverted form. The need to "step outside" for all these writers arises from the difficulty they come up against when using abstract or logical-metaphysical thought to grasp something that, being effectively in motion, inevitably tends to elude them.

Italian Geophilosophy

Before attempting a definition, though, we need to address a preliminary question, suspended until now, since the plausibility of our entire inquiry depends on it. Does such a thing as "Italian philosophy" exist? Even before answering that, is it legitimate to think of philosophy as belonging to a nation or, at least, to a territory? Or would it be more accurate to say that philosophy, like mathematics, medicine, or music, has no local features because the indispensable element of its performance lies in a universal dimension? Leaving open for the moment the most controversial problem, that of nationhood, I think it is undeniable that some connection exists between philosophy and territory. What I mean by "territory" is not so much a specific geographical area encompassed within stable boundaries, as a set of environmental, linguistic, "tonal" characteristics connoting a specific mode that is unmistakable when compared to other styles of thought. "Thinking," writes Gilles Deleuze, "is neither a line drawn between subject and object nor a revolving of one around the other. Rather, thinking takes place in the relationship of territory and the earth."[20] Deleuze actually goes farther. Not only is geography internal to philosophy, to the point that it overlaps to form a lexical compound that can be dubbed "geophilosophy," it spreads open a horizontal, or more precisely, a diagonal plane that dissects the vertical, more canonical one formed by historical sequence. Not in the sense of abstractly opposing it from an ahistorical attitude, but in the sense of modeling history itself into a "geohistorical" form, as Fernand Braudel termed it in his studies on the Mediterranean. What does this mean? That geography is not limited to providing history with elements, features, localizing foci—it is not only history's spatial com-

---

20. Gilles Deleuze and Félix Guattari, *What Is Philosophy?* trans. Hugh Tomlinson and Graham Burchell (New York: Columbia University Press, 1994), p. 85.

ponent—but something less obvious and more incisive. Geography is what tears history away from the claim of simple progression but also from the regressive cult of origins, to trace out lines of flight, undiscovered passages, and sudden diversions that tamper with the order of time by overturning the usual relationships. What we are referring to are the effects, at first sight elusive—the incidence of a milieu, a climate, an atmosphere, alluded to earlier by Nietzsche while seeking the key to the various European philosophies—that Deleuze calls "becoming," intending them as something that enters back into history but does not belong to it. Of course, since becoming stands outside the pillars of history, it should remain indeterminate; it should literally lose its conditions of existence. But it is not, in essence, historical: it obeys a different logic, one of unpredictability and surprise, deviation and infringement. Here, following on Nietzsche's *Untimely Meditations*, Deleuze picks up on something we will come across again in the course of our study, having to do with the presence of a nonhistorical element in history, like a sort of limit or point of resistance that, precisely by its "untimely" presence, challenges the process of historicization, though without interrupting it.

If the geophilosophical gaze breaks up the straight line of historical sequence, then historicity, in its turn—understood as the continuous proliferation of unrepeatable events—is refracted, and destabilizes geographical localization. This is because Deleuze's reference to the earth does not allude to the fixity of a picture frozen in time, or to the inevitability of ethnic or even anthropological roots. On the contrary, it implies a complex dialectic in which the territory is only one pole, opposed by a corresponding, simultaneous movement of deterritorialization: an outwardly-turning movement that breaks up territorial boundaries. Outside this double-pulsed oscillation, going from the center to the periphery and vice versa, there can be no true philosophy. All modern thought from Hegel to Heidegger, through Hölderlin, Fichte, and Husserl, has played a decisive role in a circuit of appropriation and expropriation in which ancient Greece has constituted the privileged object.[21] Without being able to retrace these events, we know the fatal outcome to which continental philosophy was led by the predominance of territorialization over the principle of decen-

21. On this topic, see Caterina Resta, "Il mito dell'autoctonia del pensiero (Note su Hegel, Fichte, Heidegger)," in *Geofilosofia*, ed. Marco Baldino, Luisa Bonesio, and Caterina Resta (Sondrio: Lyasis, 1996), pp. 13–37.

tralization, when Heidegger himself went so far as to state that since German is the only modern language of thought, if the French want to think, they have to do it in German.[22] In this case, the movement of belonging to the earth was absolutized over the opposite course, in the end circumscribing it within the closed borders of the national state. In his *Addresses to the German Nation* (1806), on the other hand, Johann Gottlieb Fichte had connected the viability of the *Deutschtum* to the defense of the *Ursprache* that sprang from the deep powers of the earth, united to them by an original bond, which alone would enable a true national destiny. This assumption is what allowed him to say, foreshadowing Heidegger's claim, that

the German, if only he makes us of all his advantages, can always be superior to the foreigner and understand him fully, even better than the foreigner understands himself, and can translate the foreigner to the fullest extent. On the other hand, the foreigner can never understand the true German without a thorough and extremely laborious study of the German language, and there is no doubt that he will leave what is genuinely German untranslated.[23]

Contrary to this regressive and exclusive circle inside of which European philosophy has remained trapped on more than one occasion, we must keep a firm grasp of the semantic difference between territory and nation. Geophilosophy, the territorializing—and therefore, also always deterritorialized—characterization of thought is no way identical to philosophical nationalism—or even to a strictly national variety of philosophy. I would go even further: nothing like the constant oscillation between inside and outside—brought to its greatest intensity by Hölderlin, when he identified difference from oneself as the principle that modernity needs to absorb from ancient Greece—is more opposed in principle to all forms of philosophical nationalism. All the more curious, then—curiously lazy—the evaluation that Deleuze cursorily provides of Italian philosophy compared to English, French, and German thought. It may even be dramatically true

---

22. Interview in *Der Spiegel* on May 13, 1976 ("Nur noch ein Gott kann uns helfen"); translated into English as "Only a God Can Save Us," by Lisa Harries and Joachim Neugroschel, in *Martin Heidegger and National Socialism: Questions and Answers*, ed. Gunther Neske, and Emil Kettering (St. Paul, MN: Paragon House, 1990), pp. 41–66.

23. Fichte, *Reden an die deutsche Nation*, in *Sämtliche Werke* (Berlin, 1971); English version: *Addresses to the German Nation*, trans. R. F. Jones and G. H. Turnbull (Chicago: Open Court, 1922), p. 70.

that "Italy and Spain lacked a 'milieu' for philosophy, so that their thinkers remained 'comets'; and they were inclined to burn their comets."[24] But a negative response does not follow from this, in the case of Italy, unless the different natures of territory and nation are confused when defining that lack, as Deleuze seems to do: "Italy in particular presented a set of deterritorialized cities and a maritime power that were capable of reviving the conditions for a 'miracle.' It marked the start of an incomparable philosophy. But it aborted, with its heritage passing instead to Germany (with Leibniz and Schelling)."[25] What is clear, in this brief description, is the original plurality and ultimate extroversion of Italian thought. We can agree with both these passages, but not with the judgment that connects them. The least we can say is that what resonates in Deleuze's assessment is an undue identification between estrangement and exhaustion: according to this view, the move into Europe would signal the end of Italian philosophy. But what if this escaping outside itself—its continual deterritorialization—is the most originally living feature of Italian thought?

2. The most striking thing about Deleuze's assessment is not so much the idea that Italian philosophy experienced an interruption at the end of the early modern period as that it was transferred to Germany via the direction that runs from Leibniz to idealism. Far from being original, this idea continues an interpretative tradition that culminated in the thesis championed by Bertrando Spaventa on the "circulation of European thought"; according to this theory, after anticipating the great themes of modern thought, Italian philosophy reappropriated them and brought them to their definitive fulfillment. Now, even leaving aside this appropriative outcome, one that is entirely foreign to Deleuze's view, it is difficult to ignore the contradictory assumption that separates it from the geophilosophical interpretation we have just discussed. While the latter alludes to a synchronic plurality of languages, paradigms, and styles of thought that cannot be channeled into a single current—in fact, their significance arises precisely out of their mutual difference—the transfer or "circulation" theory, no matter how it is termed, inevitably refunnels the different theoretical impulses back into a single flow channel that simultaneously incorporates them and dissolves them as such. From this point of view,

24. Deleuze, *What Is philosophy?* p. 103.
25. Ibid., p. 102.

obviously, the role of every philosophical culture does not lie so much in its originality as it does in the contribution it is able to make to the development of a thought which is universally valid precisely insofar as it is able to incorporate grammars from different origins by amalgamating them into a single blend. Clearly, what distinguishes this perspective, even before any claims to primacy are advanced, is precisely the prevalence of historical progression over geographic spatiality. To this, Deleuze opposed the nonhistorical transversality of conceptual constellations that cannot be inscribed in the chronological order of before and after, or in the logical order of cause and effect. If we assume this "differential" point of view, so to speak, then no single expression of thought can take place in another or before another in the linearity of a flow oriented in a single direction. On the contrary, each gains strength and validity precisely by infringing and laterally deviating away from it.

And yet, Spaventa's idea was based precisely on the twofold criterion of "forerunning [precorrimento]" and "proving true [inveramento]." In his inaugural lecture of 1861, "On Nationality in Philosophy," followed by a course given in Naples on Italian thought, he does acknowledge the specific quality of the various modern philosophies, but he trims them to fit their subordinate role as stages in a single process. The final outcome of this process may not yet be determined, but it is firmly anchored by the consistency of its guiding principle: "Especially after the Risorgimento," he argues, "what appear to be national philosophies—Cartesianism in France, Lockism in England, and so on—are nothing more than multiple stations through which thought passes on its immortal course. Thus, modern philosophy is not English, French, Italian, or German alone, but rather, European."[26] This means that the value each form of thought acquires is not based on its original content so much as on its vertical relationship—as a prelude or a confirmation—that connects it to whatever comes before or after it. In this framework, the role (and rank) of Italian philosophy would consist, on the one hand, in having anticipated the most significant portion of European thought, and, on the other, in having brought it to a point of synthesis that reunites it with its Renaissance origins. So if Telesio, Bruno, and Campanella are located at the head of this process, orienting it

26. Bertrando Spaventa, "Della nazionalità nella filosofia," in *Opere*, ed. Francesco Valagussa, with an afterword by Vincenzo Vitiello (Milan: Bompiani, 2008), p. 1189. All translations are by the translator of this volume, unless otherwise stated.

in the direction of its ascent, Galuppi, Gioberti, and Rosmini represent its end, developing its most vital conclusions. As Vincenzo Gioberti had already expressed in his *Primacy*, which Spaventa also countered with his secular perspective, the entire course of modern thought begins and ends in Italy. However, this is precisely the source of the contradiction that thwarts any attempt to identify a peculiar trait of Italian philosophy from within it. If Italian philosophy is "not a particular orientation of thought, but I would almost say, thought in its fullness, the totality of all orientations," then its difference lies precisely in not having one, "in that universality, in which all opposites are united"; in that "harmonious unity gathering together all aspects of the European intellect [ingegno]."[27] This is the source of the unresolved oscillation between a residue of philosophical nationalism and the universalist perspective through which Spaventa tended to diffuse it. True, for him, the transfer from Italian to European thought was never complete and residue-free: the triple circuit described by the birth, loss, and reconquest of Italian philosophy never reached its conclusion due to a congenital inability on the part of Italians to translate their cultural traits into firm civil self-awareness. And yet, despite this reservation, Italian thought is part of a unitary framework whose deeply incised contour traces out the lineaments of a national destiny.

When Giovanni Gentile later went on to provide the most complete, authoritative reconstruction of Italian thought, with much greater analytical depth and breadth of references, the result was twofold: he rid Spaventa's theory of its most extrinsic, schematic elements, while at the same time rendering it more penetrating and compelling. The epicenter of this categorial reformulation (already contained in the 1918 inaugural lecture at the University of Rome, "The Historical Character of Italian Philosophy") was precisely the idea of nation, transferred from the abstract and, in some ways more naturalistic, plane that Spaventa had kept it on to an essentially spiritualistic one. The nation is in no way a given based on certain natural prerequisites; rather, it is a spiritual body forged in the dialectic of appropriation and donation that links it to other national cultures in a continuous exchange of ideas and values. On these lines, Gentile can affirm that philosophy—like science, art, and religion—is such insofar as it is universal and international—hence, not national. Yet the fact remains

27. Ibid., p. 1198.

that it always arises out of a particular rhythm of consciousness that is most genuinely expressed in national temperaments. Through this dialectic one can and must "justify the idea, one that has already been widely debated and will remain controversial until it has been more properly understood, of an Italian philosophy, and in general, of a national philosophy."[28] If the nation is not anchored to a definite element in its ethnic roots, but is instead drawn out tautly in the never exhausted impetus of planning, it may well live beyond, and even before, its historical fulfillment. Indeed, following the principle of the actuality of every historical interpretation, just as the beginning nourishes its own development, the latter in its turn sheds new light on the former. This explains why, despite having taken an appropriate distance from a misguided and anachronistic idea of primacy, the lecture ends with the names of Dante and Gioberti. The thread that ties them together, despite all the interruptions, is what makes the Italian tradition a living force capable of endowing the Italian nation with the role it historically deserves. In this way, through the superimposition of past and present, the universal element of thought ends up identical to its particular horizon. The entire history of Italian philosophy—coextensive with its own theoretical significance—is inscribed in the heroic, prophetic dimension that runs from Dante through Machiavelli and Vico, passing through Cuoco, Mazzini, and Gioberti, to arrive at Spaventa and at Gentile's own Actualism, in a progressive spiritualization of the nation that is also a nationalization of the spirit. If the universal character of all forms of thought in this interpretative horizon can be discerned in their original national form, the specific character of Italian philosophy is to have brought this fact of destiny to the level of reflective awareness and profound vocation.

3. The direction this book takes is diametrically opposed to what we have just described: not only can Italian philosophy not be reduced to its national role, but its most authentic reason for being lies precisely in the distance it takes from that role. As we have already noted with regard to the dialectic between territorialization and deterritorialization, the intensely geophilosophical character of Italian culture comes from a land that did not correspond to a nation and, indeed, during a very long phase, a land that took form in the absence of a nation. This statement—one that goes against

28. Giovanni Gentile, "Il carattere storico della filosofia italiana," in *I problemi della scolastica e il pensiero italiano* (1913; reprint, Florence: Sansoni, 1963), p. 210.

the grain of the entire idealistic historiography—is based initially on a given that is difficult to dispute. Unlike in other European countries—in France, Spain, England, and, with a delay of two centuries, Germany—rather than accompanying or following the formation of the nation-state, the great Italian philosophy of Machiavelli, Bruno, Campanella, Galileo, and Vico preceded it by a long time. Italian philosophy neither influenced nor was influenced by the formation of the national state. It came into being under conditions of political decentralization and fragmentation far removed from the reality, or even the possibility, of unification. It formed outside the nation and the state and, thus, without the resources of a capital like Paris, London, or Madrid, which acted as geopolitical collectors for a series of intellectual experiences, gathering them into a common place of production and diffusion of Italian knowledge. The transition from medieval villages to the cities of early Humanism and the high Renaissance did not give rise to anything comparable to a territory united by a single political will.

By this, I do not mean to deny that the idea, aspiration, and prefiguration of unity ran through—and even mobilized—the culture that was created in Italy starting from the inception of its language. It is all too easy a task to cite the well-known passages on the theme in Dante, Petrarch, and Machiavelli, not to mention Foscolo, Manzoni, Mazzini, and Gioberti. Idealistic historiography has been able to collect together a conspicuous part of the Italian tradition in a crowded gallery of voices, references, and calls to a common background. And yet, it is impossible to overlook the generally rhetorical and literary character of these sorts of appeals. Nothing deep and intrinsic binds Italian philosophy to the Italian nation. If the highly developed thought of scholasticism already moved entirely outside the confines of the national culture with Thomas Aquinas, gravitating more toward Paris, Humanism as a whole had an external projection that made it an international movement in the most powerful sense of the term. Founded on the resumption of Latin and Greek, it spoke on the one hand to the world of the city-states, out of which emerged its most eminent exponents, and on the other hand, to the great European cultural centers, through a close exchange of letters, translations, and travels that crossed over the Italian borders. Eugenio Garin and his school have provided a detailed reconstruction of this intellectual emigration that poured out from Florence, Venice, and Milan as well as from Rome and Naples throughout Europe, disseminating the best of the philosophical, artistic, and literary works produced in Italy. Between the late fifteenth century and the early sixteenth century, Dante, Petrarch, and Boccaccio were translated into French, the Italian political writers quickly became an essential reference of European political thought, while Moro, Budé, and Reuchlin spread the Florentine Platonism of Ficino and Pico to central and northern Europe. All this took place during the same period the major foreign intellectuals came to Italy to refine their own culture, starting with Erasmus. For all of them—Italians and foreigners alike—Italy was anything but a nation like Spain, France, or England, which by that time had been consolidated into the forms of their respective state bodies. Without political boundaries and without a center, Italy remained a formidable land of development, dissemination, and cross-pollination of the great, single European culture whose scope and importance was not national, because it went beyond the nation. This is precisely why it was experienced as potentially universal; in other words, capable of producing arguments, languages, and images that everyone could share.

As far as philosophy proper was concerned—in reality it still lacked a technically defined status distinct from scientific, aesthetic, and anthropological knowledge—the major authors of the period, from Machiavelli to Bruno, Campanella, and Galileo, moved about in a relationship with the political and Church authorities that was tense and always troubled, in some cases going so far as to take the form of resistance and sacrifice. Without wanting to read too much into this characterization, it could well be said that, beyond the biographical profile and character of these particular individuals, this can be attributed to the lack of a stable state representative, in the absence of a national institution able to connect temperaments, insights, and theories of a rare intellectual quality into a unified plan. That this implies an element of weakness, and perhaps immaturity, compared to the experiences of European contemporaries has been an insistent topos of the historiography, not entirely without reason. The ancient, and in some ways never resolved, difference between knowledge and power, between cultural production and institutional solidity, has been a decisive hindrance to the overall growth of Italy, even beyond more specific contingencies.[29] But

29. Among the many texts on the subject, see in particular Ernesto Galli della Loggia, *L'identità italiana* (Bologna: Il Mulino, 1998); Aldo Schiavone, *Italiani senza Italia: Storia e identità* (Turin: Einaudi, 1998); Silvana Patriarca, *Italianità: La costruzione del carattere nazionale* (Rome-Bari: Laterza, 2010).

it has also led to the possibility of a thought that is more free from encumbrances and constraints; one that, in alternating phases, appears to bob back up to the surface with the strength of unused potential energy. Unlike philosophical cultures marked from the outset by their relationship to a strong, already consolidated political institution like the England of Hobbes or the France of Descartes; unlike traditions of thought engaged in constructing a state knowledge, as in the Germany of Hegel, Italian thought on politics is prestatal in its conception and, at times, is even framed in terms of resistance to the state. While Gentile saw his philosophical role as lying within the state, unlike him, Croce and Gramsci (at least during the fascist period) positioned themselves in opposition to it. Following this line of reasoning, it is no coincidence that contemporary Italian philosophy has shown a critical and sometimes antagonistic potential not commonly found in other contexts. Sometimes, in special situations and under certain conditions—in the case, for example, of a drastic transition between epochs like the one we have been experiencing for some years now—what appears to be, and is, in effect, a lack or an anomaly can transform itself into an advantage compared to more stable, well-established situations. What I want to say—but this statement will have to be examined with a fine-tooth comb—is that the lack of a profound national vocation and, until the middle of the nineteenth century, a unitary state, is precisely what has given Italian philosophy something more than (or at least different from) other philosophical traditions which have experienced a more direct identification between territory and nation. Because Italian thought did not locate itself on the perimeter of the nation, positioning itself instead at its external margins, it has from the outset traveled a road different from that of other European philosophies. For this reason, now that the time of the nation is running out—or at the very least, when its assumptions and ends are being called into question—Italian thought can face the future with greater innovative energy. This is one more facet of the Italian difference.

Another Modernity

1. But not the only one. If Italian philosophy, in its original conception, was located outside the boundaries of the nation-state, it has also remained largely foreign to the historical-conceptual horizon in which it is situated. I am referring of course to the plexus of logics, languages, and

grammars that, in direct contrast to the period preceding it, is defined by the term *modernity*.[30] This is not to say that Italian thought is premodern or, as is sometimes claimed, antimodern. Its major exponents, at least, maintain a continuous relationship with the authors, texts, and voices that make up the philosophical discourse of modernity. But they do so from a different angle of view, because Italian thought is situated on the other side of modernity, or, more precisely, along a tangent that cuts across it diagonally, without being absorbed by it. This alterity, running parallel or perpendicular to the dominant axis of the Modern, is what makes it in some way outdated [*inattuale*], apparently inadequate to understand the dynamics that were set into motion all over Europe at the close of the Middle Ages. But it is also, at the same time, what makes it capable of keeping its reserve of meaning intact—or at least still alive—at a time when these dynamics no longer seem up to the task of coping with the questions and conflicts that arose from them. This is not to say that the answers to the problems modernity bequeathed to us or hid in its folds—ones that, being structural, are often insurmountable—are to be found in Italian philosophy. What it does mean, perhaps, is that from the perspective point originating at the intersection of its constituent categories, a crosswise view is made possible from which these problems take on a different value and, consequently, open themselves up to a new interpretation.

If pressed to identify the epicenter of this alterity, I would have to locate it in a different relation to the origin. While modern philosophical culture, in its various expressions, identifies itself in a gesture of rupture with what comes before it, Italian thought not only has never severed this tie, it seeks the form and sense of its own actuality by looking to the origin.[31] We need only consider the attitude with which Descartes and Hobbes founded their discourses on the most clear-cut separation possible from common or natural experience in order to appreciate how distant Italian thought is

30. On the "logics" of modernity, see Carlo Galli, "La 'macchina' della modernità: Metafisica e contingenza nel moderno pensiero politico," in *Logiche e crisi della modernità*, ed. Carlo Galli (Bologna: Il Mulino, 1991), pp. 83–141.

31. The denial of origins theme has been addressed by Giancarlo Mazzacurati, framing it in the culture of the Italian early-modern period in contrast with the Florentine city-state tradition. See his important book, entitled *Il rinascimento dei moderni: La crisi culturale del XVI secolo e la negazione delle origini* (Bologna: Il Mulino, 1985), which has founded an entire interpretative line.

from their perspectives. The presupposition that makes the new knowledge possible is the construction of an anthropological, epistemological, and institutional threshold that provides refuge from anything originary unsubduable by reason and indeed threatening to it. Regardless of whether this pre-reflective magma is identified in an anthropic stratum that still lies too close for comfort to the animal realm, in the figurative language of magic and myth, or in a state of nature torn apart by incurable conflict, the remedy is invariably sought in a new beginning, one that is rational, artificial, and coinciding with the break with the origin. Compared to a decision of this kind, Italian philosophy took a different route right from the start. I am not only referring to Machiavelli's "return to principles [ritorno ai principii]" as a tool for restoring political life to a healthy state, or to Vico's "return [ricorso]," necessary for the reopening of a new historical cycle. Without ever turning inward in a conservative attitude, and indeed projecting itself beyond the threshold of modernity, all Italian thought, from Bruno to Leopardi, seeks in the wisdom of the ancients the keys to interpret what is closest at hand. Even Croce's principle that "past history is contemporary history" can be read along the lines of the *actuality of the originary.* The fact that even the most recent Italian philosophy elaborates on categories and dispositifs taken from the ancient world—such as empire, sanctity, or person—is further evidence of the genealogical vocation of a line of thought that, throughout its course, has tended to tune in to the constitutive traits of the present by examining them in the light of its deep roots. This obviously has nothing to do with a mythology of the origin, by which I mean the identification of an originary moment that is identifiable as such, and from which history (or a certain kind of history) is supposed to have started and to which it could return.[32] The genealogical attitude starts with the opposite assumption, that a founding moment of this sort is structurally absent. Because of this constitutive "inoriginarity" of history, the origin is always latently coeval with each historical moment. This allows it to be reactivated as a source of energy, rather than simply endured as some sort of spectral return. From this point of view, the return to the origin is anything but the restoration of a past experience, something that is irreproducible as such. Rather, it should be understood in the opposite sense: as its

32. On this topic see the two books by Francesco Erspamer, *La creazione del passato* (Palermo: Sallerio, 2009); and *Paura di cambiare: Crisi e critica del concetto di cultura* (Rome: Donzelli, 2010).

No mjeture with history.

deflagration in the future, starting from its tangency with the shifting line of the present. While reflective awareness on this question is lacking, Italian philosophy engages with it on a singularly frequent basis.

All three spheres associated with it—politics, history, and life—are involved in and somehow modified by it, giving rise to complex paradigms that leave their mark on its entire course. As regards the political sphere, unlike Hobbes, Machiavelli never cuts off the relationship with the vital substratum—both bodily and animal—that underlies human action, but rather binds the possibility of human success, although always contingent and reversible, to its enhanced maintenance in the civil world. What logically follows from this is the inexhaustibility, and indeed co-essentiality, of conflict in the order which contains it, something excluded in principle from the Hobbesian model. This is precisely where the first paradigmatic axis of Italian thought is rooted, in the highly complex figure of the *immanentization of antagonism*. The idea that conflict is constitutive of order—or to put it differently, that an order which excludes conflict is neither conceivable nor desirable—signals the emergence of an origin in history, of which it tends to seek—unsuccessfully—to rid itself. The origin cannot be eliminated by an order that, in its factual concreteness, derives from conflict and that, indeed, continues incessantly to reproduce it. This assumption is one of the fundamental, recurring vectors of all Italian philosophy, and not only its political thought. For Bruno as well, for example, the universe is founded on and moved by the encounter and tension between opposites that life perpetually generates in a continuous circuit of conjunction and disjunction. What thus emerges is a constitutive relationship between immanence and antagonism: conflict is inherent to a reality that cannot be transcended in a different dimension. When Machiavelli promises to look into the "effectual truth of things [verità effettuale delle cose]" what he is alluding to is the inevitably conflictual character of the plane of immanence, which, as such, occupies the entire space of reality. While Croce already interpreted Machiavelli as the thinker of force, for Gramsci, his icastic figure of the prince anticipated the political "party," specifically in the sense of "taking part [prendere parte]" and "being partisan [parteggiare]," which in a world traversed and modeled by conflict is inevitable. For Gramsci (parallel with Machiavelli on this point as well), who disputed the Hegelian identification between politics and state, the world of life is cut through by pervasive struggle, in a fight to the death for hegemony; whether we like it or not, we are always forced to take a position in favor of one part against the other.

Not by chance, the political debate that opened in Italy during the 1960s and 1970s—in the most theoretically innovative school of thought, Operaism—took up again, without always being aware of it, the question on the relationship between antagonism and immanence that came from Gramsci. The problem it poses is precisely the compatibility between the plane of immanence and the logic of conflict, between "inside" and "against." How can an "against" be inside what it opposes without breaking up its unity? And how can an "inside" contain what opposes it without eliminating it? These questions were framed by Italian political philosophy with an incisiveness difficult to find elsewhere. This is not to talk solely about the school of realism that extends from Gaetano Mosca to Vilfredo Pareto and Gugliemo Ferrero—according to whom we can never definitively separate reason and force, or sometimes even force and violence. It goes without saying that this dramatic awareness comes out of the tradition of Machiavelli and Vico. But what characterizes both modern and contemporary Italian philosophy is the awareness that the ontology of actuality is furrowed by alternatives that cannot be mediated and that demand a decision. This is all the more true when what is at stake in political conflict is life itself, understood as that set of impulses, desires, and needs that run through the body of individuals and populations in a form that is irreducible to the distinction between *res cogitans* and *res extensa*, reason and force, or proper and common. To capture its full spectrum, the category of biopolitics, as it has been taken up and radically developed by the most recent Italian thinkers, must be included in this framework of problems. It extends beyond the empirical or sociological interpretations it has acquired elsewhere precisely because of this capacity for mobilization—passing through the crucial intuitions of Nietzsche and Foucault, of course—that roots it in the very depths of the Italian tradition.

2. If the relationship between immanence and conflict is the most innovative and, at the same time, the most problematic trait of Italian political thought, its reflection on history, begun at a later stage, is marked by the intrinsic but equally antinomic relationship with a nonhistorical (or at least not entirely historicizable) element that nevertheless forms a part of it. One could say that the more historical knowledge gradually extends across

the entire sphere of human reality, the more a point of resistance, or contrast, is created inside it that, in this case, too, is related to the emergence of the origin. It is as if it cannot fully resolve itself in the historical dimension, thus opening up a problematic, indecipherable area in its interior. The most theoretically complex place where this second Italian paradigm, definable as the "historicization of the nonhistorical," takes on visibility is in Vico's work. Even though the latter is rightly situated at the genesis of modern thought on history, this does not cancel out an aspect that renders Vico's work inassimilable to both traditional Christian providentialism and the new philosophy of history that came out of its secularization. What differentiates Vico's vision from both involves the nexus between origin and process that, in providentialism, tends to contract all history into the initial instant of divine creation, and in secular history, tends on the contrary to dissolve the origin in the fluidity of time that issues from it. The layered structure of the *New Science* avoids both these reductions by establishing an irreducible tension between the two adjacent but noncontiguous elements of the beginning and the development. The unbridgeable gap between sacred history and secular history had already broken up the chronological order of succession, doubling the origin into two noncoinciding polarities. But secular history itself unfolds in a multiplicity of times, arising in their turn from a variety of origins that correspond to each other without ever becoming blurred. Whence the inoriginarity of history—in the sense that it does not have a single origin—and the ahistoricity of the origin, since it is spared from complete historicization. No matter what angle you look at it from, in contrast to subsequent philosophies of history, the origin is not dissolved in history, just as history is not reduced to time. In any case, what remains excluded is the full temporalization of history, the process associated with the modern conception and, in a weakened, extenuated form, with the postmodern one as well.

An even more specific element, though, destined to become a permanent feature of nineteenth-century Italian thought, is the corporeal—and thus living—character Vico assigns to the conceptually unrepresentable dimension preceding human history proper. The *ingens sylva* of the "beasts," from which human beings descend through a tortuous civilizing process, has the formless yet deformed appearance of an indistinctive bioanthropic whole that is entirely filled up and rendered amorphous by the communion of the overflowing, piled bodies of its inhabitants. In order for a specifically human history to begin, this world in common, made indistinct by the superimposition of bodies, must give way to a different form of life gradually governed by the mind and by the immunitary dispositifs that make possible a fully historical humanity. But what is crucial to our discussion is that this originary element, which is nonhistorical—and, given its purely living dimension, even incompatible with the process of historicization—never completely fades away, but rather, moves in a covert fashion, so to speak, into history itself. Out of this comes the contradictory figure—because it is arranged in two overlapping, potentially colliding layers—that marks the entire course of the *New Science*. History must always contain or curb the obscure vital power that underlies it in order to proceed along the path that divine providence and human reason trace. Nonetheless, history cannot completely squeeze the originary power dry through a process of idealization with no remains, or it would risk retreating into itself and making itself sterile, thus laying itself open to a returned barbarism. The concept of "ricorso" designates this unresolvable dialectic, defining the ultimate threshold beyond which the need for self-preservation is reversed into a new form of dissipation, and the remedy warps into a greater evil. Oblivion, or the denial of origins, is precisely what gives rise to the resurgence of the originary force on the historical scene in such a virulent form that all apparent progress is annihilated. Nothing is more deadly, for Vico, than the typically modern idea that we can sever the knot that binds history to its nonhistorical beginning, unraveling it through a process that fully temporalizes life.

If there is an element that runs through all Italian philosophy, distinguishing it from other traditions of thought, it is precisely this awareness of the problematic and, beyond a certain threshold, counterfactual nature of secularization. At the bottom of history there lies an opaque, seminatural, historically intractable element that human beings must come to terms with the moment their gaze turns toward the future, imagining that they can liberate themselves, along with the entire past, even from the uncertain point of its provenance. Vincenzo Cuoco's *Saggio storico sulla rivoluzione napoletana del 1799* (Historical essay on the Neapolitan revolution of 1799), published in Milan in 1801, is imbued with this awareness. The disaster of the 1799 revolution was caused by the pretense of translating into history a nonhistoric or prehistoric stratum that Cuoco refers to as "second nature" precisely because is too closely tied to the first for us to be able to definitively emancipate ourselves from it. Never as in that terrible case, in the form of the Bourbon reaction—but also earlier, in the geoanthropic resistance on the part of the southern Italian population irreducible to a people—had there been such a spectral reemergence of the originary in an abstract, geometrical construction that believed it could do away with it. Although expressed in their respective languages and in different contexts and horizons, the perspectives of Leopardi and de Sanctis—both highly sensitive to the influence of Vico—were no different in this respect. While for Leopardi modernity was destined to a wasting away of its vitality due to its ill-considered attempt to detach reason from the bodily impulses that determine human behavior, de Sanctis tied both the political and ethical decadence of Italian culture to the breakdown of its originary relationship with life, which he understood in a biological and natural sense as well, especially in his last writings. This devitalization formed a constitutive link between history and crisis, making crisis the very form of history. We owe the most powerful effort to historicize contemporary reality to Croce, who not only grasped the limit of history in the resistance of the "vital," but also the ultimate threshold beyond which civilization risks derailing itself, finishing prey to uncontainable forces. Even beyond contingent events of a historical and biographical nature, at the heart of this lack of balance there lies an ontological difference between history and life that Croce's system of distinctions [*distinti*] is unable to master. The whole debate on secularization that has been reopened today in Italian philosophy reproduces this question, that is, the inevitably antinomic role of tradition as that which set the Permanent into becoming by transmitting it through time. The complex relationship that Italian thought maintains today with Christianity and its corresponding confrontation with nihilism turn out, in the final analysis, to be part of the philosophically irreducible problem of the historicization of the nonhistorical.[33] A continued engagement, in other words, with the inevitable and insoluble relation between origin and history.

3. The third influential paradigm of Italian philosophy, along with the immanentization of conflict and the historicization of the nonhistorical, is the process of the *mundanization of the subject*. While the first two are related, in different ways, to the incidence of life in the constitution of knowledge, the third is the most direct expression of this intersection. We

33. I am thinking in particular of the philosophical work of Vincenzo Vitiello, a summary of which is contained in *Ripensare il Cristianesimo: De Europa* (Turin: Ananke, 2008).

have seen how Italian thought as a whole did not get caught up in the transcendental fold that characterizes the most conspicuous area of European philosophy. And also how its propensity for the nonphilosophical conveys, in terms of content, a pronounced tendency to push outside its disciplinary confines. But what disrupts the dominant line of the modern conception that reached maturity between Descartes and Kant is its *ante litteram* critique of the logic of presupposition as a constitutive structure of subjectivity. Not only does the modern subject presuppose itself with respect to the world of experience, it even presents itself to itself as presupposed. The *subiectum suppositum*, a figure posited on itself that is at the same time the substance on which it is posited, is clearly aporetic. What we have here is the construct that founds the unity of the subject on a separation between itself and its own biological substrate—or in metaphysical terms, between body and soul—crucial to the entire Western tradition. The dialectic between subjectification and subjection that Foucault called attention to— by which one only becomes a subject by subjecting oneself to someone else or to a part of oneself—is based precisely on this logic of presupposition. On these lines, in spite of the profound semantic difference that separates them, the category of the subject derives genealogically from the Roman and Christian category of the person, since this was what gave form for the first time to that curious dispositif responsible for splitting the living being into two areas, adjacent but not coextensive, one of which is declared to be personal while the other, subordinated to the first, is declared to be animal. The only way to enjoy full rights as a person is thus by dominating one's animal part or other human beings, who are thrust as a consequence into the realm of animality. The original legal definition of *persona*, one that has never been completely abandoned, is someone who is subject to objectivization by himself or herself or by others.

From the time of its Renaissance beginnings, Italian philosophy can be said to have been constructed outside this argumentative machine, and, indeed, to have provided critical ideas for its deconstruction. To begin with, it is situated on a plane different from, although not unrelated to, that of modern individualism. Of course Italian thinkers are well aware that politics is also—and at times, above all—made by individuals, as is the case for Machiavelli's prince, but in a form that can never be separated in an abstract way from the collective dynamics out of which they arise on each occasion, and with which they must nevertheless contend. Vico accentuates this common, even bodily, dimension of subjectivity; true, he subordinates it to the use of immune apparatuses aimed at self-preservation, but never to the point of breaking it up into a set of unrelated individuals who are the owners of themselves, as does the liberal tradition from John Locke to John Stuart Mill. Although partly due to the influence of contemporary French thought, the deep inspiration behind the recent return to Italian philosophy of the theme of *communitas*, in the unconcluded dialectic with *immunitas*, can be traced back to this horizon. Moreover, the theme of community, as an opening of subjectivity to its own alterity, is an integral part of nineteenth-century Italian thought. A significant instance of this current is represented by Gentile's final, dramatic work. The idea that the individual contains the community in itself, *in interiore homine*, in an irreducible relationship with its other, or even with its enemy, is certainly an ambiguous formulation, since it seems to re-interiorize the subjectivity externalized in action. But action, understood in its most extreme sense, is inseparable from a movement of desubjectivization in the open space of the world. The category of "praxis," as it was taken up and radicalized by Gramsci, only acquires meaning by overcoming the assumed separation between subject and object and in its external reversal. Of course behind this mundanization of thought there lies Marx and a particular interpretation of Hegel that enriched Italian philosophical culture from de Sanctis to Spaventa all the way to Croce. Not that there ever lacked an impetus going back to the very foundation of the Italian tradition, one that was destined to reformulate and fluidify, so to speak, the more rigid elements of the Hegelian legacy in an original way.

At the origin of this simultaneous passage outside and through the subject there stands the thought of Giordano Bruno. But he brings an even more radical element, furnished by his explicit, insistent criticism of the category of person (both human and divine) in favor of infinite life. His rejection of the presupposed separation between body and soul, spirit and nature, subject and object, was allied with the idea of a living cosmos without center or boundaries. Rather than excluding subjectivity, it is introduced and integrated into the regenerative process of the world in a form that only Baruch Spinoza—the most "Italian" of modern philosophers—would later advance with a similar force toward the philosophy of the impersonal. It is no coincidence that Gentile's genealogy of immanence, which has recently returned to spark Italian debate, stemmed from both these thinkers. At its core stands the definition of forms of life not as "bare life"—which is unthinkable as such except as a negative archetype— but rather understood in both their singular and common dimensions at the same time. Our attention needs to be focused on this point because of the effects it has on the discourse as a whole. The fact that the axis of Italian philosophy can be identified in the relation between life and form means that the inevitably open question of subjectivity is hardly excluded from it. Subjectivity is not replaced; it is deconstructed and reconstructed as a category of life which, in its turn, is always determined by its particular configurations. Unlike what has happened elsewhere, in Italian thought life has never been understood as an undifferentiated or independent mode of a biological or metaphysical type. The reason there has never been a specific "philosophy of life" in Italy, analogous to the nineteenth-century ones commonly referred to by this name, is because the entirety of Italian thought is traversed and determined by it. And also, because life has always been thought about both in relation to and in confrontation with the categories of history and politics. This means that life is not an alternative to subjectivity, but rather, constitutive of subjectivity. How could politics and, even more, history arise in a world devoid of subjects defined, within the plane of immanence, by their own living singularity? The problem for future philosophy, rather, is how to conceive of a subject free from the ancient, yet continually reproduced, dispositif that separates it from its own bodily substance, and at the same time renew the subject's constitutive link with the community. The reopening of a dialogue with Italian philosophy responds to this need as well.

PASSAGE 1: THE VERTIGO OF HUMANISM

Before entering the great laboratory of modern Italian philosophy, let's pause for a moment on its threshold—on the shifting line that introduces us to it but at the same time distances us from it in a dialectic whose significance we have yet to fully grasp. I am referring to that complex movement of ideas, philological practices, and cultural transfers that took the name of "Humanism," a term that, despite its apparent clarity, harbors an elusive and enigmatic kernel. What is at stake in the term, above and beyond any specific content, is its relation to philosophy—whether such a relation exists at all, strongly questioned by a broad-based, diverse cultural front. It may seem paradoxical—but symptomatic of a deep fracture in the corpus of contemporary knowledge—that this philosophical demoting of humanism loomed up precisely in the dramatic years straddling the Second World War, when it seemed that all European philosophy sought to reposition itself in relation to it: Jacques Maritain's *Integral Humanism* came out in 1934, *Existentialism Is a Humanism* by Sartre appeared in 1946, while Heidegger's "Letter on Humanism" dates from 1947.[34] The semantic, but also conceptual, difference that arose from this stems from the fact that, on the one hand, none of these texts that in varying degrees were decisive for the fate of nineteenth-century reflection took as its direct object the Italian culture of the early Renaissance. On the other hand, the great historiographical essays on the topic beginning with Eugenio Garin's *Italian Humanism*, first published in the German edition in the same year as Heidegger's "Letter on Humanism,"[35] did not take a specifically theoretical slant. It almost seems as if philosophy could only pose the question of *humanitas* by diverting its gaze away from the period when it had first been raised with all the intensity of an astonishing discovery. There are also books, located in an area halfway between history and theory, so to speak, such as *The Individual and the Cosmos in Renaissance Philosophy*, by Ernst Cassirer, or *Studies in Renaissance Thought*, by Paul Oskar Kristeller,[36] that tend, without undervaluing the Aristotelian and Platonic traditions,

34. Jacques Maritain, *Humanisme integral* (Paris: Aubier, 1934); Jean-Paul Sartre, *L'existentialisme est un humanisme* (Paris: Nagel, 1946); Martin Heidegger, "Brief über den 'Humanismus,'" in *Wegmarken*, in *Gesamtausgabe*, vol. 9 (Frankfurt am Main, 1976).

35. Eugenio Garin, *Die italienische Humanismus* (Bern: Francke, 1947).

36. Ernest Cassirer, *Individuum und Kosmos in der Philosophie der Renaissance* (Leipzig:

to deny that Humanism has a truly philosophical character, following an interpretative line dating back to Hegel. In his *Lectures on the History of Philosophy*, when Hegel decreed that it was only in the sixteenth and seventeenth centuries that "the genuine philosophy re-appeared, which seeks to grasp the truth as truth,"[37] the rupture between Humanism and philosophy was now sanctioned with a clarity that was destined to provide a model for those that followed: "Such endeavours are, however, connected rather with the history of literature and culture, and with the advancement of the same; we do not find originality in this philosophic work, nor can we recognize therein any forward step."[38]

In the most theoretically engaged text of the ones just mentioned, when Heidegger makes explicit reference to Italian Humanism, he remains basically within the same hermeneutic horizon: "all mere 'humanist' association and revitalization ('renaissances') remain suspended in the margins of historicality."[39] The Italian culture of the Renaissance, for him, is nothing more than a late revival of the Roman tradition of *humanitas*, which in turn is nothing but a spurious and conceptually frayed reintroduction of the classical model of the Greek *paideia*: "The so-called Renaissance of the fourteenth and fifteenth centuries in Italy is a *renascentia romanitatis*. Because *romanitas* is what matters, it is concerned with *humanitas* and therefore with Greek *paideia*. But Greek civilization is always seen in its later form and this itself is seen from a Roman point of view."[40] It is hard to explain such a blatant undervaluation of an epochal transition that, no matter how you want to characterize it, remains the incunabulum of modern knowledge. A number of interpretations have appeared. The first is ideological, in the sense that Heidegger's antihumanistic polemic is believed to

Teubner, 1927); Paul Oskar Kristeller, *Studies in Renaissance Thought*, vols. 1–4 (Rome: Edizioni di Storia e Letteratura, 1956).

37. G. W. F. Hegel, *Vorlesungen über die Geschichte der Philosophie*, in *Werke*, vols. 18–20 (Frankfurt am Main: Suhrkamp, 1970); English version: *Lectures on the History of Philosophy*, vol. 3 of *Medieval and Modern Philosophy*, trans. E. S. Haldane and Frances H. Simson (Lincoln: University of Nebraska, 1995), p. 161.

38. Ibid., p. 110.

39. Martin Heidegger, *Hölderins Hymne "Der Ister,"* in *Gesamtausgabe*, vol. 53 (1984); English version: *Hölderin's Hymn "The Ister,"* trans. William McNeill and Julia Davis (Bloomington: Indiana University Press, 1996), pp. 124–25.

40. Heidegger, "Letter on Humanism," in *Pathmarks*, trans. Frank A. Capuzzi (Cambridge: Cambridge University Press, 1998), pp. 239–76. This quote p. 244.

be somehow linked to the opposition between the original Greek culture
and the Latin tradition set up by the cultural politics of Nazism, in order
to construct their own genealogy as an alternative to the heritage of Rome.
But this explanation clashes on several points. To begin with, there was the
urgent need of the philosopher to distance himself as far as possible from
the defeated Nazi regime during that period. Moreover, a few years earlier,
in the essay on "Plato's Doctrine of Truth"—whose publication, not surprisingly, was opposed by Rosenberg and even Goebbels—he had included
the Nazi eugenics cult for the care of the body in his criticism of humanistic pedagogy.[41] But what definitively clears this first hypothesis from the
field is that the essential inspiration for the crude declaration on the death
of Renaissance culture that Heidegger made in the first of his seminars on
Hölderlin dates back to the years when he was preparing *Being and Time*
and the courses on Dilthey given in 1925:[42] a period, in other words, when
he was still entirely sheltered from any ideological pressure.

But even the thesis endorsed by Heidegger himself that points to
the constructively metaphysical character of all humanisms of Roman
origin is not without problems of a historical and hermeneutical nature. When he connects it to an essentialistic definition of man, we are
hard pressed to recognize it in that manifesto of Italian Humanism—
the famous oration by Pico della Mirandola, later called *De hominis
dignitate*—whose most innovative *pointe* with respect to the tradition
that preceded it lies precisely in denying that man has an essence, or a
predefined place, on the scale of beings. How are we to see an essentialist
definition of man in a creature who possesses "no fixed seat nor features
proper to [him]self nor endowment peculiar to [him] alone [nec cer-
tam sedem, nec propriam faciem, nec munus ullum peculiare]," to cite
Pico's famous words?[43] The impression we get is that Heidegger fails to
grasp the empty point, the missing pigeonhole, the semantic vertigo be-

41. Heidegger, *Platons Lehre von der Wahrheit*, in *Wegmarken*; English version: "Plato's
Doctrine of Truth," trans. Thomas Sheehan, in *Pathmarks* (Cambridge: Cambridge University Press, 1998), pp. 155–82.

42. See Heidegger, *Sein und Zeit*, in *Gesamtausgabe*, vol. 2 (Frankfurt am Main: Klostermann, 1977); English version: *Being and Time*, trans. John Macquarrie and Edward Rob-
inson (Oxford: Blackwell, 1962).

43. Pico della Mirandola, *On the Dignity of Man*, trans. Charles Glenn Wallis (Indianapolis, IN: Hackett, 1998), p. 4.

hind the Promethean impetus of what is defined as Humanism, based on which it is impossible for human beings to define themselves positively as such; whence the need to qualify themselves in relation to that which, being more or less than human, decenters them, pushing them beyond themselves. That Heidegger reduces this constitutive alterity to an implication, itself metaphysical in nature, in the animal sphere, on the basis of the classical definition of man as the *animal rationale*,[44] only further complicates things, since both Montaigne and Descartes, heirs for different reasons to the humanist tradition, explicitly reject its relevance. Montaigne, criticizing the custom of deriving the meaning of one term from that of another term that is often even less salient, assures us that "I know better what is man than I know what is animal";[45] while Descartes, also asking himself about the nature of human beings, rejects in his turn the use of the expression "rational animal": "because then I would have to inquire what 'animal' and 'rational' mean. And thus from one question I would slide into many more difficult ones."[46]

So now what? Although not entirely implausible, if none of these interpretations are able to pinpoint the underlying reason, the philosophical assumption, behind Heidegger's prejudice, where are we to look? If I had to give a short answer to this question, I would say that Heidegger's criticism of historical humanism expressed his urgency to replace the category of "factical life [das faktische Leben]"—which he amply elaborated on during the previous years, and which became increasingly central to his thought from the 1930s on—with that of language. Of course, what we are talking about are categorial blocks, as well as lexical horizons, that overlap or even alternate with each other throughout the course of Heidegger's work, with no real interruption. But for an author with his kind of mastery over his conceptual apparatus, even a shift of emphasis is undoubtedly significant, especially in a text like the "Letter," which marked a turning point, serving as a vehicle for theoretical reconfiguration as well as strategic repo-

44. Heidegger, "Letter," p. 249.

45. Michel de Montaigne, *Essais*, in *Oeuvres complètes* (Paris: Gallimard, 1962); English version: *The Complete Essays of Montaigne*, trans. Donald Frame (Stanford, CA: Stanford University Press, 2002), p. 819.

46. Réné Descartes, *Meditazioni metafisiche sulla filosofia prima*, in *Opere filosofiche* (Turin: UTET, 1969), p. 204; English version: *Meditations, Objections, and Replies*, trans. Roger Ariew and Donald A. Cress (Indianapolis, IN: Hackett, 2008), p. 14.

sitioning after the historic and personal defeat. Following this line of reasoning, it seems to me that the drastic rupture it imposes between human and animal—further developed in the lectures on the "basic concepts of metaphysics" (*Die Grundbegriffe der Metaphysik*) in the opposition between "man creator of the world" and "animal poor of the world"[47]—makes sense as a whole only in the context of a gradual detachment from the semantics of *bios* and its replacement with the primacy of language. The reason why man appears to Heidegger to plunge into the aphasic realm of the animal when he is thought of in humanistic terms can be located in the fact that he does not feel "claimed by being. Only from that claim 'has' he found that wherein his essence dwells. Only from this dwelling does he 'have' 'language' as the home that preserves the ecstatic for his essence."[48] The error of all biologisms resides in the forgetfulness of this character. Adjoining a soul, a mind, or a spirit to corporeality, as Heidegger believes all humanisms have done, does not overcome this error and even exacerbates it, since they fall back into the same proximity with the nonhuman that they sought to leave behind. That is because the indissoluble connection that human beings have with speech is the only thing that makes *homo* truly *humanus*, unlike stones, plants, and above all animals, which do not cease to be such even when they are given a human face: "Because plants and animals are lodged in the respective environments but are never placed freely into the clearing of being which alone is 'world,' they lack language."[49] In opposition to a humanist tradition that measures the "dignity" of the human by our ability to integrate within us all other creatures—from the animal to the angelic—Heidegger chooses the opposite path of placing the human near the disembodied essence of the divine, even if it means dissolving all bodily ties with the naturalness of the living being.

An indirect confirmation of the reconstruction I am proposing can be found in another text dedicated to Italian Humanism, and specifically to Heidegger's interpretation of it: Ernesto Grassi's *Heidegger and*

47. Martin Heidegger, *Die Grundbegriffe der Metaphysik: Welt-Endlichkeit-Einsamkeit*, in *Gesamtausgabe*, vols. 19–30 (1983); English version: *The Fundamental Concepts of Metaphysics: World, Finitude, Solitude*, trans. William McNeill and Nicholas Walker (Bloomington: Indiana University Press, 1995).

48. Heidegger, "Letter," p. 247.

49. Ibid., p. 248.

the Question of Renaissance Humanism.[50] An expert connoisseur of the humanist tradition, Grassi moved to Germany in the 1930s with the quasi-institutional task of building a bridge between German and Italian culture. With this purpose in view, in 1939, under the patronage of the Reale Accademia d'Italia, he was assigned the task of founding the Institut Studia Humanitatis in Berlin, aimed at promoting knowledge of Humanism and the Renaissance. When the institute was inaugurated two years later, Grassi started up a publishing venture. Along with Walter Otto and Karl Reinhardt, he created the annual *Geistige Überlieferung* (Intellectual tradition), which published Heidegger's essay on Plato. This was accomplished in spite of the difficulties mentioned earlier and not without the intervention of Giuseppe Bottai and Mussolini himself. When the difficulties continued to mount on the part of Nazi leaders determined to break any relationship with the Latin tradition, Grasssi took refuge in Switzerland, where, at the Francke publishing house in Berne, he founded *Überlieferung und Auftrag* (Tradition and order) with Wilhelm Szilasi, a former student of Heidegger who took his place while he was banned from teaching. The series subsequently republished Heidegger's essay on Plato together with the "Letter on Humanism."[51]

Placed in the delicate position of having to disseminate the humanist tradition that Heidegger had attacked, but without wanting to depart from his teachings (which Grassi always remained faithful to), he chose the only way open to him—no doubt a very difficult one—by crafting an interpretation of humanism that was compatible with Heidegger's philosophy, although contrary to his negative assessment of it. It should be immediately pointed out that, despite some inevitable straining due to his conciliatory aims—oscillating between a humanistic reading of Heidegger and a Heideggerian interpretation of humanism—he was right on at least two points. First of all, contrary to the movement that was committed in principle to denying any philosophical significance to humanist culture at all, he rightly claimed that it had a precise theoretical component. At the same

50. Ernesto Grassi, *Heidegger and the Question of Renaissance Humanism*, trans. Ulrich Hemel-John Michael Krois, Center for Medieval and Early Renaissance Studies (Binghamton, NY: State University of New York Press, 1983).

51. This biographical and political series of events is revisited in detail by Franco Volpi in his introduction to Heidegger's "Letter on Humanism," in *Lettera sull' "umanismo,"* ed. and trans. Franco Volpi (Milan: Adelphi, 1995), pp. 11–27.

time, in contrast to Cassirer and Kristeller, but also to Gentile and Garin, rather than seeing it as a sort of forerunner to modern philosophy coming out of Cartesianism and arriving at idealism, he located it in a distinctly alternative horizon. His definition—a rather problematic one, to be sure— although coming from another angle and with a reversed hermeneutic aim, brings into clear visibility Heidegger's claim for the primacy of language that we saw orienting his interpretation of Humanism in a polemical direction. Without questioning its premise, and indeed, staying strictly within its limits, Grassi adapted his object of study to Heidegger's interpretation by identifying the philosophical significance of Humanism, so resolutely denied by Heidegger, specifically in the centrality of speech. This is what makes Grassi's move so original and yet problematic at the same time. Unlike the prevalent reading originating with Burckhardt that sees the most important contribution of Humanism in the development of a new image of the human being, he emphasized its ontological and hermeneutic tone, thus inscribing it within the same theoretical sphere as Heideggerian philosophy: what stands at the center of the Italian Humanist culture is not, as is generally believed, the question of the human, but that of *Lichtung*—the originary clearing in which the world comes to light through the revelation of the poetic word. In this way Humanism not only escapes from the metaphysical current that underlies the rationalistic conception, it also opens up another avenue of access to modern philosophy. Unlike the traditional doctrine of beings, which excludes from their understanding the tools of poetic language—metaphor, imagination, *ingenium*—Humanism seeks it out in the interpretation of texts. This means that Being—even prior to beings—has an intrinsically linguistic constitution; it is *esse dictum*, because it is revealed only through the historicity of speech. From this point of view, poetry and literature in general not only have a revelatory, epiphanic role, they are also constitutive of the community and its historical institutions.

Grassi naturally places Dante at the origin of this tradition. While Dante still adhered to Scholastic metaphysics in the universalism of *De monarchia*, he definitively freed himself from them with the *Convivio*, proclaiming the constitutive function of the vernacular as the only language capable of founding a national tradition. Before him, in his *Epistles*, Albertino Mussato had identified the essence of poetry in the essential unveiling of its age: as the prefiguration of events or acts aimed at the construction of a forthcoming civilization, in the same way that in recounting the heroic past of his people, Homer had simultaneously sketched out their possible future. All Humanism—from Petrarch's *Canzoniere* to Boccaccio's *Genealogy*, from Bruni's *Orations* to Pontano's *Dialogues*, through Salutati and Landino, Guarino and Poliziano—replaced the substantial entity of *res* with the creative power of *verba*; the metaphysical fixedness of *essentiae* with the inventive acuity of *ingenium*; the abstract rigidity of logic with the contagious plasticity of *imaginatio*. But it was Vico above all who gave the entire humanistic knowledge the unity of an extraordinary philosophical narrative, far removed and opposite to dry Cartesian rationalism. In Grassi's reconstruction, the *New Science* is neither a theory of humankind nor a theory of history, but a poetic description, and therefore a theoretical reformulation, of the original deforestation of the primordial forest out of which human civilization originated, in a sense that is no different from the one Heidegger gave to the presencing of the world in the open space of the *Lichtung*. This way—concludes the author—a different, more problematic beginning is superimposed over but also juxtaposed with the canonical start of modern thought, one that is later destined to join up with the Romantic philosophy of Novalis, the Schlegel brothers, and Schelling; but above all, with the anonymous "Entwurf des ältesten Systemsprogramm desdeutschen Idealismus," in which poetry and myth become inscribed in the very heart of philosophical practice.

How much of this can really be found in Italian humanistic culture and how much was projected by Grassi's chosen angle of perspective is not always clear. Certainly, his claim that this tradition has a philosophical tonality in contrast with the dominant axis of modern philosophy is not without foundation. What remains problematic is the exclusively rhetorical and linguistic horizon that Grassi tends to attribute to it, in such a way that he ends up expelling the vector of reflection on the human that had lent its very name to humanism. Not surprisingly, he is forced to exclude the only unquestionably philosophical segment, the Platonic and Neoplatonic school which, together with the Aristotelian one, had dedicated its conceptual creativity precisely to the interpretation of *humanitas*. While Ficino's *Platonic Theology* does nothing but lead thought to the rational definition of entities and to the aprioric validity of causal logic, Grassi goes so far as to maintain that in *On the Dignity of Man*, "Pico locates man exclusively within the framework of traditional ontology: the problems which arise out of this location do not lead to any 'new' advances in thought."[52] That this judgment was influenced by a desire to adhere to the Heideggerian paradigm, biased now in order to recuperate the very same humanism that Heidegger had rejected, is all too clear. But is this passage opened up by Grassi—starting from the primacy of language—the only one we have for penetrating into the innermost meaningful core of what is gathered around the name of the human?

Perhaps, sixty years after Heidegger's "Letter," the question of humanism could even be considered closed. If, in its historical origin as well as in its trans-epochal significance, it refers to a human model of education, one based on the exchange of those long letters that for some time now we have been accustomed to calling books, then we might well say that it has doubly failed. For one thing, because what happened in Europe between the 1930s and the 1940s, even without wanting to push too far ahead, seems to have made a clean sweep of the exchange of letters that linked one generation to another through the centuries. And then, in an age when the messages that count circumnavigate far greater distances at far greater speeds, the medium of letters has exhausted its role in forging national consciousness. From this point of view, the neohumanist revival, rising out of the still smoldering rubble of the post–World War II period, maintains the tone of an immediate reaction—one that is certainly understandable and even called-for—against those who sought to wipe out all traces of humanity, but it is not sufficient to revitalize a means of communication that is by now exhausted.

Yet, the historical obsolescence of the humanist medium—and of humanism itself as an intercultural medium—does not take away our interest in that decisive stretch of European culture that developed in Italy between the fourteenth and sixteenth centuries. True, for the first time since late antiquity, it was Humanism that posed the largely classical question regarding the *eruditio et institutio in bonas artes*, mainly used to distinguish a *homo* who was essentially *humanus* from a *barbarus*; except for later being forced to acknowledge that one is often simply the civil face of the other, as it appeared in ancient Rome from the perplexing affinity between literary activities and a taste for blood in the arena. But alongside this more

---

52. Ernesto Grassi, *Einführung in philosophische Probleme des Humanismus* (Darmstadt: Wissenschaftliche Buchgesellschaft, 1986); English version: *Renaissance Humanism: Studies in Philosophy and Poetics*, Medieval and Renaissance Texts and Studies (Binghamton: State University of New York Press, 1988), p. 119.

canonical pedagogical function, for those who know how to question it closely, humanistic culture seems to safeguard another, less obvious side, almost like a last letter that never reached its destination. I am referring specifically to that empty, "perforated" representation of the human being with literally no form that Pico's text, with conscious antinomy, seeks to represent. When he defines man—thereby removing him from all definitions—as a "work of indeterminate form [indiscretae opus imaginis]," to whom God assigned "no fixed seat, no form of thy very own, no gift peculiarly thine," so that he can freely choose at will, Pico was taking an extraordinarily important first step that led far beyond the many late-medieval and prehumanistic texts *de dignitate, excellentia et nobilitate hominis* that seem to anticipate him to the letter. Because what is at stake in these expressions is not only the traditional place of the human at the midpoint of a hierarchy that has at its ends the angel and the beast, nor even the figure of the "microcosm," or the *minor mundus*, understood as the embodiment, inside oneself, of all the expressions of the universe. On the contrary, it is the breaking of the classical scheme in favor of a new dynamic that has at its center the transition from being to becoming: human beings are nothing other than what they become, or better, what they intend to "make" of themselves. In this way, Pico takes his place both before and after the modern semantics of *subiectum*—understood as a permanently constituted or presupposed entity—making the human a creature with the perennial ability to fabricate itself. This transition is referred to in Pico's narrative in the divine "fabrication" of a man capable in turn of becoming "molder and maker" of himself so that he can "sculpt" himself into whatever shape he prefers ("ut tui ipsius quasi arbitrarius honorariusque plastes et factor in quam malueris tute formam effingas").[53]

Peter Sloterdijk has recently argued that in order to grasp this aspect— situated on the thin margin along which humanism extends beyond itself— we must leave the ecstatic place to which we were led by Heidegger;[54] or at least, cross through it in a different direction from the hyperhumanistic one, all things considered, that he embarked on in defense of the ontologi-

53. Pico, *Oration*, pp. 4–5.

54. I am referring to the extraordinary essays by Peter Sloterdijk in the collection *Nicht gerettet: Versuche nach Heidegger* (Frankfurt am Main: Suhrkamp, 2001); Italian version: *Non siamo ancora stati salvati: Saggi dopo Heidegger* (Milan, 2004). My comments on the "end" of humanism also allude to this work.

cal absoluteness of *Dasein*. To do this, we need to break the dual prohibition
that Heidegger issued against anthropology and technology in favor of the
absolute primacy of language. Because it is precisely our anthropo-technics
and not our linguistic capacity that is the most extreme vector of meaning
that, in a dizzying semantic transposition, connects the lexicon of the not-
yet modern *Oration* to our fate as postmodern animals. This is not say that
language is not one of the tools we have given ourselves in order to gain access to our essential condition. But it was not the first or the most important
of them. Before speech, though not independently of it, the *homo humanus*, or *sapiens* if you prefer, did, in fact, forge themselves through technology. First of all, using the hard technique of hitting and throwing, of stone
and fire; and then, the soft technique of gestures and symbols. In the same
way, before language, humans had to inhabit another "home," another anthropic shell capable of sheltering them from the ruling powers. Similarly,
before educating themselves, humans had to tame the animals with whom,
for a long time, they shared the same type of life, and even before that, the
same experience of life as such, in a form in which the essential difference
between living species was still very tenuous. From this point of view, the
controversial expression, a very recent one after all, that "we descend from
animals" should be interpreted in the sense that human beings emerge from
something prehuman that is not human as we know it now, but not completely different from us either, since we have been able to go beyond ourselves through technics into a dimension that breaks down the confines of
the environment, opening ourselves to the limitlessness of the world. In this
oscillation, in this infinite trembling, between what humans no longer are
and what they are yet to be, lies the vertigo of humanism—the original flight
of sense that, much more that any possible sense, constitutes its most indelible philosophical trace.

To say that we remain inside it—that the question of humanism is
still our question—would go too far, perhaps. Or, conversely, it might be
overly simplistic with regard to what has happened over the last five hundred years, and especially, the last fifty. But we have certainly not left its
shadow, or, to be more precise, its other side. To argue that technics, the
capacity for the animal-human's altered self-fabrication, stands at the origin—not only at the end—of the human experience may seem obvious
today. It certainly was not so, however, more than half a millennium ago.
Of course that formation, or transformation, which at the time seemed

to concern only the human soul now involves our very body—that bio-determined complex in which we can no longer distinguish body from soul. Likewise, the idea that the human being contains within it all species in heaven and earth—according to the ancient mythologem of the microcosm—has been literally flipped inside out, in the extroversion of the human onto our external space. To put it briefly: if once the world was a globe made in the measure of the human being, today it is the humans who are globalizing themselves. But the identification between what human beings are and what they can become—what we called the question of anthropo-technics that now also takes the form of biotechnics—comes precisely from that fold in European culture located, like an enigma yet to be deciphered, between the Middle Ages and the modern era. Of course, after more than a century of full-blown philosophical diffidence toward technics, often still interpreted today as the supreme threat to human beings, it is not easy to recognize a first heralding of it in that series of letters handed down to us by the Humanists—who were certainly unaware of the fact that the "lector" (*Lesung*, reading) *de homine* could, sooner or later, also become the "selector" (*Auslegung*, interpretation) *hominis*. But even a possibility of this sort was implicit in the limitless freedom to which Italian Humanism had, in its depths and heights, bound our fragile dignity.

The Power of the Origin

The Order of Conflict

1. The relationship between Machiavelli and philosophy is one of those problems that comes up continually for discussion without ever getting resolved. Although some critics have called attention to how extraneous (or at least heterogeneous) the Florentine's work is to the canonical forms of philosophical language, there is no denying the interest and even fascination his thought has held, sometimes for those same critics. What has philosophy sought—or what has it glimpsed—in a writer it has generally kept outside its disciplinary boundaries? And why, except for some rare instances that can be linked with the names of Spinoza and Nietzsche, did the same discipline expel from its corpus a text whose importance it nevertheless dimly perceived? Probably the only way to steer clear of these sorts of conundrums is to shift our aim: instead of focusing our attention on the philosophical character of Machiavelli's work, we might do better to examine the inability of modern philosophy to take on the radical challenge his thought posed to it, in a form that was somehow congenial to the character of Italian thought. Part of what I am referring to is the hybridization of theoretical reflection that takes place with lexicons of different provenance: the political lexicon, in Machiavelli's case, or the literary one of his plays. But I am also referring to a more long-term attitude, which touches on the relationship of philosophy to the outside world. Instead of being closed off in a self-referential loop, entirely occupied with the nature of consciousness or forms of knowledge, the thought that arose from the Italian Renaissance was characterized

from the outset by a propensity toward what we might call the nonphilosophical: meaning, on the one hand, the experience of common people;
and, on the other, that of the public sphere. But with the caveat that this
exteriority to philosophy—to what is defined as such in other places—must
be taken as a specific modality of philosophy: more than a nonphilosophy, it
is a philosophy capable of entering into direct relationship with its own life
horizon. For this reason it has the capacity to establish a strong, at times exclusive link with the actuality of the present: to make itself an act of thought
itself, or thought in action, as part of a theory that is entirely absorbed by
the materiality of its object. The upshot of all this—in Machiavelli's case but
also with regard to other Italian authors influenced by him—was a philosophy that was non-neutral, and indeed completely foreign to the principle
of neutralization around which modern political philosophy was gradually
being constructed. This is a partisan [*di parte*] philosophy: not only does it
participate in the issues posed by its living present as they arise, it is also partial in choosing from the fields imposed by its times.

The general diffidence of philosophy toward Machiavelli stems—
perhaps even more than from its unconventional contents—from this infringement of a model of knowledge gathered about itself and about the
formulation of its own methodological assumptions. While this type of
knowledge, starting from its modern beginnings, was established as an
ordered set of abstract protocols intended to represent the real and facilitate its domination, Machiavelli flipped the relation of dominance—and
precedence—between theory and practice, thrusting the concrete into the
very heart of reflection.[1] Instead of seeking, pointlessly, to subdue or medi-
ate the real by preemptively adapting it to his own expressive modes, and
without being concerned about contradicting himself, Machiavelli allowed
his thought to be permeated with the real until he assumed it as such, with
all its inherently antinomic qualities.[2] This is the source of the incongrui-

1. On this topic, see Louis Althusser, "Machiavel et nous," in *Écrits philosophiques et politiques*, vol. 2 (Paris: Stock/Imec, 1995); English edition: *Machiavelli and Us*, trans. Gregory
Elliott (London: Verso, 1999). Althusser's interpretation of Machiavelli has been critically
reconstructed by Vittorio Morfino, "La storia come 'revoca permanente del fatto compiuto':
Machiavelli nell'ultimo Althusser," in *La varia natura, le molteplici cagioni: Studi su Machiavelli*, ed. Riccardo Caporali (Cesena, 2007), pp. 125–41.

2. For an interpretation along similar lines, see Gennaro M. Barbuto, *Antinomie della
politica: Saggio su Machiavelli* (Naples: Liguori, 2007).

ties—between the principle of the invariance of times, and the principle of perpetual change, for example—that lend such force to his writings, precisely because they reproduce an enigmatic trait of that same reality. The relation between universal and singular is inverted in the same way as it is for theory and practice. What dominates the scene laid out on the dry, terse pages of Machiavelli's text is not the regularity of general laws, but the contingency of unpredictable events. Not limited to simply disrupting the represented reality, they penetrate the very order of representation, destabilizing it; especially its inclination for a presupposed unification of what, due to its irreducibly multiple nature, tends to constantly overstep the boundaries of the picture.[3] Hence the impression of both vacillation and excess conveyed by a text like Machiavelli's, always on the verge of overflowing beyond its own discursive limits by dragging into its semantic vortex institutions and powers, bodies and passions, individuals and multitudes. Like something that presses up against it, threatening its very status, this incipient precipice—this deaf struggle, this semantic drift—is what modern knowledge perceived to be inassimilable.

Opposed to this formless and disquieting substance that can be traced to the figure of the origin, modern knowledge offered the creation of a new beginning: a rational, artificial beginning intended to wipe out all traces of the origin. To establish itself in a verifiable and functionally effective form—a project uniting Hobbes and Descartes and continuing until Kant—the new philosophy had to situate itself on a different, more advanced plane with respect to the seemingly ungovernable matter that seethed up inside it. Only after having defined the origin in its negativity—as state of nature, feral body, primal conflict—and thus casting it outside its own borders, could the new philosophy keep the world safe from the persistent challenge that it posed. This assumption—that there is something else, something earlier, with respect to what presents itself from the outset as the only factual reality—is precisely what Machiavelli radically questioned. Unlike the "moderns," he does not seek an unquestionable point of departure, a new theoretical skeleton key he can use to

3. A similar approach can be seen in Filippo Del Lucchese, Luca Sartorello, and Stefano Visentin, eds., *Machiavelli: Immaginazione e contingenza* (Pisa, 2006); Giorgio Inglese, *Per Machiavelli: L'arte dello stato, la cognizione delle storie* (Rome: Carocci, 2006); Carlo Galli, "Il volto demoniaco del potere: Alcuni momenti della fortuna continentale di Machiavelli," in *La varia natura, le molte cagioni*, ed. Caporali, pp. 35–59.

construct a different scenario against which to measure the existing one; because this foundational space is already fully occupied, and defaced in its claims to governance, by the inescapable presence of an origin that is coextensive with the entire process it has engendered. Thus—by projecting it into its "afterward," by continuously reactualizing it—Machiavelli strips the origin of any foundational character, whether metaphysical or epistemological in nature. It is not a chronologically identifiable point in time, or even a first cause, that gives rise to a series of events that are dependent on it. If so, if it were possible to trace the chain of causes and effects back to a principle of divine or human order capable of determining the next step, it would be easy to know it ahead of time. But that is exactly what does not happen, because every occurrence can radically change the picture it is introduced into as well as call into question the interpretation of the events preceding it. To maintain that politics is originary, in Machiavelli, is tantamount to saying that it has no origin. It means that there is nothing pre-political, like a state of nature, for example, that politics can take over from, relegating it to an immemorial past. Politics occupies the entire horizon of the real: there is nothing before it or after it, neither a preordained beginning nor a foreseeable end. This is also because the present—which entirely captures Machiavelli's attention—is certainly not the work of an individual subject, or, much less, of individuals united in a founding covenant; rather, it is the momentary, always reversible outcome of a clash between powers who take turns in dominating. Political actors—their options and destiny—are simply the result of power relations, natural phenomena, and contingent elements that inscribe the actors in a given horizon where they may play the cards they are dealt, but never to the point of mastering the situation completely. The classic theme of fortune in its contrasting relation with virtue [*virtù*] expresses to what extent vision, power, but also knowledge, are inherent in the set of circumstances they traverse, without ever being able to thoroughly control them. For this reason, there never will be a panorama available to political actors, a sort of bird's-eye view capable of illuminating the entire scene at once. When Machiavelli says in a famous passage that in order to get to know something you need to put yourself on a different level from it,[4] he is far from suggesting that knowledge is somehow independent from its object;

4. The reference is to Machiavelli's dedication in *The Prince*, trans. and ed. Quentin Skinner and Russell Price (Cambridge: Cambridge University Press, 1988), p. 3.

on the contrary, what he is referring to is the dialectic that binds them irrevocably together. From this point of view—anticipating a recurring trait of Italian thought in this respect as well—a defining feature of political knowledge, like any other kind of knowledge, is its inevitable opacity. Far from casting the light of its own self-evidence onto reality, political knowledge is destined to absorb the shadows and the ripples, the contrasts and the folds, the upsurges and the failures of the real. On these lines, Machiavelli's thought is not, nor did it ever strive to be, a political philosophy—in the sense of a philosophical foundation of politics. Rather, it is a radical reflection on existence in its inevitably conflictual dimension.

2. This means that there is no area of human life that is removed from the necessity of politics. Without politics—its instruments, its logic, its orders—neither individuals nor collective aggregates could withstand the flurry of accidents that ceaselessly beat down upon them. They wouldn't know how to divert the force of impact onto other targets or channel it between embankments capable of containing its destructive violence. But the relationship between life and politics does not stop here—at the protection that the latter affords the former. It also needs to be viewed from the perspective of its complementary opposite: if politics is indeed the necessary form of life, then life, in its turn, is the exclusive subject matter of politics. This applies equally to the formation of knowledge and to the phenomenology of power: to avoid being slowly drained and turning inward on themselves, both must establish a biunivocal, productive relationship with the world of life.[5] They must make life their object, but equally, their source. They, too, must become vitalized—springing from life and directed toward life. When Machiavelli speaks of the "free mode of life [vivere libero]," or claims that "a republic has a fuller life" than a principality,[6] we must take these words in their most intensely literal sense: there are political forms, institutions, and regimes more capable than others of staying alive because they have commingled with life from the outset—with the needs, impulses, and desires of life. From this point of view, contrary to what has been claimed, in Machiavellian politics there is always something more than mere techniques for the preservation of power. Not be-

5. See M. Zanardi, "Il corpo rigenerato," in *Il Centauro* 1982 (50): 56–86.
6. Niccolò Machiavelli, *Discourses on Livy*, trans. Julia Conaway Bondanella and Peter Bondanella (Oxford: Oxford University Press, 1977), p. 282.

cause the state does not tend naturally to preserve itself, but because to do so—to keep itself stable—it must change at the same speed as its context, which is itself in perpetual change: it must regenerate itself by going back to the source of its life. Between one and the other—between power and life—there is never an absolute distance, a radical gap. Just as there can be no life that is utterly bare, devoid of any formal qualification, confined to a pre-political universe; in the same way, there is no power so absolute, so locked into its own orbit, that it relates to life only from above and outside it. No matter how isolated or careful it may be—all the more so in these cases—power sinks its roots into a natural, instinctive world that is no different in its consistency from the animal world. The image of the centaur and the definition of the prince as being halfway between a fox and a lion are figural depictions of how inextricably intertwined they are. The animal is not the lowest level to which a human being regresses as it moves away from its divine status, as humanistic anthropology would have it; nor is it a provisional, primitive state to be definitively surpassed by the political order, as the modern order would have it. The animal is the bedrock of natural energy in every person from which we draw our capacity to defend ourselves and the drive to prevail over others, our subtle intelligence [*ingegno*], and primogenial vigor. Between humanity and animality there is no such abyss as there is in Hobbes separating the "wolves" in the state of nature from the subjects in the civil state: the wolf is part of the human, the same way nature is part of civilization. As a matter of fact, the effort, or the temptation, to split this combination of form and force, power [*potere*] and potency [*potenza*], is exactly what produces the sometimes irreversible crisis of the political body. The only way to save itself is by going back to the origin where its regenerative capacity is still preserved intact by life. To grasp the most acute point of Machiavelli's thought—one that has deeply penetrated the corpus of Italian philosophy—we must not lose sight of the ontological connection between origin, life, and change. As we have said, in spite of the constant reminder of the origin and the recurring theme of the "return to principles" or of "going back to the beginnings," they do not lead to a theory of preservation. Instead, they open up thought on innovation, as expressed in one of the most well-known passages in the *Discourses*:

Changes which bring such bodies back to their principles are healthy. The ones that have the best organization and the longest lives are, however, those that can renew themselves often through their own institutions, or that come to such a renewal through some circumstance outside these institutions. And it is clearer than light itself that if they do not renew themselves, these bodies will not endure. The method of renewing them is, as was stated, to bring them back to their principles.[7]

The return to the beginning, like a ricochet movement, coincides with the drive toward the new. Freed of any regressive mythology, the origin is the moment when—skipping over the present current—the past projects life into the free and open space of its future.

But to understand the literally "biopolitical" segment of Machiavelli's thought at its deepest level, we must shift the focus of our analysis onto an underlying plane; namely, the continuous use he makes of the biological lexicon in his description of the different political regimes. This certainly anachronistic reference to a contemporary term is not meant to argue that his work is an early example of the treatises on government that, starting in a later period, began to take the material life of subjects and populations as the object of their knowledge. Michel Foucault and his school have rightly excluded this possibility, identifying in the Machiavellian prince, if anything, the paradigm against which the new knowledge took shape in contrast to it.[8] This difference especially highlights the even more intrinsic relation between biomedical language and political language that causes them to be superimposed in Machiavelli's text. It could be said that, for him, life cannot yet be an object of governance on the part of politics because politics is itself already conceived in terms of life. Indeed, in this original indistinguishability—in a knowledge not *on* life (which is soon to arise) but *of* life, inseparable from the vital substratum of its object—there may very well lie the still unexplored possibility of something like an affirmative biopolitics. Without getting prematurely into a topic that will be more clearly formulated later on, let's pause for a moment on this immediately biological characterization of the political order, since it defines what differentiates Machiavelli from the earlier humanistic tradition as well as from the full-fledged modern tradition. There is no question that the roots of the state-body metaphor go back to very distant times, something we need not return to in detail. But the crucial point is the fact that the Florentine sec-

7. Ibid., p. 246.

8. See Michel Foucault, *Sécurité, territoire, population* (Paris: Gallimard, 2004); English edition: *Security, Territory, Population: Lectures at the College de France 1977–78*, ed. Michel Senellart, trans. Graham Burchell (New York: Palgrave Macmillan, 2009), pp. 55 ff.

retary appropriated the metaphor specifically in order to change it, pointing it in a direction that was entirely alien to it. It is widely known that Machiavelli adopted Hippocratic medical terminology that came to him via Galen, especially with regard to the theory of the opposing humors, and the generation and corruption of states. According to this theory, like other mixed bodies, political bodies are subject to the changes and upheavals that all natural beings are subject to. This dynamic variation—which calls more on physiology than anatomy—marks a first, important deviation from the primarily static functioning attributed to the organismic metaphor: what matters now is not so much the arrangement of the bodily organs so much as how they function in terms of metamorphosis.[9]

But this early, already significant deviation from the classical model is joined by a second, even more influential one involving the relationship between the various parts of the body. Unlike the humanistic literature on the prince, but deviating also from the modern literature on the sovereign state, the Machiavellian body politic does not present significant hierarchical distinctions between the head—or the "soul," as Hobbes preferred to call it[10]—and the other members. For the English philosopher, the body is distinctly separate from the soul, which unifies and governs it, however, since without the soul's command, the body would go to pieces. For Machiavelli, the body is instead a unified whole whose health derives from the relation between its different parts, so that a body with "more parts" has "greater life."[11] But the decisive element of differentiation—in this case, too, from both the literature of the Renaissance and from that of the seventeenth century—is to be found elsewhere. It resides in the absolutely unprecedented way this relationship is conceived: not in the immobile, reassuring terms of harmony, but rather, in the shifting, risk-laden terms of conflict. Here, too, the way Machiavelli arrives at this extreme outcome is by a semantic rotation in the biological vocabulary. Since its initial formulation, and

9. On this topic see especially M. Gaille-Nikodimov, *Conflit civil et liberté: La politique-machiavélienne entre histoire et médecine* (Paris: Champion, 2004); as well as S. D'Alessio, *Tra la vita e la morte: Declinazioni della libertà in Machiavelli e Hobbes*, in *Tolleranza e libertà*, ed. V. Dini (Milan: Elèuthera, 2001), pp. 41–66.

10. See Thomas Hobbes, *Leviathan*, in *The English Works*, ed. William Molesworth, vol. 3 (London: John Bohn, 1839).

11. Niccolò Machiavelli, *The Art of War*, trans. Henry Neville (1675) (Bedmore, VA: Wilder, 2008), p. 60.

throughout its history, the organismic metaphor of the state-body had been employed to extol the harmony between the parts, in order to legitimate whichever regime best guaranteed it. Machiavelli turned this significance on its head: as in the Galenic theory of the humors, in the city, too, the health of the body politic does not stem from the prevalence of one humor over another but from their balanced opposition. A body is healthy not when one of its humors is being drained by the dominance of an opposing humor, but only when that humor is able to resist its opposite with equal vitality. Only this dynamic equilibrium between opposing forces ensures the body the growth it requires in order not to weaken and eventually perish. With a final, sensational innovation, reducing the number of humors from the four contained in the Galenic model to only two—defined as the desire of the Grandi to dominate the people, and that of the people to resist the Grandi—he gives even more emphasis to the constitutive role of discord. Of course, to remain productive, to not lead the body into complete self-destruction, discord cannot go beyond civil limits by degenerating into personal or privatistic forms. But the risk of explosion—from too much stasis—is no smaller than the danger of implosion. The role of politics is to govern the conflictual tension arising naturally from the different interests at play. But without tension there can be no politics at all. The number associated with politics—when life is at stake—is not One, but Two.

It is here—in his development of a completely new theory of conflict, now viewed not as a residue or opposite of order, but as a form of order—that Machiavelli opens up a whole new horizon of meaning to political thought. It seems to me that there is general agreement on this point in the literature on Machiavelli.[12] But I think it is possible, and necessary, to take it a step further; one that can provide an answer to the question we began with regarding Machiavelli's specific contribution to the field of philosophy. I am referring to the problematic, and in some ways even antinomic, relationship between antagonism and immanence that is to be found, in different forms, in other phases of Italian thought. The problem of this relationship lies in the fact that the plane of immanence is at once enabled and undermined by its conflictual makeup. It is enabled in the sense that conflict does not precede order, as it does in Hobbes, or follow it, as it does in counterrevolution-

12. See Filippo Del Lucchese, "'Disputare' e 'combattere': Modi del conflitto nel pensiero politico di Machiavelli," *Filosofia Politica* 1 (2001): 1–95; and Roberto Esposito, *Ordinee conflitto: Machiavelli e la letteratura politica del Rinascimento italiano* (Naples: Liguori, 1984).

ary philosophies. But nor can it be said that conflict assails order from the outside, starting from a point that is transcendental to it. On the contrary, like its very mode of being, conflict is inherent in order. Hence the immanence of one with respect to the other. Order, in Machiavelli, is inherently conflictual; just as, when it has not degenerated, conflict is prescribed by institutional mechanisms designed for that purpose. This is the same integrated relationship that exists between form and force: just as form cannot exist without a force that gives life to it, so every force, to act productively, must acquire a formal determination. From this point of view, the only modern philosopher who can be assimilated to Machiavelli's thought, notwithstanding all their differences, is Spinoza, who, not surprisingly, makes use of the Florentine's work to argue against Hobbesian monism. For Spinoza, too, as for his "acutissimus" Florentine predecessor, the clash between the two social parts can never be eliminated, because it is inherent in the constituted order. And for him, too, the preservation of the body, far from being the result of a sum of renunciations—as in Hobbes's theory—is proportional to the sum of the forces that compose it. In a horizon in which politics tends to coincide with ontology, for both, power [*potere*] is inseparable from potency [*potenza*]; but not to the point that one is entirely identified with the other. This is the source of the problem that neither thinker is able to resolve completely. For both Spinoza and Machiavelli, although the logic of antagonism is inscribed in the plane of immanence, there is always a point beyond which they enter into potential friction. This is the moment when conflict degenerates into private or direct economic interests, thereby losing its political valence and sliding toward civil war, situated on the outer edge of the system. When antagonism rises beyond a certain threshold, it is liable to lacerate the very plane of immanence that encompasses it, resulting in the need for a new momentum of transcendence capable of creating a new order. Only when seen in this light can we grasp the full significance of the theory of the prince in Machiavelli's work. In philosophical terms, it expresses the extreme outcome as well as the breaking point of the antinomic relationship between antagonism and immanence.

3. At this point the dissonant element in Machiavelli's thought—his essential inassimilability on the part of modern philosophical thought—is plainly evident. Given that modern political philosophy identified its center of gravity in the sovereign dispositif of the neutralization of conflict,

how could it do anything except frontally negate a conception that viewed conflict as the fuel of political action? Bodin's charge against Machiavelli, that he had "profaned the sacred mysteries of political philosophy,"[13] and, perhaps even more significantly, Hobbes's deafening silence on his Florentine predecessor, are absolutely explicit in this regard. What gets called into question by Machiavelli's opting for discord is the category of sovereignty around which the entire theory of modern politics pivoted. According to sovereignty theory, the only way to safeguard the relationship between human beings from the dissolutive risk that threatens them is to abolish the relationship as such, replacing it with an artificial order governed from a single point of command. The new European thought—despite substantial internal differences in the ways sovereignty was instituted and in the extent of its powers—converged in this rigidly immunitary assumption: human life must be defended from its common origin, first by a theory and then by a practice aimed at emptying it of its natural substance. This line of reasoning reveals a clear theological/political implication: since only a single God can put an end to polytheist turmoil, in the same way, only a single sovereign is able to rid the state body of the scourge of conflict. The Hobbesian theory of representation, according to which one Person alone is authorized by all the others to act forever in their name, is simply the secularization of a dispositif with evident theological roots whose effects of meaning are still being felt today. From this point of view, the thread of continuity that through the category of sovereignty, although diversely formulated, ties together through time theoreticians of absolutism like Hobbes, liberal writers like Locke, and democratic ones like Rousseau, proves stronger than their undeniably substantial differences.

The difference that separates Machiavelli from these thinkers is not just a matter of content, though: it is a different paradigm altogether. What distinguishes it at first sight, more than the presence of any given elements, is the absence of a state body that can be identified as the scope of sovereign power. This absence, both historical and conceptual in nature, has rightly been spoken about in terms of the late entrance of Italy's political culture into a thoroughly modern dimension comparable to those of other European countries. But this void—of a state and of any plausible plan for national unification—was an extraordinary place for Machiavelli to form a

13. Jean Bodin, *Les six livres de la République* (Geneva, 1577), unpaginated preface.

thought free from constraining assumptions. We know the interpretive tradition inaugurated by Hegel, who viewed Machiavelli's work as the early form of a theory of state that remained undeveloped due to unfavorable historical conditions, only to be reworked and perfected by later authors. My view is that this fails to fully grasp the peculiarity of Machiavelli's vision. Not only was the Florentine's perspective heterogeneous to the incipient theory of sovereignty and to the secularized political theology that formed its necessary foundation in terms of political monism, it followed a completely different paradigmatic orbit. In its place, Machiavelli developed a binary-type ontology: what lies at the origin—the same origin to which the political body must return when its life force wanes—is not the consistency of a single organizing principle, but rather, an unexhausted struggle between opposing powers [*potenze*]. The form society takes in its normal configuration is discord—not between individuals, as in the Hobbesian state of nature, but between aggregates of people moved by diverse, conflicting desires. The political clash that Machiavelli sees played out before him between the Grandi and the Popolari—foreshadowed in its clearest form by the Roman republic—merely expresses this ineluctable struggle. There is no need to imagine some sort of artificial overhaul for society (nor would it make any sense to Machiavelli) because there is no way to avoid the recurrence of the origin—or in other words, the return of our own conflictual nature.

As we have seen, what can be done is to adopt a type of regime that is able to stabilize this dynamic, by pulling together into a single node the poles of conflict and order that only appear to alternate. We know that this conflictual order, or ordered conflict, is identified by Machiavelli in the constitutional form of the "mixed state." While this form is explicitly rejected by Bodin and Hobbes—for being ineffective and even inherently contradictory—the mixed state is accepted and even appreciated by Italian authors of Machiavelli's time like Savonarola, Guicciardini, and Giannotti. But only as long as it works to foster harmony between the parts. This need for stabilization had already been fulfilled, for that matter, by the mixed constitution of the Aristotelian type that was revived by the humanistic tradition, mediated through Polybius and Cicero. According to this tradition, to prevent disorder and change, it was a question of uniting the three traditional forms of government around a middle point, with the right balancing of powers. Machiavelli's intention was diametrically opposed to this organic design. In sharp contrast to a political geometry governed by the

primacy of the center, his focus shifted to its extremes, reduced, at least in
the crucial texts, from three to two, and defined by their oppositional attitude toward each other: the desire of the one to dominate is matched by
an equal tendency on the part of the other not to allow itself to be domi-
nated. The power of the former is met by the resistance of the latter, and
vice versa, in an endless circuit. Rather than being viewed as a neutralizing
machine, the mixture is seen as the institutionally regulated production of
conflict. It is theorized specifically in virtue of its conflict-producing mechanism, not in spite of it. This is because only conflict allows for the renewal
and replacement without which the political body tends to crystallize in the
domination of one part over the other, leading first to corruption and then
to deflagration. From this angle, alongside and within the immanentization
of conflict, another one of Machiavelli's "discoveries" becomes clearly visible: the prevalence of the founding moment over the time of established
institution. Not that he undervalues duration compared to event, or form
compared to force. Only the durability of an institution over time proves
the rightness of the power that modeled it. Similarly, the goodness of the
law is demonstrated by its ability to overcome the violence out of which it
inevitably arises, by integrating it. But institution, form, and law function
to the extent that they always leave a gap open to the advent of a power
not founded upon anything and precisely for this reason able to establish a
new order.[14] The theory of the new prince, in its apparent dissimilarity to
the republican logic of the *Discourses*, must also be understood in these in-
stitutive and constituent terms, pushed out of the plane of immanence by
the exceptionality of a situation that is otherwise ungovernable. When the
rule of law is no longer able to renew itself, because it is exhausted, the only
way to regain its lost strength is to reactivate the potency [*potenza*] of the
origin, with a leap in the dark. Of course, this holds true only as long as it
provides itself with a political subjectivity capable of embodying its vitality
and productive drive in the vortex of the crisis.

It is precisely against this primacy of the constituent over the constituted—of the event over the form, of the instant over the duration—that the
ideators of sovereignty move together as one. To begin with, sovereignty is
distinguished by the three qualities—absoluteness, perpetuity, and indivis-
ibility—that most contradict Machiavelli's bipolar dynamics; and second, its

14. See especially Miguel Vatter, *Between Form and Event: Machiavelli's Theory of Political Freedom* (Norwell, MA: Kluwer, 2000).

normative epicenter is based on prohibiting any return to the origin. Its institution—valid once and for all—serves to ward off the literally catastrophic possibility of the civic order plunging once again into the state of nature out of which it had emerged by definitively eradicating it. If the constituted power was revocable—this is Hobbes's thesis—what it would find again at its external borders is the savage chaos of the prepolitical community, not the source that fuels its constituent power. In this scenario, the immunitary cordon that separates order from its opposite would be broken, and conflict would become generalized in the fight to the death of all against all. As it did before the state, and after it, politics would burst its banks and overflow into a permanent war. Machiavelli escapes this powerful logical device even before it gets constructed, by using a vocabulary that cannot be fully understood by his Florentine contemporaries or by his modern critics. Its basis is a rejection of the presupposed identification between politics and state. If there can be politics only in the state—not before it or after it—then politics will eventually turn inward on itself and dry up. Entirely concentrated in the hands of the sovereign, it will be reduced to obedience to a set of laws intended to exhaust politics for the benefit of the supreme good of security. Machiavelli's reach outside this neutralizing dispositif remains irreducible. Of course, it can be seen as a measure of how backward Italy was in creating a unitary state, which is no doubt also true. But perhaps, in an era like ours, when even the most powerful of Leviathans is showing signs of fatigue, this "pre-statal" politics points to something that reaches beyond the state.

The Infinite Life

1. If there is a pivot around which Giordano Bruno's entire thought seems to rotate like a circle in which theology, cosmology, and anthropology pass seamlessly through one another, it is his critique of the idea of personhood. Pressed by the inquisitors, when he admits that he indeed "had doubts about the name 'person' as applied to the Son and the Holy Spirit; not conceiving these two persons to be distinct from the Father,"[15] not only

---

15. See Luigi Firpo, *Il processo di Giordano Bruno*, ed. Diego Quaglioni (Rome: Salerno, 1993), p. 170; for an English translation of the inquisition transcript see William Thayer, "The Trial, Opinions, and Death of Giordano Bruno," in *Atlantic Monthly* (March 1890), pp. 289–310. This quote appears on p. 296.

does he challenge the dogmatic foundation of the mysteries of the Trinity and the Incarnation, he also opens up a radical perspective whose scope we are only now beginning to appreciate. His attempt to legitimize his position in the face of his inquisitors by appealing to the authority of St. Augustine—to whom Bruno attributed his own distrust of a term that, according to the saint, was newly coined and not contained in Scripture—only emphasizes the absolute originality of his philosophical theses. He was a known supporter of the Arian and Sabellian heresies, and according to a certainly plausible hypothesis, he also supported an amalgamation of the effective position of Augustine with the philological critique launched by Lorenzo Valla against the equating of *persona* and *substantia* that Boethius had established.[16] But neither of these circumstances suffice to explain away or curb the explosive effect caused by Bruno's denial. His refusal to sanction the category of person not only implied a negation of the mediatory role of Christ between the finite and the infinite, but also the very notion of a personal God; which is to say, a deity characterized essentially by the attribute of will. The consequence of this position—on the theological plane and transferred from there to the cosmological and anthropological planes—is truly astonishing. Bruno argues that if God, somehow separating himself from himself, had decided to create a world external to him—or at least, based on the thesis later advanced by Leibniz, had chosen the best among possible worlds—then the world that was created would be the only one; just as its inhabitants would be the only ones to claim the title of creatures made in the image and likeness of the Creator. But it is just this—the uniqueness of the world and the personal identity of the human—that Bruno disputed even before he came into contact with the Copernican theory.

This chronological note is important for us so as not to lose sight of the real cause-and-effect connections that structure the complex formation of Bruno's thought.[17] The rift in the theological order, which would push him toward a decidedly post-Christian side, preceded the cosmological one—although the latter eventually had the effect of strengthening the former in its turn. At its root lies the modal identification between possibility and reality, potency [*potenza*] and act [*atto*]. If "the power to create implies

16. See the detailed reconstruction on the entire question by Michele Ciliberto, in *Giordano Bruno: Il teatro della vita* (Milan, 2007), especially pp. 33 ff.

17. See Alfonso Ingegno, *Cosmologia e filosofia nel pensiero di Giordano Bruno* (Milan: La Nuova Italia, 1978).

the power to be created [il posser fare pone il posser esser fatto],"[18] then what exists is not the arbitrary product of a single will, but the completed totality of what could occur. For God to imagine a distinction between himself and his object, or even between himself as knower and himself as known—as the paradigm of person entails—would introduce untenable elements of insufficiency and dissociation into his highly simple intelligence. If this were the case, as Nicholas of Cusa maintained, the world would be the fruit of the intratrinitarian relationship between the three Persons and not, as Bruno believed, a product of the clearly impersonal potency of God. Moreover, it would be the object of a sovereign decision by a hidden god who was waiting to be revealed by the coming of his Son, rather than the immediate manifestation of that god's presence. But this is exactly what Bruno's "political theology" rejected. For him, the self-realization of the divine is not a Person but the world. God, he says, "needs the world as much as the world needs God," just as "God would be nothing if the world did not exist."[19] But then, since there is no God that precedes the world, this means the world has no starting point; or, which comes to the same thing, its beginning continues without interruption—it coincides with the entire lifespan of the world.

It is all too evident that this work of de-Christianization—which Bruno did not intend as a frontal rejection of theology, but as a reconciliation with its first and most authentic meaning—is refracted through his conception of the cosmos. Since the universe is not the chosen object of any creationist design but the externalization of a spiritual principle without beginning or end, none of its points can be taken as center—or all of them have to be assumed in the same way, with no hierarchical distinction between high and low, above and below, or inside and outside. Any grain of sand, from this perspective, is as much the center as the biggest of planets. The other consequence of a view like this, one that goes well beyond the Copernican system, because it knocks the bottom out of its still-centered topology, is that there is no real distinction between what can be

18. *Le opere italiane di Giordano Bruno*, vol. 1, ed. Paolo de Lagarde (Göttingen, 1888), p. 322; English version: *On the Infinite Universe and Worlds* (Venice, 1584), second dialogue. Online version available at the Positive Atheism Magazine Web site, www.positiveatheism.org/hist/brunoiuwo.htm#IUWTOC (accessed June 10, 2012).

19. Angelo Mercati, *Il sommario del processo di G. Bruno* (Vatican City: Biblioteca Apostolica Vaticana, 1942), p. 79.

called soul and an equally infinite matter that is pervaded with soul in its simultaneously corporeal and incorporeal body. The name Bruno reserves for this—with such frequency and intensity that, more than a simple category, it becomes the foundational cornerstone of his thought—is Life. Life as a whole, inseparable into form and content, soul and matter, or spirit and nature. An inexhaustible substance running through and animating all parts of reality that inextricably connects God and the world. This is what Bruno means in the *De immenso* when he sees life in every part: there is no place in the universe that is not animated, and the same spiritual matter underlies every living being. Along with the traditional opposition between transcendence and immanence—understood by Bruno as two faces of the same coin—the equally codified oppositions between potency and act, subject and object, sense and intellect, also fall away. This does not mean that he loses sight of the difference between the planes and lines that cut through the real, articulating it into its irreducible multiplicity. On the contrary, his system could be said to be the first modern ontology of difference and plurality, starting with regard to the distinction between finite and infinite, continually upheld by Bruno against any sort of mediation. But also when he says that the soul is all in every part of a body, he does not mean that it expresses itself everywhere in the same proportion and intensity. The soul does indeed run through all matter, and since no body is extraneous to the cosmic principle of life, it can be said about all things that "if they are not animals, they are animated."[20] But rather than excluding difference, this makes it more acute through the figure of contrareity. From this point of view, at a structural level, the affinity with Machiavelli's lexicon is stronger than the similarities in content relating to the civil role of religion. Without opposites, and the tension they continuously regenerate, there would be no life. Life is the perennial impulse that joins and then once again separates the polarities that clash from time to time on the horizontal and vertical planes. Except that while life, when viewed from the angle of each individual thing, appears to be characterized by difference—or contrareity—when viewed from the perspective of the whole, it appears as the totality.[21]

20. Giordano Bruno, *De la causa, principio e uno*, in *Dialoghi italiani: Dialoghi metafisici e dialoghi morali*, ed. Giovanni Gentile and Giovanni Aquilecchia (Florence: Sansoni, [1958]), vol. 1, p. 243.

21. On this theme, see Eugenio Canone, *Magia dei contrari: Cinque studi su Giordano Bruno* (Rome, 2005).

If this connection gets lost, so do the whole and the part, namely, that vital principle by which "if indeed there be no perturbation, there beseemeth neither passion for perpetuity nor fear of dissolution."[22] This famous passage from *On the Infinite Universe and Worlds* is particularly important because it somehow seems to foreshadow, or, in the most radically philosophical sense of the term, at least motivate Bruno's ultimate sacrifice. I am not referring simply to such an absolute identification between philosophy and life—in the specific sense this time of his particular life history—that renouncing one entails giving up the other. Rather, I am alluding to the recurrent character of Italian philosophy, which, unlike other traditions that are less likely to force the theoretical circle of self-reflection, tends to incorporate thought into life, making it, in the most literal sense of the word, *living*. Bruno takes this attitude one extreme step further, of course, and ends up including in it that which ultimately puts an end to its development. He makes death an act, the most vital act of all, because it is tied inextricably to defending a philosophy that coincides with life: "We shall discover that neither we ourselves nor any substance doth suffer death; for nothing is in fact diminished in its substance, but all things wandering through infinite space undergo change of aspect."[23] Against the immunitary philosophies aimed at preserving life—even at the cost of subordinating it to a sovereign power who promises to protect it— Bruno ties its meaning to the artesian well force of a movement designed to push it beyond itself. To the point of coming up against its opposite, since this opposite, on certain occasions, may safeguard its most authentic meaning. That is why the principle of life—life as beginning and end of the being—has no "fear of dissolution." Because that loss is an integral part of its own unstoppable flow. Life is not a scarce resource that must be defended and preserved at all costs, but a power [*potenza*] so abundant that not even death can consume it definitively, transmuting it instead into another form of the same living substance.

2. The eccentricity or obliquity of Bruno's place in relation to the pillars of modern philosophy is not confined to his criticism—implicit during his whole life, and even in his death—of the conservative, immunitary-type paradigm. Above and beyond the obvious content of his thought, what set

22. Bruno, *On the Infinite Universe and Worlds*, fourth dialogue.
23. Ibid., fifth dialogue.

him apart are the vocabulary and tone of a work entirely irreducible to the mechanistic and geometrical turn that European philosophical reflection took as a whole during the late Renaissance. A glance at any of Bruno's *Dialogues* suffices to recognize the signs of a distance that was destined to widen even further as his hermetic and kabbalistic interests continued to expand. How can we compare these feverish pages—teeming with intensely powerful images and expressions at once coarse and sublime—with the understated and rigorous prose of the new modern philosophy? It was as if Bruno wanted to keep a door open—a channel for transfer and contamination between the languages of reason and sense, deduction and narration, logos and myth—that elsewhere had been hermetically sealed in the interest of furthering the project of the complete mathematization of the world. Descartes, Mersenne, Hobbes—but even Galileo and Kepler—by now stood on the other side of that line dividing modern knowledge from its humanistic roots. Even before Frances Yates dragged Bruno's entire oeuvre into the esoteric circle of magic, Cassirer and Koyré,[24] albeit in different ways, had already decreed the backward character of his conceptual lexicon, because it was inadequate for exactly these formal canons: too dissimilar, and even lacking in form, to be able to be aligned with a scientific approach that had surpassed it in both method and merit.

The most perceptive critical literature has long challenged this type of approach, opting instead for a historical/conceptual genealogy less prone to preestablished periodizations—and with a different attention to the lateral deviations, broken paths, and sudden detours that opened up the founding of the Modern to a plurality of differing and even opposing possibilities.[25] As we have seen with Machiavelli, and will see with Vico, what at first sight appear to be backward elements or inadequacies can be shown to be passageways which, by crossing diagonally through modernity, end up opening onto a perspectival horizon that may even lie beyond it. But, in any case, if we still wondered what it is that distances Bruno from the

24. Frances A. Yates, *Giordano Bruno and the Hermetic Tradition* (London: Routledge, 1964); Ernst Cassirer, *The Individual and the Cosmos in Renaissance Philosophy*, trans. Mario Domandi (New York: Harper and Row, 1963); Alexandre Koyré, *From the Closed World to the Infinite Universe* (Baltimore: Johns Hopkins University Press, 1957).

25. On this topic, see Biagio de Giovanni, "Lo spazio della vita tra G. Bruno e T. Campanella," *Il Centauro* 11–12 (1984): 3–32; and his "L'infinito di Bruno," *Il Centauro* 16 (1986): 3–21.

new philosophy, we would have to look at the empty spot that, in its reflection, occupies the category of subject. We have already seen how in the theological sphere the divine subjectivity was replaced by—and therefore also deprived of—the natural process of the world's self-generation. Nothing less than a personal God—one provided with the qualities of will and self-determination, that is—could be at its origin. And, indeed, that very origin—understood as the infratemporal, or extratemporal, instant of *creatio ex nihilo*—is dissolved, or stretched out, along the course of a process that is literally without subject because it cannot be separated from its object. Now this identity between subject and object—or, to express it differently, between transcendence and immanence—that breaks down the divine personality, turning it inside out, also applies to the human personality. Here, too, what is at stake is the conception and the very figure of the origin. Just as God does not precede the world, so the human subject is not a premise to the cosmic process that presides over its temporary constitution: the subject is not posited on itself in a form that places it prior to its own position, as is the case for the Cartesian ego.

Thus, just as Machiavelli broke down the sovereign neutralization of conflict, another Italian author is responsible for the early deconstruction of the presupposition of the subject. Human beings are but a part—a very modest and certainly not a privileged part—of the living substance that makes up the universe. We are a simple transitional segment, an intriguing and particular one to be sure, between one phase of cosmic evolution and another. The human is a juncture inside the infinite stream of life between one configuration that could be defined as preindividual, and another that could be called postindividual, or at least transindividual. Obviously, since the subject is not assumed prior to life, this means that the construction of knowledge does not rest on a self-evident foundation, as is the case for the knowledge we refer to as modern. The reason is clear: for Bruno there is no point of distinction that cleanly separates the chaotic world of sense experience from the crystalline and ordered world of the intellect. There isn't even a dividing line between the self and the world that the self knows. For Bruno, just as for Machiavelli before him, although in a different way, the knowing subject is not external to the process of knowing or to its object. And indeed, the more the knowing subject rises in degree and quality, the more it is invaded by its object, until losing its own contours altogether. The myth of the hunter Actaeon in *The Heroic Enthusiasts*, devoured by his own dogs for having contemplated the naked body of the goddess Diana, signifies precisely this dialectic, not only between lover and beloved, but also between someone invaded by the sacred fire of knowledge and that which, finally grasped, takes possession of the knower in its turn: "Actaeon, 'the greater hunter saw,' he understood as much as was possible, and became the hunted. He went out for prey, and this hunter became himself the prey, by the operation of the intellect converting the things learned into itself."[26] Similarly to how the beloved absorbs the lover into himself or herself until desire has been consumed, so the known object sucks into itself the identity of the subject, thereby altering its constitution.

This explains why the use of a new method ensuring a priori certainty and performative effectiveness cannot possibly transform the order of knowledge in a radical way. Quite the opposite: any knowledge that claims to be new, like Bruno's, is so only to the extent that it reinstates a founding relation with its own original roots. So it is true—as Hans Blumenberg's superb interpretation concludes[27]—that Bruno's work escapes the paradigm of secularization. Because it doesn't start from a Christian philosophy of history, it doesn't even approach a philosophy of progress culminating in an Enlightenment-type outcome: light, for the Nolan, is not an eruption that suddenly explodes, canceling out the darkness, but rather the partial and temporary legacy left by the withdrawal of a shadow that is always on the verge of returning and lengthening across the earth. Like every other element, light does not exist without its opposite; in fact, it was born from darkness. But just as Bruno's philosophy does not fit into the scheme of secularization, it also protrudes outside modernity as a process of self-legitimization, as Blumenberg maintains, in the sense that it doesn't envisage or theorize a point of radical rupture with the past. In the same way that the origin of the cosmos continues without interruption until our time, knowledge will be truly renewed only if it can be rejoined to the ancient wisdom, especially the Egyptian, that precedes the Christian-European era. While the latter is but one of countless civilizations gener-

26. Giordano Bruno, *De gli eroici furori*, in *Dialoghi italiani*, vol. 2, p. 1007; English version: *The Heroic Enthusiasts: An Ethical Poem (1887–1889), Books I and II*, trans. L. Williams (Forgotten Books, 2007), p. 68.

27. See Hans Blumenberg, *Die Legitimität der Neuzeit* (Frankfurt am Main: Suhrkamp, 1974); English version: *The Legitimacy of the Modern Age*, trans. Robert M. Wallace (Cambridge, MA: MIT Press, 1983).

ated along the wheel of time—and therefore no more privileged than any other knowledge from non-European or even other possible worlds—the *prisca theologia* and Egyptian knowledge are conceived by Bruno as a drawbridge toward a future situated beyond the modern age. While the dogma of the Incarnation—with the fatal category of the person at its core—has been a sort of metaphysical guarantee for the human being as the master of all nature, by referring to a more ancient knowledge, says Bruno, the primacy of infinite Life will be restored, placing the human being in a different but no higher position than that of all other living beings.

3. These latter observations, inscribed in the furrow separating Bruno from the most influential register of modern thought, trace out an equally problematic relationship with Humanism—which goes to show that distance from the former in no way signifies slavish adherence to the latter. While his deviation from the main lines of the new philosophy did not, in short, take the form of a return to an era that in many ways had run its course, neither did it exclude a relation with some of its constitutive elements: specifically, that of civic engagement, typical of all Italian philosophy—recognizable particularly in the theory that Machiavelli had developed earlier on the political function of religion and in the consequent rejection of Lutheran quietism. Bruno's position on Florentine Neoplatonism, on the other hand, is a different and more complex matter. While his proximity to Marsilio Ficino on some topics, especially those involving Hermeticism, is so marked as to allow his enemies to speak of plagiarism, Bruno remained steadfast in his rejection of their Christian interpretation: not for fear that it would diminish the place of human beings in the universe, but, on the contrary, because it would provide a transcendental safeguard for legitimizing human primacy. This is exactly where the school of thought combining humanism and Christianity that culminated in Pico's *Oration* ultimately led: as we have seen, the conception of the Creation performed by a personal God transmitted the same characteristics that were attributed to the Creator—namely, will and self-determination—to the human creature. Once human beings were invested with these prerogatives, in Pico's narrative, they seemed entirely free to choose their own place in the ascending scale leading from *ferinitas* to *divinitas*. Based on a choice that was in no way predetermined and that placed humans above every other being, whether living or non-

living, they could fashion themselves in any form they liked, ranging from the bestial to the divine.

Now, this is exactly the point from which Bruno takes his distance. The possibility of *deificatio*, with the removal of the human from any proximity to the animal, was made possible in the Neoplatonic model by the clear primacy of the soul, or reason, over the body. The individual soul, in its essential difference from its somatic dwelling, was what made it possible to sever the animal root that put man in touch with God. This is the opposite of the increasingly defined thesis maintained by Bruno, who, in opposition to the paradigm of personal identity, recognized in the indissolubility of the relation between body and soul the necessity of the relation between the human and the animal. The point of departure lies in the emphasis he allots to the body compared to the Platonic tradition, but this can be equally applied to the whole of modern philosophy from Descartes to Heidegger, passing through Kant and Hegel. It comes to the fore not only in certain stylistic or biographical traits expressed in Bruno's forceful polemic against Petrarchan spiritualism, but also in a precise doctrine, albeit with some vacillations, culminating in his denial of the immortality of the individual soul. To begin with, in opposition to the presupposed division between a rational part and another, corporeal part that is subordinated to it, Bruno affirmed the indissolubility of the two: the one can never escape the presence, or even the hold, of the other. Not only that, but in a certain sense he inverts the relation of dominance, steering it away from the advantage that the soul has in the Platonic and Christian tradition and orienting it toward the body. True, according to the principle of the transmigration of the soul that he espouses, the behavior of the soul in the past decides which body it will be placed in next; but it is the conformation of the chosen body that establishes the terms within which the soul can then act. By using the body it comes to inhabit as an expressive device, the soul is molded and in some way redefined by it in the realm of its effective performative possibilities. Prior to souls, then, bodies—their anatomical composition, their physiological activity, their biological quality—are what make the difference between different individuals, and even between different living species.

In short, what for the humanistic tradition was an essence becomes for Bruno determined by nature. If the difference between human beings as well as between the human and all other living species is measured by what their bodies are able to accomplish, this means that the order of cause and effect is altered. Compared to all the other inhabitants of the universe, it is not that they have the kind of body they have because they are human; rather, they are human because they have that kind of body. The ensuing inversion, as far as classical anthropology is concerned, is evident. It could be said that the whole process of anthropogenesis is impacted by this reversal and reconfigured in a way that brings into play not only the relationship between nature and history, but also that between life and technics. As has been noted by others, the civilizing function that Bruno attributes to the hand in this dynamic is decisive.[28] While in *The Expulsion of the Triumphant Beast* the hand is still in some ways subordinate to the guidance of the intellect, in *The Cabala of Pegasus* it becomes the driving force of the hominization process. By opening up access to the higher activities, the hand projects human beings into the world of history. But what is most striking is the distance, and the inversion, this view takes from the Aristotelian theory of origin, although without bringing it any closer to the teleological ideas associated with Calvinism. While Aristotle places the role of the hand in a teleological horizon, defined by the superior destiny that humans were assigned from the outset, and Calvinism considers it a means of redemption from sin through work, the Italian philosopher identifies in it the biodetermined passage from the sphere of nature to the sphere of culture—not in the sense of their opposition, but rather, as an intrinsic relationship that makes one the continuation of the other: the hand is the natural vector along which life encounters technics, or to be more precise, where it recognizes its originally technological character. Unlike what the new modern philosophies were theorizing, the artifactual is not something additional or alternative to nature, created by humans to free themselves from their bodily constraints; rather, it is their very effect, transferred from the realm of necessity to the never definitively attained realm of freedom. This is where the break from both Aristotelian and Neoplatonic finalism occurs: humans do not have a hand because they are what they are (in other words, human); rather, they are what they are because, having hands, they

28. For more on the topic of the hand in Bruno see Aniello Montano, *La mente e la mano: Aspetti e storicità del sapere e del primato del fare in Giordano Bruno* (Naples: La Città del Sole, 2000); Fulvio Papi, *Antropologia e civiltà nel pensiero del nolano* (Naples, 2006); Nuccio Ordine, *Contro il Vangelo armato: Giordano Bruno, Ronsard e la religione* (Milan: Cortina, 2007).

can make the anthropic leap that enables them to perform actions that other living beings are incapable of carrying out. The diversity arising from this is not one of essence, but of potency [*potenza*], thus rendering the human a different animal from the others in terms of aptitudes and skills, but without signaling the ontological primacy of the human.

The relationship between the human and the animal may well represent the most disruptive element in Bruno's philosophy; perhaps Nietzsche is the only other author in all of Western thought to have taken it to such a radical degree.[29] In *The Cabala of Pegasus*, he has the ass Onorio tell us that "Fate not only fails to differentiate the human body from the [body of the] ass, and the body of the animals from the body of things thought to be without soul, but even in the genus of spiritual matter Fate treats the asinine soul no differently than the human, and the spirit that constitutes those so-called animals than what is found in all things."[30] In this rightly famous passage, Bruno does not stop at juxtaposing species whose biological structure is similar in many aspects, like that of humans and higher mammals; he brings them all back to a single substance out of which all things, even inanimate ones, arise. This is not a marginal theme or an underground artery: it is the deep core of his reflection that, from one dialogue to the next, drives his thought beyond its own limits. The animal is not only homologous with the human, it forms a part of it; just as the human in its turn is part of the animal world.[31] The animal is also its past and its future, since the principle of metamorphosis, mentioned by Bruno when recounting his own life history, makes the human soul "the same in specific and generic essence as that of flies, sea oysters, and plants, and of anything whatsoever that one finds animated or having a soul."[32] Of course, once the immortality of the individual soul has been negated in the endless loop of metasomatism, there still remains a difference of principle between the souls of humans and those of beasts: while the former keep their memory

29. See the recent book by Vanessa Lemm, *Nietzsche's Animal Philosophy: Culture, Politics, and the Animality of the Human Being* (New York: Fordham University Press, 2009).

30. Giordano Bruno, *Cabala del cavallo Pegaseo*, in *Dialoghi italiani*, vol. 2, p. 883; English version: *The Cabala of Pegasus*, trans. Sidney L. Sondergard and Madison U. Sowell (New Haven, CT: Yale University Press, 2002), p. 54.

31. For more specifically on asininity, see Nuccio Ordine, *La cabala dell'asino: Asinità e conoscenza in Giordano Bruno* (Naples: Liguori, 1996).

32. Bruno, *Cabala*, p. 56.

of their previous lives, the latter do not. But they are still made of the same vital substance, which they return to as fragments of the universal spirit from whence they had all come. Rarely in the corpus of ancient and modern philosophy has an author pushed so far ahead in the identification of the principle of life that the very lineaments of the human are dissolved in it, together with all the prejudices and claims of primacy of one civilization over another. The fact that a view of this sort was created within—and at the same time against—a movement of ideas called "humanism" is further testament to the antinomic force that characterizes Italian thought: a force that situates it outside the most recognized confines of modern thought, but also, and for the same reason, close to our contemporary world.

The Body of History

1. Can Vico's thought be connected to that of Machiavelli and Bruno along a path that describes the foundational trait of Italian philosophy? Before answering yes to this question, we need to be careful not to lose sight of the specificity of their works, life histories, and languages, all of which are too closely tied to their particular circumstances to allow them to be located on the same orbital trajectory. On a purely textual level, moreover, Vico never made reference to Bruno, and on several occasions he even launched a firm critique against Machiavelli. And yet, it doesn't seem to me that this puts the question to rest. If they are read against the backdrop of the philosophical knowledge of their times, several common characteristics come into view. To begin with, their choice to use the vernacular is something that goes far beyond a mere stylistic option. Vivid images, poetic inventions, and expressions drawn from nonphilosophical lexicons like those of medicine, magic, and myth make them equidistant from the formalized language of modern philosophy.[33] But this shared lexical anomaly, often interpreted in terms of conceptual backwardness, conveys an even more significant affinity with regard to the question of the origin, a

33. On Vico's linguistic heterogeneity, see Enrico Nuzzo, *Tra ordine della storia e storicità: Saggi sui saperi della storia in Vico* (Rome: Edizioni di Storia e Letteratura, 2001), pp. 46 ff. By the same author and on similar themes, this time regarding Bruno, see "Le figure metaforiche nel linguaggio filosofico di Giordano Bruno," in *La mente di Giordano Bruno*, ed. Fabrizio Meroi (Florence: Olschki, 2004), with an introduction by Michele Ciliberto, pp. 13–60.

decisive one from all points of view. For each of these three Italian authors, regardless of how we may construe the origin, it is not to be located in the founding will of a group of subjects; but rather, in the depths of an animal life that breaks through the confines of human consciousness, connecting it with something preceding it and going beyond it. On another level, this also applies to the beginning of knowledge: understood less as a point of light destined to suddenly illuminate the world, and more as a process internal to the inquiring object and, therefore, enshrouded in the opacity of its historical depth. The shared concrete, corporeal, material language adopted by these authors is simply their way of translating into the present of knowledge that vast area of pre-reflexive experience out of which it arose; and from which it cannot detach itself, unless it is willing to close itself off in some abstract, arid jargon. From this angle, too, then, the origin, with all the energy and violence it bears with it, is not an archaic moment confined to a past that would better be abandoned, but the hollowed out bedrock underlying all of human history, forever ready to rise to the surface the instant we presume to rid ourselves of it.

Of course the reference to history as such only applies to Vico. While it is true that Machiavelli and Bruno also look at human affairs in terms of evolution, their approach does not open up a fully historical horizon. Despite the emphasis on contingency and chance, the image of the wheel of time that both use alludes to a circular repetition that ends up crushing the novelty of the present onto the predefined tracing of the past: in the short course of one's life, it is only given to extraordinary individuals to experience a destiny different from what has been preordained. It was Vico who introduced human life into the complex and dramatic dimension of history, thus projecting himself not only beyond the Italian culture of the late Renaissance, but also beyond the dominant vectors in the philosophical discourse of modernity; to begin with, certainly beyond the Cartesian project, halted at the exact relation between truth and consciousness, but also beyond the natural law jurists represented by Grotius, Selden, and Pufendorf, and beyond the political philosophy of Hobbes, Locke, and Spinoza. While the natural law jurists generally made beginning and development coincide in their definition of a state of nature, as Vico saw it, by explaining the course of history as a senseless interweaving of utility and necessity, the political philosophers lost any general criterion for interpreting it. What gets lost in both cases is the relationship between the form of history and its origin: which is exactly the subject of that singular genealogy to which Vico devoted his greatest work. However, what makes it unique to European philosophical culture when compared to the knowledge of his time is not only what may well be called "the invention of history," but, above all, its irreducibility to the Enlightenment and idealist philosophies of history that were soon to occupy the field.[34] This inassimilability is predicated partly on his Christian orthodoxy, but primarily on his dissonance with the canon of providential history established by Augustine along a path that led to Bossuet. His deviation from this theological model is exactly what also removed the Viconian paradigm from its secularization in historicist terms, so to speak.

The point of contention lies in his rejection of the linearity that characterized both the Augustinian paradigm and its modern transvaluation, albeit in differing and opposing forms: for the former, in terms of transcendence; and for the latter, in terms of immanence. While Augustine brought profane history back to sacred history, modern historicism reversed the terms of their unification, incorporating the salvific core of sacred history into the telos of profane history. To Augustine's complete theologizing of history, historicism responded by fully temporalizing history. While in the first, all of history was concentrated and seemingly resolved in the instant of origin; in the second, the origin, understood as the beginning of the sequence of events, is what gets embedded, and thus dissolved, in history. Now, the disruptive and even disconcerting character of Vico's theory lies precisely in its protrusion outside both these interpretive schemes. For him, sacred history neither subsumes profane history nor is resolved in it. There remains an unbridgeable gap between the two that simultaneously incites and curbs historical development.[35] While sacred history unfolds seamlessly into a form that cannot be defined as historical in all respects, precisely because it coincides entirely with the divine principle, profane history arises only subsequently, without ever reuniting with sacred history.[36] Although profane history is also initially set into motion by Providence—according to an eternal ideal order that the human mind

---

34. On this topic, see Mario Papini, *Il geroglifico della storia* (Bologna: Cappelli, 1984).

35. See Biagio de Giovanni, "Sul cominciamento della storia in Vico," in *Luoghi del pensare*, ed. Enrica Lisciani (Milan: Petrini, 2005), pp. 13–29.

36. On the question of the different "histories" in Vico, see Paolo Rossi, *I segni del tempo: Storia della terra e storia delle nazioni da Hooke a Vico* (Milan: Feltrinelli, 1979).

strives to reconstruct—it is incapable of adhering fully to that order and is indeed cyclically inclined to deviate from it in a catastrophic fashion. But an even more unsettling consequence of the Viconian paradigm is the following: if the start of profane history does not coincide with that of sacred history, it means that its beginning is located precisely at the point where time splits into two diverging branches that are destined to never again intersect. Constitutively external to the sacred temporality that precedes it, the origin of our history turns out to be outside the time from which it nevertheless arose. Now it is this externality of time to the origin—both prior and subsequent to it—that distances Vico's thought from the complete temporalization of history back to which one of the most powerful immune devices of modernity can be traced: there is a moment of history that does not belong to time and that, precisely for this reason, can literally suck history into its temporal void as soon as we think we can rid ourselves of the origin once and for all.

The decentralization this asymmetry causes to the entire Viconian theory of history is clear. Not only is history split structurally into two levels—one metaphysical and the other empirical—running on parallel planes; but the empirical plane, the only one on which human beings can effectively act, multiplies into several temporalities that are distinguished from one another by the different relationship each has to the origin. The hermeneutic perspective also has to be adapted continually to the multiplicity of the material, so as to take different angles when viewing different objects: ages, customs, languages. But the most complicating factor resides in the fact that the origin itself, on which the entire spectrum of differences depends, is opaque to our gaze, since it is impenetrable to all historically formed knowledges, and, even more so, to the logical/systematic and deductive one that has taken the upper hand in modernity. Not because of its rather obvious inadequacy (how can the language of reason grasp something that infinitely precedes it?), but primarily because of the nature of the origin, which is ungraspable in itself. That the origin is "prehistoric"—situated prior to history—must be understood in the literal sense that it is not representable by any of the historically formed languages. It always comes before the beginning—the secondary, derivative one that the historically formed languages are able to glimpse from time to time, imagining that they have captured it at last. It comes earlier than the earliest; it precedes every predecessor; it antedates every antecedent.

This continuous retreat of the origin—not only with respect to the gaze that tries in vain to bring it into focus, but also with regard to the originary character of the origin itself—is the most difficult yet most astonishing aspect of the Viconian genealogy. Like Nietzsche's genealogy, and later Foucault's—although in ways that are hardly comparable—Vico's genealogy also rests on an empty spot around which the entire discourse seems to gravitate. The genealogical, properly speaking, is knowledge about the origin, but about an origin that is structurally ungraspable. On these lines, because any historiography would be blind without it, genealogy is just as necessary as it is impossible. Indeed, what is necessary is exactly its impossibility.

2. But Vico does not stop at simply signaling the unrepresentability of the origin. He makes an ingenious attempt to give expression to it. He tries to represent this unrepresentability, in a contradictory fashion, of course. How? First of all, by giving up on expressive means that hinder or distort its expression—starting with the logical/deductive language used by the philosophy of his time that was held to be the only one adequate for the realm of thought.[37] If there is no general method of investigation, since "doctrines must take their beginning from that of the matters of which they treat,"[38] we must adopt a language that is akin to its object. This is the completely unprecedented undertaking that Vico embarks upon in his laborious composition of *The New Science*. Already laid out in the metaphysical image serving as frontispiece to the entire text, it is most clearly discernible in the sections on the contiguous and not always distinguishable ages of men and heroes. Two aspects qualify it: the abundant use of classical myth; and the intended archaism of words, which are removed from their more usual meaning and brought back to their etymon, sometimes in an imaginative fashion—even arriving unabashedly at onomatopoeia—in a sort of degree-zero regression. In the far less extensive section dedicated to the age of men, however, a different tonal register is adopted, where the language of myth

37. On the irreducibility of Vico's language to the language of reason see Stephan Otto and Vincenzo Vitiello, *La memoria e il sacro* (Naples: La Città del Sole, 2001); Vitiello has condensed his complex interpretation of Vico in *Vico: Storia, linguaggio, natura* (Rome: Edizioni di Storia e Letteratura, 2008).

38. Giambattista Vico, *The New Science* (1744), trans. Thomas Goddard Bergin and Max Harold Fisch (Ithaca, NY: Cornell University Press, 1948), § 314, p. 82.

seems to give ground, gradually, to the language of reason, although never exiting the stage altogether, as if to signal that the process of the rationalization of the world is always incomplete and amply reversible.

But then, if this is the procedure he adopts, how does Vico relate to the scene of the origin, which, retreating further and further away from every possible representation, is seated in the heart of the Unrepresentable? He chooses the logically destabilizing route of naming it through its opposite—of filling in its irreducible absence by an overflowing presence. In any case, how else can something that eludes representation be represented except by turning it into its opposite? This is the only way to give voice to its constitutive antinomy—to express all of its inexpressibility. This is how that semantic gash, that void of meaning inscribed in the order of discourse by the origin, is traced back, with a brilliant symbolic inversion, to the highly dense figure of the body.[39] Originally there is nothing but body: "From body is born time; and from body and from time, which is measured with the motion of body . . . comes chance."[40] This point is worth noting: at the origin of time—before time, in other words—there was no contingency of chance; there was only the intrusive density of the body. This is the first break in that process of total temporalization to which the concept of history was soon to be led by modern philosophical reflection. There is something—the prehistoric beginning of history—that protrudes from the empty dimension of time and the abstractness of its linear motion. From there, from that corpulent, heavy substance, everything—the sky, the world, human beings, knowledge, and power—have their start. At their wellspring, human minds "were not in the least abstract, refined, or spiritualized, because they were entirely immersed in the senses, buffeted by the passions, buried in the body."[41] So, whoever wants to form a picture of their origin must take root in the dark, seething matter of the primordial world,

---

39. On the semantics of the body in Vico, see Biagio de Giovanni, "'Corpo' e 'ragione' in Spinoza e Vico," in Roberto Esposito et al., *Divenire della ragione moderna* (Naples: Liguori, 1981), pp. 93–165.

40. "Vico's Reprehension of the Metaphysics of René Descartes, Benedict Spinoza, and John Locke," trans. and commentary by Donald Phillip Verene, in *Giambattista Vico: Keys to the New Science; Translations, Commentaries, and Essays*, trans. and ed. Thora Ilin Bayer and Donald Phillip Verene (Ithaca, NY: Cornell University Press, 2009), pp. 179–98. This quote appears on p. 182.

41. Vico, *New Science*, § 378, p. 106.

running backward through the phylogenetic process of hominization. Moreover, in so doing, Vico will simply be indulging a primitive attitude of our mind, which being "immersed and buried in the body, . . . naturally inclines to take notice of bodily things, and finds the effort to attend to itself too laborious; just as the bodily eye sees all objects outside itself but needs a mirror to see itself.[42] Not surprisingly, "in all languages the greater part of the expressions relating to inanimate things are formed by metaphor from the human body and its parts and from the human senses and passions."[43] Thus "head," "eyes," "mouth," "tooth," "arm," "foot," "heart," and all the other parts of the body are terms used metaphorically to describe natural elements, inanimate objects, and abstract ideas. This is because the origin of life itself, in all its expressions—material and ideal, sensory and cognitive, emotional and intellectual—is embedded in that corporeal magma from which it can never fully detach itself. In its beginnings and in its development, this is none other than the living body, the life of the body— even when life tends to separate from the body by acceding to a spiritual dimension. It is significant that at a time when modern knowledge, at least since Descartes, had situated itself at a conspicuous distance from the body, Vico—like Machiavelli and Bruno—kept it steadily in view. For him, the "doctrines," like their "matters," are completely constituted, traversed, and determined by the dense and material presence of bodies: by their position, relation, and proportion.

The *New Science* itself, the story it narrates, takes its cue from the "vast bodies" of the giants who wandered ceaselessly through the great forest that grew after the universal flood.[44] Never has the knot between body and beginning been so tightly bound as in these creatures. After the divine punishment, life began to germinate once again in beings who were entirely identified with their bodies. As would never happen again, they were all body and only body. But the reference to the body does not suffice, as such, to convey the originary condition. If, with Vico, we penetrate into the dense vegetation of the forest out of which everything began, we come across something—as in an excess of meaning—that oversteps the boundaries of the body, and that is part and parcel of this trespassing; to wit, its collective character, which is irreducible to the individual-

42. Ibid, § 331, p. 85.
43. Ibid., § 405, p. 116.
44. Ibid., § 520, p. 160.

ity of separate organisms. What qualifies the bodies of the giants—their brute bestiality—is not only their hyperbolic, disproportionate, overflowing quantity, but the overflowing itself, the absence of constitutive limits. The body of the giants is so enormous that it oversteps its boundaries. As a matter of fact, they became the way they were—gigantic, that is—because of the abnormal exertion of their muscles required to break through the impenetrability of the forest; and from the salts in the sea water, which made them "excessively big in brawn and bone," until they attained a "gigantic stature."[45] The decisive element in this account is the excessiveness that precludes form. Their life is certainly characterized by their body, but by a body that resists any form: it is formless, unformed, deformed. Not a "form of life," but a life without form, just as one would imagine for beings "destitute of any human custom and deprived of any human speech, and so in a state of wild animals."[46] This is another way for Vico to force representation—to represent its very unrepresentability rather than its content. All the elements in the picture, starting from gigantism, are intended to break through it, to project it beyond the limits of its frame, toward a horizon without ends/terms [*termini*], one that is literally "endless/exterminated" [*sterminato*]. Rather than a *mundus*, it is an *immundus*, in both the ethical and spatial senses of the word. As the "wetness" of the forest alludes to a flooding that overflows the river banks,[47] in the same way, the "beasts" that populate it are the biological product of flesh that is no longer contained within the confines of the body—of an ultrabody that seeps out of its semantic profile. In the same way, their wandering aimlessly without direction is the sign of a decentering so irremediable that it unhinges any perspectival distance between background and foreground, confusing the perspectives by endlessly multiplying them.

Nothing conveys the world of the forest better than "confusion."[48] It confuses—fuses together—the elements that compose it, thus depriving them of their proper differential status. This is because, in its excess beyond representation, it represents the very opposite of difference—namely the indifference that erases the distinction between the one and the other,

---

45. Ibid., § 369, p. 101.

46. Ibid., § 62, p. 34.

47. Ibid., § 62, p. 34; § 540, p. 169.

48. For more on the forest, the classic book by Enzo Paci, *Ingens sylva: Saggio su Vico* (Milan: Mondadori, 1949), is required reading.

positive and negative, human and animal. The people who inhabit the forest are not solely human, but neither are they purely animal, because they do not fall within the genealogical enclosure of a single species. In their extralegal life, in their blind wandering, they are unable to trace a specific line or to transmit a clear genetic identity along a generational strand. Neither *ghenos* nor *ethnos* identifies them or grants them some membership, place, or proper being. Not only is the proper—like individuality, difference, and discontinuity—what they are not, it is also their antonym, since what characterizes them is precisely its contrary, which is to say, the improper. Or, even more profoundly, the *common*. It is precisely this element in the body and beyond the body of the giant that represents the unrepresentable origin of the nonhuman, of a human defined by its not being such, or by its being other than itself: human-beast or beast-human. And "savage communism [ferina comunità]," "nefarious holding of women and property in common [nefaria comunione]," is defined by Vico using a term—as has been rightly noted[49]—never used elsewhere with the same meaning of trespassing and mixture. Unlike the *civitas*, but also the *societas* of the archaic families, the *communitas* of the human-beasts is confusion of human seeds, of women, and of blood. It is here—in this "disbelonging" of each with respect to the all, in this lack of distinction that causes bodies to be confused with one another and humors to be mixed—that life has its beginnings, expressing its expansive potency to the maximum. But it is also the place where the expansion of life degenerates: it escapes out of its genus, to get lost in its own otherness, in the irretrievable alterity of each "proper." This is the ambivalence recalled by the unpresentable antinomy of the origin— the historical inconsistency of a body so full of itself that it is swallowed up by its own lack of distinction. In a key paragraph of the *New Science*, the chaos of the origin, represented in the form of a limitless all, suddenly precipitates into a semantic void that has the appearance of nothingness: the theological poets "imagined it as Orcus, a misshapen monster which devoured all things, because men in this infamous community [infame comunione] did not have the proper form of men, and were swallowed up by the void because through the uncertainty of offspring they left nothing

49. Gennaro Carillo, *Origine e genealogia dell'ordine* (Naples: Editoriale Scientifica, 2000), p. 210. Carillo was the first critic to recognize the constitutive function of the *communitas/immunitas* dialectic in Vico. For "ferina comunità" see § 17; for "nefaria comunione" § 16.

of themselves. This [chaos] was later taken by the physicists as the prime matter of natural things, which, formless itself, is greedy for forms and devours all forms."[50]

3. However, the self-dissolutive drift of the originary community does not definitively preclude the possibility of history—on the contrary, it is precisely what makes history possible. For Vico, properly human history arises out of the exhaustion of an origin incapable of making itself the effective beginning of a permanent process. Besides, how could the formless and promiscuous *communitas* ever have transformed itself into *civitas* or *societas* if the *munus* that constitutes *communitas* bears with it a principle of internal dissipation that bars it from any consolidation? In order to allow the transition from that "before," refractory to its own representation, to an "after"—to start a continuous line of historical sequence—there must be an event that has the force and clarity of a new beginning. In Vico's narrative strategy, the flash of lightning that breaks up the darkness of the forest, ripping the giants from their unreflective lives, responds to this need. It has a distinctly theological/political flavor, in the sense that the terror it provokes in the humans opens the world to the possibility of both religion and politics. From their juncture originates the decisive figure of the *auctoritas*, without whose ordering impulse, "human society cannot stand for a moment."[51] It releases an opposite, propulsive impulse, diametrically opposed to the chaotic and disorderly impulse of the originary community. While the latter is full of body to the point of exploding, authority is directed toward the mind: in order to be interpreted, it presupposes or produces the first emancipation from the immediacy of the senses. While the forest is characterized by a mixing of individuals, genera, and species—and therefore by the absence of boundaries—*auctoritas* decides: it cuts the earth's surface with the sword or with the plow, sectioning it into different areas. Finally, if the originary community was devoid of forms—as a *zoe* that has not yet reached the determinateness of the *bios*—authority puts life back into shape, educating how "to bring forth in a certain way the form of the human soul which had been completely submerged in the vast bodies of the giants."[52] If we wanted to trace all these procedures to a sin-

---

50. Ibid., § 688, p. 232.
51. Ibid., § 1100, p. 379.
52. Ibid., § 520, p. 160.

gle dispositif, one that is opposite in its logic and its effects to the dissolutive semantics of *communitas*, we can only return to that of immunization, already mentioned on several occasions. From this angle, Vico not only shows himself to be at the height of modern self-reflection, he also captures an essential element of it with a radicalism equal to that of Hobbes: if life seeks to preserve itself—this is the thesis of both thinkers—it must compress its corporeal power [*potenza*] into apparatuses of command and obedience designed to protect it from its own excess. This need is fulfilled by *conatus*: "For the giants, confined under the mountains by the frightful religion of the thunderbolts, learned to restrain their bestial habit of wandering wild through the great forest of the earth."[53] In a word, the establishment of order is dependent on a dual process, parallel and criss-crossing, of restraint and abstraction: on the one hand, it keeps life contained within stable forms; and on the other, it releases life from its primitive corporeal bond, freeing it for higher activities of an intellectual type. If we go back over the process of social differentiation—initially generated by the protection afforded by the "heroes" to the "miserable," threatened by the "impious" who were left in the extralegal state—what can be recognized in its crucial moments is the self-preservational dialectic of human history. Both the salvific function of the "restraint" placed by Vico at the center of all the theological/political hubs of civilization, and the equally constitutive function of fear that initially triggers it, confirm the starkly immunitary direction embarked on by human history at the twilight of the originary community. It is based on the biopolitical exchange between protection and salvation: "These refugees were received by the heroes under the just law of protection, by which they preserved their natural lives under the obligation of serving the heroes as day laborers."[54] Outside this first circle there is only death for those who do not submit to the law of the strong. Once *bios* has arisen out of the opaque background of *zoe*, it can only develop inside the armed enclosure of established order. The gradual process of humanization—inaugurated by Hercules setting fire to the Nemean forest—does not wipe out the hierarchical demarcation that separates groups of humans who are granted different degrees of mastery over each other. Their correspondence to the different phases of ancient Roman law—from the secretization of the laws to their communication to the plebs—indi-

53. Ibid., § 504, p. 153.
54. Ibid., § 555, p. 176.

cates the universalistic direction that the process of civilization took, but also the coercive sort of bond that it involved.[55] The full right of the *patres* presupposes the submission of all those who remained under their hand, until, through a series of transitions that cannot be reduced to a single path, that bond seems to have yielded. Its disappearance, or its loosening, at least, is testified by the advent of popular monarchies, "by which the monarchs seek to make their subjects all equal" and "whereby sovereigns humble the powerful and thus keep the masses safe and free from oppressions" while keeping "the multitude satisfied and content as regards the necessaries of life and the enjoyment of popular liberty."[56] This is the ultimate point attainable by modern history, when "a complete humanity seems to be spread abroad through all nations, for a few great monarchs rule over this world of peoples."[57] With it, the originary, despotic regime seems to reverse itself in the full satisfaction of vital needs. The necessity for the protection of life appears to be reconciled with its facilitated development, offering order with freedom, force with legitimacy, and power [*potere*] with right [*diritto*]. The gap between ideal, eternal history and real history is minimized by an immunitary procedure designed to eliminate the now isolated and dispersed remains of the ancient savage community.

And yet, as we know, this is not Vico's last word on the subject. *The New Science* does not close with the certainty that conditions will be equaled and humanity will be unconditionally developed. There is a critical point where this progression is abruptly reversed into its opposite, opening up a catastrophic scenario that in Viconian language takes the celebrated name of "recourse." This is not just a snag in the process that shows up to delay a still achievable outcome, but a structural imbalance that calls into question all the results obtained up to that point. Contrary to how it might have appeared, the crisis is not a hitch that at some point interrupts an otherwise completed process, but something that has marked it indelibly since its beginning. This means that, rather than coming from the outside, it is implicit in its very machinery—that is to say, in that general immunitary mechanism designed to protect against the dissolutive effects of the originary community. Of course, without it, without those "stern re-

55. On the ambivalence of the civilizing process in Vico, see Riccardo Caporali, *Heroes gentium: Sapienza e politica in Vico* (Bologna: Il Mulino, 1992).

56. Vico, *New Science*, § 1008, p. 341; translation slightly adapted to reflect the original.

57. Ibid., § 1089, p. 371.

straints of frightful religions,"[58] prearranged by Providence to block the energy expenditure of the forest, history would never have existed—life itself would have been irretrievably consumed, as the great political philosophy of the moderns saw so clearly. But the extraordinary intuition that places the thought of Vico outside and beyond theirs is that the process of immunization is not viable ad infinitum, because it bears within itself a negative force that is destined, at some point, to turn against itself, thereby blocking the life that it is ordered to safeguard. This ultramodern awareness, so to speak, is strikingly clear not only in the conclusion of the work but in all its decisive passages. It is true that left to itself—to its corporeal excess, to the promiscuous confusion of its members—the *communitas* does not last; it does not create history. But this does not imply that its absolute opposite—total immunization—leads to a lesser risk, if not of explosion, of implosion of the body politic in which it inheres. This is because, by putting life out of danger from the excess of the "common," it inevitably creates a hypertrophy of the "proper." The threat that weighs on the process of civilization from the beginning is in fact identified by Vico in the difference between individual interests and collective interest—in the anything but hypothetical possibility that the proper might diverge so radically from the common so as to annihilate it.

This particularistic and appropriative drift, in a world secularized by the dissolution of the theological/political bond, is parallel and consequent to the progressive separation of the mind from the body. The violent erasure of the originary forest, as well as being a reduction of the *communitas*, marks a progressive abstraction from its bodily content. All of history, both ancient and modern, is involved in its practices and forms of knowledge. Both are subjected to a progressive process of formalization, or spiritualization, which is allied with the acceleration of the immunitary dynamic. Human history immunizes itself from the ungovernable effects of the bodily impulses—instincts, senses, passions. But this separation from the body—intended to save and strengthen life—ends up distancing it from its own vital content, from its energetic source and constitutive energy. For this reason, with the rise of the barbarism of reflection, the extreme remedy foreseen by Providence is a return to the basic needs of the body, to the prime "utilities of life."[59] Vico's response to the immunitary crisis—

58. Ibid., § 554, p. 175.
59. Ibid., § 699, p. 236.

like a kind of autoimmune disease caused by an excess of the proper—is a forced return to common elements, which had never really entirely disappeared. The "multitude" mentioned earlier—heir to the Roman plebs in their resistance to the order of the optimates and as the new subject of the popular republics—bears its imprint not only in its collective conformation but also in a corporeality rooted in the animal. Fittingly, it was Nessus the centaur—the bearer in his very body of the hybridization between the species—who with his blood infected the hero that had set the immune process in motion by setting fire to the forest. But the tragic character of human history lies in the fact that the multitude, once it has been emancipated and has become the subject of its own destiny, loses its common vocation in the interest of individual utility. This is how that delicate balance between community and immunity that provided the only possibility of survival for our species was disrupted. Vico is perhaps the only philosopher who (expressed in his own language, naturally) glimpsed both the historical necessity of this connection and the possibility of its catastrophic unraveling. The supreme risk does not lie, as the "moderns" believed, in the dissipation of a life driven beyond itself by its common passion. Rather, it lies in its inversion into an opposite condition which, by separating life from the body, causes its original substance to be lost. Both community and immunity, divided by their opposite, bring life to the brink of the precipice. They come up against "barbarism": from which community directly originates, and which immunity reactivates in an even more threatening form, if that were possible. The only remaining option to prevent us from plunging backward is to keep our eyes on the line of tangency that simultaneously separates and connects them, making one the irreducible content of the other. Along that tangent, perilously "in time," is where human history runs.

PASSAGE II: IN THE VORTEX OF THE *BATTLE*

We have seen how diverse authors like Machiavelli, Vico, and Bruno are connected in a single horizon by their common engagement with an origin that is not only unattainable—since it is both left behind and projected ahead—but also ambivalent, charged with vital energy and yet bearing an obscure threat. If pressed to identify a symbolic representation of it in Italian Renaissance art, I wouldn't hesitate to choose the legendary *Battle of Anghiari*, painted by Leonardo da Vinci in the Hall of the Great Council in the Palazzo Vecchio in Florence. The first reason for my choice lies in the premature and definitive disappearance of the work. Like the painting by Michelangelo, depicting the Battle of Cascina, that was supposed to flank it—and that never came to light, except in a preparatory cartoon that was soon destroyed—it deteriorated while still being painted, practically dissolving away. Walled up after only a few decades by Giorgio Vasari during the renovations to the room—which from then on became the Hall of the Five Hundred—all traces of the painting have been lost to us. Although it cannot be completely excluded that whatever may remain of it lies hidden in a hollow space in the wall, it is in any case invisible to our eyes. Even the causes of its deterioration are not entirely clear. While probably due to a misguided use of what is known as the encaustic technique described by Pliny, and which turned out to be unsuitable for the tall wall height, other sources blame it on poor paint materials or defective plaster. Whatever the cause may be, the fact remains that even before disappearing into nothingness the painting had already been abandoned by its creator, who limited himself to painting only the central scene of the total fifty-six-by-twenty-three-foot space and left all the rest unfinished. While it is true that Leonardo left for Milan in May 1506—the work had been started more than two years previously—this doesn't entirely explain his decision to leave unfinished a work that had been commissioned and partially paid for by the Chancellery of the Republic, especially seeing as it had garnered intense interest from the outset, to the extent of being defined by Benvenuto Cellini, along with the drawing by Michelangelo, as "the school of the world." Especially striking is the contrast between the absence of the painting and the number of reproductions that for more than a century continually retransmitted its image—even by artists of the caliber of Peter Paul Rubens, to whom we owe the last and most famous reworking of the painting, shown in Figure 6, which was copied in its turn from a previous sixteenth-century copy. On the basis of a late source, but one of questionable credibility, the original cartoon by Leonardo supposedly stayed in Florence, specifically in the Palazzo Medici Riccardi, until the end of the eighteenth century. But it is more likely that it had been dismembered by the artist himself into smaller partial cartoons, some of which were brought to France where they could have been seen by Rubens.

1. Leonardo da Vinci, study of a horseman from the *Battle of Anghiari*. Pen and ink with watercolor highlights on prepared pink paper. Paris, Musée du Louvre. (Photo by Jean-Gilles Berizzi / RMN / Archivi Alinari, Florence.)

Although the only thing that remains to us of the original painting—unfinished, dissolved, dispersed—are copies of differing value and faithfulness, there are, however, a series of sketches, even closer to the original, in the form of preparatory materials in the artist's hand, that give an idea of what it must have been like. Essentially, these are five drawings, now in the Gallerie dell'Accademia in Venice, depicting the central scene that was actually painted; a few sketches of horses rearing or galloping, presumably intended for the parts that were never executed, now kept in the Royal Library at Windsor and in the British Museum in London; two head studies of three of the horsemen, preserved in the Szépmüvészeti Múzeum of Budapest; and a full, stylized figure, archived at the Institut de France. Taken all together, the impression given by these drawings is both extraordinary and disconcerting. It is as if there were a spark in each of them, a flash of the future painting—the uncontrollability of the galloping horses, the fragility of the vanquished riders, the animal ferocity of the faces—but in a form that is irreducible to the compositional unity of a single subject. Not surprisingly, the attempts made by critics to link them together into a whole expressive of the entire work have been unsuccessful, proving inadequate on the one hand and forced on the other. Either way, they fail to present us with the ultimate meaning—which is to say, the first meaning—of what was intended to be their final result. This instead remains covered and removed from visibility by a wall that is not only material—like the one some people believe still protects it today and keeps it from our view. Crushed or torn, somewhere between even more originary fragments and subsequent copies, the origin—the originality—of the text, its overwhelming truth, remains obscured, enveloped in a thick fog. Unless its truth consists precisely in this obscurity—in a void of figuration that is also the figuration of a void: a vortex that sucks representation itself into its blind spot. If this were indeed the case, then the unrepresentable that so many have attempted to reveal by means of new and invariably inadequate reproductions would not only be the obstacle—the wall of invisibility that hides the painting—it would also, somehow, be its secret content. This would suggest that Leonardo tried to paint something so elusive, or even so terrible, that it escapes representation—that it must necessarily remain unfinished, before being swallowed up into nothingness.

Truth be told, something of the sort was said about Leonardo's entire oeuvre, starting with Baldassare Castiglione, who faulted him for having "set himself to study philosophy; in which he has such strange conceptions and new chimeras, that he could not with all his painter's art depict them."[60] Even today Martin Kemp still recalls for us the legend—more than just that in reality—that Leonardo was apparently "unable to complete projects,"[61] and enumerates his unfinished works, from the *Adoration of the Magi* to the equestrian monuments. I think the question, as a whole, must be referred back to the complex relationship that the artist established between painting and ideation. On the one hand, we know that for Leonardo painting was not only an expressive instrument, it was the very form of thought itself: a kind of "thought in images" or "thinking imagination." Expressed in various ways and with different results, this holds true for all classical Italian philosophy, from Machiavelli to Leopardi, through Bruno, Galileo, Campanella, and Vico. Moreover, this overlapping between painting and idea, image and word, is never perfect. They never manage to be completely superimposed, and indeed, always cause one to stick out of the other: as if, in their parallel progress—demonstrated in Leonardo's creative output by the captions that accompany his drawings and by the figures that illustrate his written texts—painting and idea reached a point of friction such as to always push one farther ahead of the other, leading the artist to interrupt the work or derail it onto a different track than originally planned. It is almost as if he struggled to translate the complexity of his own thought onto paper; or, conversely, as if its complexity went beyond his limits, pushing him beyond his first ideation. Along these lines, one could say that the furthest point of Leonardo's genius does not lie, as is sometimes assumed, in the perfect correspondence between painting and philosophy—"la peinture pour philosophie," as Valéry used to say[62]—but in the margin that, in connecting one to the other, continues to separate them nonetheless. It is in this "shared division [condivisione]" that the innermost secrets of Leonardo's art must be sought. If this is indeed the case, then his grandiose failure to complete projects clearly does not ensue primarily from historical and environmental contingencies, but from the fact that he "saw" things that cannot be

60. Baldassare Castiglione, *The Book of the Courtier*, trans. Leonard Eckstein Opdycke (New York: Charles Scribner's Sons 1903), p. 117.

61. Martin Kemp, *Leonardo* (Oxford: Oxford University Press, 2004), p. v.

62. Paul Valéry, "Léonard et les philosophes," in *Variété III* (Paris: Gallimard, 1949), p. 171.

thought or thought things that cannot be expressed. What underlies it is the continuously renewed attempt, or temptation, to represent the Unrepresentable: something that stands beyond its own conceivability, like the coincidence of origin and end, creation and dissolution, or life and death. This was put to the test most powerfully in his deluge drawings and paintings, which represent the simultaneously catastrophic and sublime arrival point of Leonardo's grand adventure. If it is true that in the end, in their bare, mute depiction, the word—all words—definitively retreat before the dissolutive and self-dissolutive force of painting, this opens up a secret path through which the artist can directly confront the Ineffable. Let's not forget that the *Deluge* series dates from the same years as the *Virgin and Child with Saint Anne*, *Saint John the Baptist*, and the *Monna Lisa*, almost as if, after being pursued for a long time, the two sides of the origin—the radiant and the horrific—finally appeared to him together.

At the core of the *Deluge* series there is neither more nor less than the representation of nothingness, of the annihilation ensuing from the final victory of energy over matter, which tries in vain to hold it back with its own force of gravity. I can not think of any other way of defining the literally impracticable idea of painting the wind or air, subjected in its turn to the dispersive pressure of the waters. When his contemporaries observed that it was impossible for Leonardo to represent what he came to imagine, they were alluding specifically to this dematerializing impulse, which caused the still harmonious perspective of Brunelleschi and Alberti to explode, but, by its uncontrollable swirling vortex, also vanquished and pierced through the figure itself. The outcome of this Heraclitean struggle between the elements—water against earth, air against water, fire against air—is the dissolution of the very representation that attempts to portray it. At "the end of nature," the world returns to the chaos that existed before the creation; the light of day is extinguished, or blinded, in the primordial night. The end of everything is none other than the explosion of the uncontainable fury of the origin, projected into the future. Its force wipes out all endings and breaks down all backgrounds—the same one that binds together into one natural law the potency of life and the impulse of death. This is the Unrepresentable that Leonardo seeks in the eye of the cyclone, the enigma that all his paintings jealously guard: the identity between origin and end, creation and destruction, freedom and violence.

It is within this frame of reference that the *Battle* should be interpreted. We know that the painting depicted a scene from the battle won by the Florentines alongside their papal allies against the Milanese army on June 29, 1440, at Anghiari, near Arezzo. Like the *Battle of Cascina*, which Michelangelo was commissioned to paint to commemorate the victorious battle against the Pisans that had been fought in Cascina on July 28, 1364, the *Battle of Anghiari* was intended to celebrate the valor of the Florentine troops, who at that time were still engaged in a long war of uncertain outcome against Pisa. Machiavelli's attendance at the signing of the contract awarding Leonardo the commission from the Chancellery, as one of the two witnesses, lends even more political importance to the event. And yet, specifically at this level, there is something that does not quite fit. I am not referring particularly to Machiavelli's role—which some historians believe to have been much smaller, performed instead by his superior in rank, Marcello Virgilio Adriani[63]—since, in any case, seeing that his relationship with Leonardo dated back to 1502 when they held different offices as members of Cesare Borgia's retinue, there is no doubt that he contributed in some way to documenting the battle.[64] But this is exactly where the first wrinkle appears. As we know, Machiavelli speaks about the Battle of Anghiari in the *Florentine Histories*, but in completely different tones from the extreme, exaggerated ones used in the painting. His version is entirely understated given the scale of the battle, which in his account was brought to a close without even a single fatality.[65] In reality, things were quite different, as we know from all the chronicles of the time: it was a bloody conflict with hundreds of dead,

63. See A. Cecchi, "Niccolò Machiavelli o Marcello Virgilio Adriani? Sul programma e l'assetto compositivo delle 'Battaglie' di Leonardo e Michelangelo per la Sala del Maggior Consiglio in Palazzo Vecchio," in *Prospettiva* 83–84 (1996): 102–15.

64. On the relationship between Leonardo and Machiavelli, in addition to the classic book by Roger D. Masters, *Fortune Is a River: Leonardo da Vinci and Niccolò Machiavelli's Magnificent Dream to Change the Course of Florentine History* (New York: Free Press, 1998), see also the excellent doctoral dissertation by Marco Versiero, "Il dono della libertà e l'ambizione dei tiranni: La scienza del potere di Leonardo da Vinci, tra arte e filosofia," University of Naples, 2007–8), whose conclusions have been partially published in his article "Dall'eternità del mondo al governo delle città: Leonardo da Vinci, 'dopo Machiavelli,'" in *Dopo Machiavelli/Aprèes Machiavelli*, ed. Lorenzo Bianchi and Alberto Postigliola (Naples: Liguori, 2008), pp. 33–52.

65. See Machiavelli, *Istorie fiorentine*, in *Tutte le opere*, ed. Mario Martelli (Florence: Sansoni, 1971), p. 763.

wounded, and prisoners, one that Machiavelli sought to reduce to a harmless skirmish in order to substantiate his claim that mercenary troops were of little value, and to promote the need for citizen militias. But this discrepancy in tone compared to Machiavelli's reconstruction casts doubt on the idea championed by Nicolai Rubinstein that Leonardo shared the same view as his friend.[66] Nothing suggests that the painting contains a clear ideological message or even an apologetic intention of some sort toward the republican model versus the monocratic Milanese model. The artist's move to the court of Ludovico il Moro and later to the French court would be difficult to explain otherwise. When Leonardo speaks of "popular" government, moreover, his comments are never sparing in cutting irony about a view of politics, and of human nature itself, that he considered unrealistic.

Moreover, a close analysis of the painting, at least as it can be imagined by cross-comparing the preparatory sketches and later copies of it, supports this nonpartisan interpretation of the work. The portion that was actually painted—portraying the skirmish between the two pairs of riders for what appears to be the conquest of the Milan standard captured by the Florentines—does not suggest a strong ideological choice in favor of one of the battling parties, just as it does not seem oriented, as a whole or in its individual parts, toward a historical description of the event. A comparison with panels of wedding chests and headboards, but also with the "battles" by Paolo Uccello or Piero della Francesca—all precedents for Leonardo's work—highlights the irreducible difference of his painting. It is true that Piero della Francesca had already abandoned the old panoramic perspective showing the entire battlefield in favor of close-ups focusing on individual clashes. But nothing comparable to Leonardo's frantic "tangle," as Vasari once described it, alluding to the unravelable interpenetration between the various subjects, human and animal, that compose it. In the *Battle*, the historicity of the event seems to be passed over for the benefit of another, more originary and savage scene that, notwithstanding its harsh realism, is situated outside any fixed space-time coordinates.[67] The absence

66. See Nicolai Rubinstein, "Machiavelli and the Mural Decoration of the Hall of the Great Council of Florence," in *Musagetes: Festschrift für Wolfram Prinz* (Berlin: Mann, 1991), pp. 275–85.

67. See also Peter Meller, "La battaglia di Anghiari," in *Leonardo: Una carriera di pittore*, ed. Pietro C. Marani (Florence: Giunti Martello, 1985), pp. 130–36.

2. Leonardo da Vinci, study of battle with horsemen and foot soldiers for the *Battle of Anghiari*. Pen and ink, 1503. Venice, Gallerie dell'Accademia. (PhotoserviceElecta / Bohm, by permission of the Italian Ministry of Cultural Heritage and Activities.)

3. Leonardo da Vinci, study for the head of two warriors for the *Battle of Anghiari*. Metalpoint, black and red chalk, 1503–4. Budapest, Szépmüvészeti Múzeum. (Foto Art Resource / Scala, Florence.)

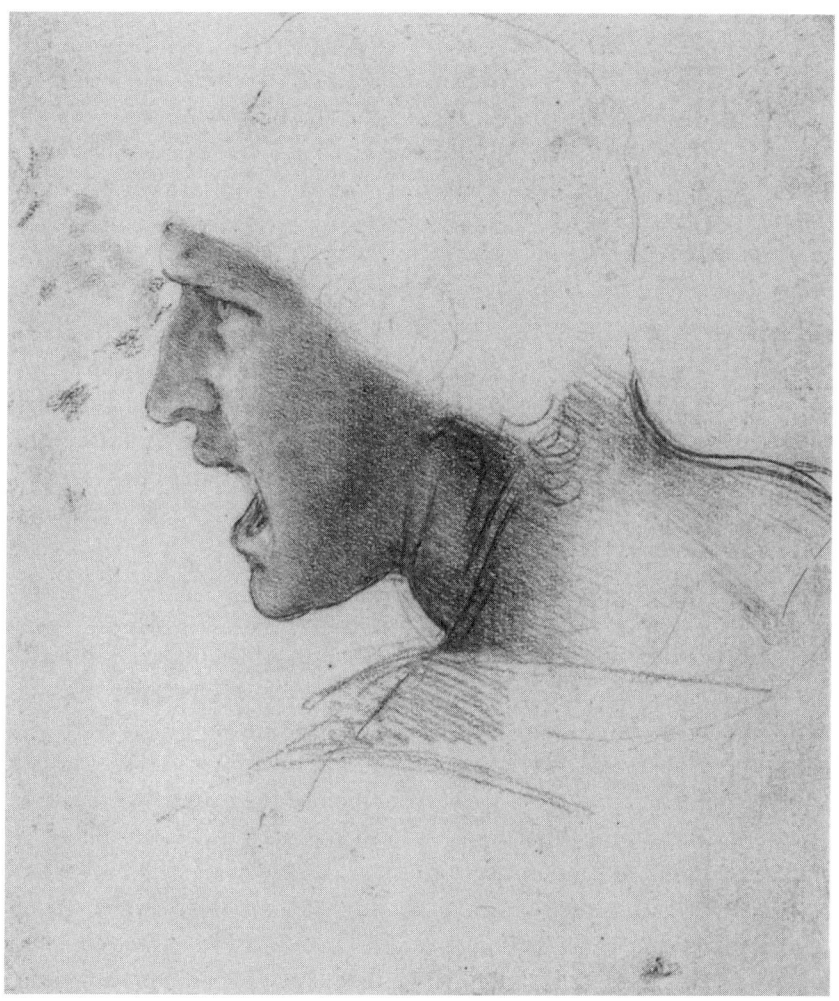

4. Leonardo da Vinci, study for the head of a soldier for the *Battle of Anghiari*. Red chalk, 1503–4. Budapest, Szépmüvészeti Múzeum. (Foto Art Resource / Scala, Florence.)

of any clearly visible heraldic emblems, particularly the Florentine lily and the Milanese snake which are plainly noticeable in other earlier paintings, shows that Leonardo's intention was not celebratory or documentary in nature. The absence of bridles and bits on the horses as well as boots and spurs on the riders, which were arbitrarily added to some of the later copies, augments the metahistorical feeling: the *Battle for the Standard* sparks no memory of a particular event that occurred at a given time, but rather, something more archaic and primordial, rooted in an otherwise originary stratum that, precisely for this reason, seems to extend its reach all the way to us. Even the literary sources, also known to Leonardo, like the manuscript poem *Trophaeum Anglaricum* by Leonardo Dati, consisting of five hundred Latin hexameters in praise of the victors, and the *Decadi* by Flavio Biondo, do not seem to have left any obvious traces in his conception of the work. As far as they are concerned, too, it is almost as if Leonardo had worked more by subtraction than by addition. Particularly striking is the lack of precise contextual references or even simple recognizable elements. Even the object of the skirmish—the battle flag—appears to be hidden and almost pushed out of the picture by an irresistible force. At the center, there isn't the struggle of the Florentines against other people who are identifiable as enemies, but rather, Struggle as such. It is an absolute and therefore irreducible contest—with no subjects or objects other than the unleashing of its force. There is no particular event, or even less, a clear confrontation between actors positioned on opposing fronts. But rather, a vortex or a whirlwind, an eye of the cyclone that sucks humans and beasts into the same bottomless abyss, just as they are, enmeshed in an inextricable tangle.

A different, influential view has been advanced by Frank Zöllner. In an interpretation of some interest, he identifies the two riders on the left, intent on defending the banner, as the two condottieri from Perugia on the payroll of the Visconti, Niccolò and Francesco Piccinino; while the other two, facing them from the right, are identified as the opposing leaders, Lodovico Scarampo and Piergiampaolo Orsini.[68] It must be said that this identification, previously advanced by Cecil Gould,[69] and taken for granted by most critics, reverses the original testimony of Vasari, endorsed

---

68. Frank Zöllner, "La *Battaglia di Anghiari* di Leonardo da Vinci, tra mitologia e politica," *Lettura Vinciana* 37 (April 18, 1997) (Florence: Giunti, 1998).

69. See Cecil Gould, "Leonardo's Great Battle–Piece: A Conjectural Reconstruction," in *Art Bulletin* 2 (1954): 117–29.

5. Anonymous, copy of the *Battle of Anghiari* (*Tavola Doria*). Oil on panel, 1504–6. Private collection.

6. Peter Paul Rubens, copy of the *Battle of Anghiari*. Black pencil, pen, ink, white lead, and watercolor, ca. 1603. Paris, Musée du Louvre. (Photos Lessing / Contrasto.)

instead by Kemp,[70] according to which the Florentine captains are on the left and the Milanese on the right. What seems even more questionable is the ideological character that Zöllner charges the work with. On the basis of a complex set of signs and allusions, both internal and external to the painting—and reconstructed solely from subsequent reproductions—he argues that Leonardo represented the bestial violence of the Visconti mercenaries in the two riders on the left, and the valor mixed with prudence of the Florentine condottieri in those on the right. The exaggerated facial features and animal ornaments—especially the ram depicted on Francesco Piccinino's chest and the lionine hilt of his sword—are supposedly a reference to the martial iconography of the god of war; while the armor of the second rider, especially Scarampo's helmet with the dragon and Orsini's with the visor, are from Minervan iconography. The distorted, menacing features of the face in relief on the visor that would appear to contradict this whole line of reasoning is explained away by the assimilation between the figure of Minerva and the portrait of Alexander the Great consequent to the circulation of coins engraved on one side with the face of the goddess and on the other with the word *Alexandros*. This supposedly explains the overlapping between the two iconographies, which, taken together, symbolize the virile but rational courage traditionally attributed to the Florentines. Zöllner's conclusion, already implicit in his premises, does not disappoint: "The antithesis evoked in the painting of the Battle of Anghiari between the mercenaries battling with brute force in the name of Mars and the Florentines who fight with "prudence" corresponds precisely to the political and military reality of the post-1500 years."[71]

This argument is feeble, to say the least;[72] partly due to the cumbersomeness of its logical steps—culminating in the iconological superimpo-

---

70. See Martin Kemp, *Leonardo da Vinci: The Marvellous Works of Nature and Man* (Oxford: Oxford University Press, 2007), p. 253.

71. Zöllner, "La *Battaglia di Anghiari*," p. 28.

72. This was already maintained by Marani, in *Leonardo*, p. 299; and by Edoardo Villata, "Leonardo e gli uomini di lettere," in *Leonardo da Vinci: La vera immagine*, ed. Vanna Arrighi, Anna Bellinazzi, Edoardo Villata (Florence: Giunti, 2005), p. 195. Versiero, *Il dono della libertà*, pp. 456 ff., expresses the same opinion, with additional, compelling points worthy of consideration. A more nuanced position is offered by A. Perissa Torrini in "La *Battaglia di Anghiari*," in *La mente di Leonardo (al tempo della "Battaglia di Anghiari")*, ed. Carlo Pedretti (Florence: Giunti, 2006), pp. 49–61.

sition of Minerva and Alexander—but primarily to the figural comparison of the characters portrayed. It may very well be that the ones on the left are the Milanese condottieri, as shown by the red headpiece of Niccolò Piccinino and the ram on the chest of Francesco, the heraldic family emblem. But this attribution is exactly what weakens the martial significance that the critic attributes to this insignia. As has been convincingly argued,[73] monsters and wild-animal heads were normally used as ornaments for arms, and before that, they appeared in relief on coats of arms of the time, so assigning them an ideological connotation is highly debatable. That is not all: the two figures on the left—especially the first one, contorted in an animalistic posture that ends up overlapping the head of the rider onto that of his own horse and creating a centaur-like effect—are highly expressive of bestial violence. But the bearing of the two riders who are closing in on them from the right—one of whom is attempting to pierce his opponent's face with a spear before the latter can cut the enemy hand gripping the standard—appears no less aggressive. The attitude of the footmen rolling on the ground, intent on keeping themselves alive while sending the other to their death are equally aggressive for that matter. What comes to the foreground, from whichever side you look at the scene, and regardless of the protagonists' identity, is precisely this reciprocity: the inseparability of attack and defense, "offendere e difendere," already united in a fragment by the artist into a single semantic node.[74] Regardless of Machiavelli's role in assigning the work, never as in this case do we find the Machiavellian theme of the inevitability of antagonism return with such force: this is the coexistence of opposites, later picked up on by Bruno (already expressed in a different form by Pico) as the original source of life;[75] but also, by necessity, as the uncontrollable drive toward death. In his book on painting, while describing how to depict a battle,

73. From G. Dalli Regoli, "Riflessioni intorno alla *Battaglia di Anghiari*: Una nota sui 'nichi' di Leonardo," in *La mente di Leonardo*, p. 82.

74. Cited from Leonardo da Vinci, *Scritti scelti*, ed. Anna Maria Brizio (Turin, 1966), p. 68.

75. See S. Toussaint, "Leonardo filosofo dei contrari: Appunti sul 'chaos,'" in *Leonardo e Pico: Analogie, contatti, confronti*, ed. Fabio Frosini (Florence, 2005), pp. 13–35. The originary and insuperable character of *polemos* is central to the philosophical work of Umberto Curi. See his *Pólemos: Filosofia della guerra* (Turin, 2000); and his previous work *Endiadi: Figure della duplicità* (1995; reprint, Milan, 2002).

when Leonardo places "the victors," "the conquered and beaten," "the living," and "the dead" all in the same sphere,[76] his intention is to identify conflict as the sole protagonist of the painting, without any value distinction between one or the other: as if they were all swept up in the current in which "the curves of life become the curves of death,"[77] seeing as we have always made "our lives with the death of others."[78] This, and no other, is the originary truth that the *Battle*, in its very "disfaction [dissfazione]," simultaneously reveals and guards.

But there is more. In the end, if knowing the historical identity of the four horsemen is not that important, because what dominates the scene is conflict as such, this means that the role of the men in the painting is diminished. As a matter of fact, in his theoretical text on depicting battles, the artist himself had stated, "The further amidst the swirling mass just described that the combatants are, the less will they be visible and the less difference will there be in their lights and shadows."[79] The description recalls the *Deluge* paintings which, in their apocalyptic violence, may well be considered the point that precipitates the human vortex painted in the *Battle*; however, with the difference that in the flood scenes, human beings have been swept away and eliminated by the raging force of nature. In his "Of Representing the Deluge" Leonardo had situated the people—the last survivors before the End—on the edge of the scene, describing them as perched in the trees for shelter from the violence of the waves, with their hands over their eyes to avoid witnessing their own destruction, intent on killing each other, or even on committing suicide in order to avoid unbearable pain. It would be difficult to conceive of a more radical repudiation of the humanistic ideal of domination over reality, which was still in full ex-

76. Leonardo da Vinci, *Libro di pittura*, ed. Carlo Pedretti, annotated transcription by Carlo Vecce (Florence, 1995), vol. 1, p. 207; English version: *The Book on Painting*, in *The Notebooks of Leonardo da Vinci: Complete*, vol. 1., trans. Jean Paul Richter (1888) (Seattle: Pacific Publishing Studio, 2010), pp. 96–97.

77. Kenneth Clark, "Leonardo e le curve della vita," *XVII Lettura Vinciana* (15 April 1977), Florence 1979, p. 15.

78. Leonardo da Vinci, MS H (Institut de France), f 89v, cited in Giuseppina Fumagalli, *Leonardo, omosanza lettere* (Florence, 1939), p. 337.

79. Leonardo da Vinci, *On Painting: An Anthology of Writings*, trans. Martin Kemp and Margaret Walker (New Haven, CT: Yale University Press, 1989), p. 229.

pansion during those years. But Nature's "percussion" is only the first of the antihumanistic vectors launched by Leonardo—which in the context of our genealogy, cannot fail to remind us of Leopardi, above and beyond all the differences that separate them.[80] The other, also destined for a Leopardian outcome, although not unrelated to Bruno's criticism of anthropocentrism, regards the relation with the animal and vegetal worlds, conceived as both contiguous and contrastive at the same time. As the people carried away by the flood cling tightly to the trees, terrified as they escape, they are entirely similar to animals, from whom they soon become indistinguishable: "Again, you might have seen on many of the hill-tops terrified animals of different kinds, collected together and subdued to tameness, in company with men and women who had fled with their children. . . . Huge branches of great oaks loaded with men were seen borne through the air by the impetuous fury of the winds."[81]

Leonardo's attention to the animal world runs throughout all his works, both literary and pictorial. For him, human beings are not only similar to animals in life and death, they share the same nature in the most powerful sense that they, too, are animals. And this holds true on both the behaviorial and the morphogenetic planes. The distinction between these two aspects, initially established in Aristotle's *Historia animalium* and included in Albert the Great's *De animalibus*, had gradually faded into a scientific and literary tradition that accentuated now one now the other.[82] In his anatomical and physiological studies especially, but also in his mechanical ones like those on flight, Leonardo focused specifically on the middle segment, on the metamorphically crossed forms between human and animal. His lion heads, illustrating passions escaped from the control of reason, are the most widely known physiognomic examples. They point to the formation of a heterodox anthropozoological culture in contrast to the spiritualistic current that from the theologized Platonic school of human-

---

80. The reference is cited in Cesare Luporini, *La mente di Leonardo* (Florence: Sansoni, 1953; reprint, Florence: Le Lettere, 1997), pp. 27–28.

81. Leonardo da Vinci, "Of Representing the Deluge (607–609)," in *Notebooks*, vol. 5, pp. 97–98.

82. See D. Laurenza, "Uomini bestiali: Leonardo da Vinci e le sue fonti," *Micrologus* 8 (2000): 581–98; as well as M. Verserio, "Metafore zoomorfe e dissimulazione della duplicità: La politica delle immagini in Niccolò Machiavelli e Leonardo da Vinci," *Studi Filosofici* 27 (2004): 101–25.

ism to the full-blown antihumanism of Heidegger sought the divine aspect of human beings in the ontological distance separating them in some essential way from the animal. From this perspective, Leonardo focused his exploration particularly on the human-horse relation. In a study contemporary to the *Battle*, he not only compared equine and human legs, he drew a limb made of bone that is part human and part horse, adding by way of explanation that "to make the bone structure of the horse and that of man equal, you will put the man on tiptoe in the figuration of the legs."[83] In other drawings, the comparison of anatomy and expression moves to the head or to other parts of the body, arriving at a sort of figural indistinguishability that by humanizing the beast simultaneously bestializes the human.

This attitude is at its unsurpassed apex in the *Battle for the Standard*. The figure of the centaur warrior is recognizable in the first character on the left, especially in the copy by Rubens. It offers a strikingly forceful compendium of the associated iconographical characteristics, not only in the way the man's head is perfectly superimposed onto that of the animal's, creating the effect of a single body that is half animal and half human; but also in the contortion of the body, spasmodically twisted around on itself in a way that is no different from the tentacles of the octopus depicted on the horseman's shoulder. Apart from the canonical source, Isidore of Seville's *Etymologiae*—according to which "in bello velut unum corpus equorum et hominum viderentur [as they rushed into battle, the horses and men seemed to have one body; 11.3.37]"—it is difficult not to think of the Machiavellian centaur, also portrayed in its dual nature as rational and feral. Although there is no direct documentation for this allusion, the reference alone should make us cautious about accepting a univocal reading of Leonardo's painting like the one presented earlier, by Zöllner. To identify the two characters on the left who are more explicitly bestialized as Milanese logically presupposes an entirely negative opinion of human-animal metamorphosis. The centaur—identified as Francesco Piccinino—would be a figurative representation of the primordial origin that, coming prior to the oppositional distinction between human and animal, could only bring with it violence and destruction. But this way what remains in the shadows is his other vital, energetic side—in the artist's conception, always

83. D. Laurenza, "Uomini bestiali," p. 594.

connected to the first—which Machiavelli, once again, had theorized by assigning a positive function as well to the centaur figure: that of constitutive force.[84] If Leonardo ever espoused the same ambivalent connotations, then the two "feral" horsemen could just as well be the Florentine leaders, victorious precisely because of the introjected animal characteristics.

But another, even more relevant question remains unresolved. This concerns not the animalization of the human, but the humanization of the animal; in other words, the other face of the centaur metamorphosis. In that "pazzia bestialissima [most bestial madness]" of war—as Leonardo expressed himself in terms to be taken literally—just as human beings driven by hatred take on the appearance of horses, in the same way, horses can acquire human attitudes by participating in clashes with the same unbridled passions as the horsemen who mount them. As Vasari had already noted about the *Battle*: "In it, anger, disdain, and vindictiveness are displayed no less by the horsemen than by their horses, two of which with forelegs intertwined are battling with their teeth no less fiercely than their riders are fighting for the standard."[85] But, if the transformation of human into animal cannot be interpreted solely in negative tones, the human metamorphosis of the animal has equally ambivalent connotations. To understand them we must go back to Leonardo's idea about the aggressive—indeed, decidedly destructive—nature of human beings who have always lived by the death of others: by the death of the animals they eat, but also by the death of the other human beings they savagely compete with, seized by an uncontrollable desire "to deal death and grief and labour and wars and fury to every living thing."[86] Now it is this infraspecies aggressivity of human beings that defines the threshold differentiating us from animals—concealed by all forms of humanism behind the claim of our resemblance to the divine—over whom humans nevertheless declare themselves to be lords and masters. While animals—as the author writes in a piece dedicated to "man

84. On this topic, see G. Mario Anselmi and Paolo Faziou, *Machiavelli: L'asino e le bestie* (Bologna: Clueb, 1984).

85. Leonardo da Vinci, *Libro di pittura*, vol. 1, p. 218; translated from the Italian. This quote is not found in the English version.

86. Giorgio Vasari, *Vita di Leonardo da Vinci, pittore e scultore fiorentino*, in *Le vite de' più eccellenti pittori, scultori e architettori* (Florence, 1975), vol. 4, pp. 31–33; English version: *The Lives of the Artists*, trans. Julia Conaway Bondanella and Peter Bondanella (Oxford: Oxford University Press, 1991), p. 295.

as king of the beasts"—do not eat specimens of their own kind, unless they are mad or they are animals of prey who may go so far as to devour their own children, you, humans "besides thy children devourest father, mother, brothers and friends; nor is this enough for thee, but thou goest to the chase on the islands of others, taking other men and [cutting off their member and testicles,] thou fattenest, and chasest them down thy own throat."[87] Leonardo had already elsewhere expressed a kind of preference toward animals over humans—for example when he observed, "Man has much power of discourse which for the most part is vain and false; animals have but little but it is useful and true and a small truth is better than a great lie."[88] If we take this to its conclusion—in every way extreme—one cannot help thinking that, for Leonardo, instead of the animal corrupting the human, according to the current theory that has been repeated in successive waves throughout the course of civilization, it is rather humans who have managed to corrupt animals by transmitting our homocidal fury to them. If this is the case, then the "monster" is not the man with the bestial features that critics have also seen in the *Battle*, but the beast with the human features. The artist had written something not far from this in his "Prophecy on the Cruelty of Man," concluding with a question—an abysmal one in all respects—about the precipice opened up under our feet: "Oh world, why dost thou not open and engulf them in the fissures of thy vast abyss and caverns, and no longer display in the sight of heaven such a cruel and ruthless monster!"[89] The vortex of the *Battle* comes to mind even more readily than that of the deluge. Maybe this is the hidden origin, the most disturbing truth that lies bricked up behind the wall in the Palazzo Vecchio: not the risk that human beings will be bestialized, but the anything but remote possibility that the animal will be humanized.

87. Leonardo, *Notebooks*, trans. Richter vol. 2, p. 365. See also M. Verserio, "Per un lessico politico di Leonardo da Vinci," in *Bruniana e Campanelliana* 15, no. 1 (2009):121–34.

88. Ibid., p. 296.

89. Ibid., p. 365 [trans. note: slightly adapted based on the original].

Philosophy / Life

History and Unhistory

1. While the work of Machiavelli, Bruno, and Vico is eccentric to the general categorial framework of the early modern period, the chasm that opened up between Italian thought of the nineteenth century and the contemporary European philosophy is no less wide. The fact that the authors I will be discussing—Vincenzo Cuoco, Giacomo Leopardi, and Francesco de Sanctis—are not philosophers in the strict sense of the term is not contingent, or accidental, but rather an integral part of the question. The slash mark connecting and disconnecting the two words of this chapter's title alludes, on the one hand, to the persistent centrality of the category of "life" in nineteenth-century Italian culture; and, on the other, to its difficult relationship with the thought that seeks to examine it. It is a thought that can only get a grasp on its object, one might say, by stepping back and turning around on itself—deconstructing itself as a philosophical language to take up residence in a different discipline, which in these cases means history, poetry, and literary criticism. More than an explicit philosophy of life, what emerges from the pages of these authors is its dramatic problematicity: its necessity and, simultaneously, its impracticability as such. Hence a double movement of withdrawal and reconstitution, of deviation and reconnection at another level. In the first instance, there is the explicitly stated perception that the philosophical language is inadequate to express a reality—whether historical, natural, or biological—that exceeds it from all sides. And thus its retreat in favor of different lexical spheres that are more

responsive to the encounter with the real. But this is only the first step in an even more complex undertaking: as soon as the break with the philosophical dimension has been signaled by putting other languages into action, it is re-created inside these languages, forcing their semantic capacity to the utmost of their expressive potential.

Cuoco's relationship to the horizon of history is inscribed within this dialectic—at once constitutive and deconstructive—of the paradigm that he himself first establishes. On the one hand we can say that his "Historical Essay on the Neapolitan Revolution" marks the beginning of modern reflection on the character and significance of the historical event as such. But—and here it diverges from other experiences of contemporary European culture—without ever taking on the form of a philosophy of history. History, understood as the slow, or sudden, transformation of things and people, achieves its specificity, and even its effectiveness, by removing itself from any ideal pattern superimposed on it. This applies equally to past history—to historiography, in other words—and to the concrete unfolding of current history. Rarely is history, as it really unfolds, the direct consequence of an abstract philosophical project; and when this does happen, its effects are often far from fortunate. A glaring example of this is the "modern" event par excellence—the French Revolution: "It was believed that the French Revolution was the work of philosophy," Cuoco warns, "while philosophy did nothing less than ruin it"[1] when it dug an ever-widening ditch between "ideas" and "things" without understanding that "the things could have been kept without keeping the ideas."[2] But it is primarily the Neapolitan Revolution, which Cuoco took as his main object of study, that provided the most dramatic example of the unwillingness of history to be guided by a philosophy, especially one arriving from somewhere else. His celebrated dictum, endlessly repeated, is that the failure of the Neapolitan Revolution stemmed from its pretension of adapting a model imported from France to a material that was totally refractory to it. Rather than descend into the depths of the history in which the Neapolitan intellectuals were nonetheless immersed; rather than comprehend and respect its irreducible specificity, they imagined they could force it into an abstract schema that was completely incapable of containing it, and they were submerged by it.

1. Vincenzo Cuoco, *Saggio storico sulla rivoluzione di Napoli*, ed. Antonino De Francesco (Manduria-Rome: Lacaita, 1998), p. 335.

2. Ibid., p. 339.

But what, exactly, is there in the depths of history? What is history made of in its ultimate, innermost core? Cuoco's answer to this question points to the set of characteristics, needs, and customs that indelibly mark the historical life of different peoples. This is what he defined, in the fragments on Mario Pagano's draft constitution, as "a second nature," one that was destined to overlap the first, even in the eyes of its leading actors, almost to the point of being identical with it. However, in the same passage, and speaking specifically about the process of naturalizing what is also historical, the author argues that "constitutions must be made for people as they are, and how they will always be, riddled with shortcomings and riddled with mistakes. Because it is no more credible that they want to dispense with customs they believe to be second nature in order to follow our institutions—which they consider arbitrary and variable—than it is reasonable for a shoemaker to expect that the foot of someone who has made a shoe too short be shortened."[3] The reference here to the eternity of certain attitudes, confirmed and condensed by the biological metaphor, alludes to something that, while internal to history, does not coincide with it and tends to resist it. It is as if Cuoco had absorbed, although not entirely adopted, the naturalistic interpretation that leads people to believe their conditions are stable or even unchangeable. This idea is what locates him along a perspectival axis that is different from the historicist model, although not entirely unrelated to it. Of course, for him, all reality is penetrated and even essentially characterized by its historicity. The essential dimension of human beings is not spatial—as it still was for the classical episteme—but temporal. This means that there is no transcendental standpoint from which the meaning of a single experience can be universalized separately from its peculiar traits. But the latter, although internal to the historical perspective, do not always fully adhere to it. Indeed, they sometimes carry an unhistorical residue—or at least one that is not immediately historicizable—which Cuoco on several occasions calls by the name of "nature": "What cannot be done by a legislator who loves the nation and follows nature instead of a system?"[4] "But observe the order of nature from the other side, and you will see that she has shown us the remedies for all the evils that the philosophers fear."[5] "Finally, the last difficulty comes from those

3. Vincenzo Cuoco, "Frammenti di lettere dirette a Vincenzo Russo," in *Saggio storico*, p. 516.

4. Ibid., p. 520.

5. Ibid., p. 528.

who seek in all things that uniformity which, the closer it comes to the rightness of human beings, the more distant it is to that of nature."[6]

Even his insistent reference to Vico, as "a man too superior to his age,"[7] which opened up the discussion on historical knowledge, needs to be understood in this context: not only as intimately dramatic but also as theoretically complex. Not surprisingly, Cuoco recalls that, according to Vico's doctrine, "the last of the social laws has its reason in nature."[8] Like his predecessor, although differently from him, Cuoco's radical adoption of the horizon of history is exactly what shows that not everything is historical—or, put another way, that history is not fully identical with temporal sequence. Only, in his case, what is not completely historicizable is not, as we have seen for Vico, the origin of history. It is not the unrepresentable event that precedes history, thereby making it possible, but its deeper content, its most intrinsic fabric. In its "quasi"-natural constitution, superimposed almost indistinguishably onto the "first nature," it is composed of a bio-anthropic substance that is dense, heavy, and amorphous, and that seems immobile simply because it moves at a different, much slower pace compared to the will of the people who seek to speed it up and who, in the end, are sucked into it and swallowed up by it. Here—in this complex conception of historical time splayed into two, noncoinciding, sometimes juxtaposed layers—is to be found an original reflection on history, on its organic relationship with the unhistorical, that it would be truly simplistic to interpret solely as a form of conservative moderatism. Life, in its material grain, protrudes out of the progressive dimension of history, setting a limit or a point of internal contrast for it, making its practicality problematic and risky. The Real, given its sticky, opaque character—this vital protrusion, or fault line—cannot be entirely diluted and absorbed into the historical flow. For Vico, too, history has a body, a material that is irreducible to the geometries of reason, sometimes stopping it in its tracks. And when reason imagines it can "idealize" history beyond a certain extent, it bends it on itself, in a turn with potentially catastrophic consequences.

6. Ibid., p. 537.

7. Vincenzo Cuoco, "Abbozzi di lettere a Jean Marie De Gérando sulla filosofia vichiana," in Cuoco, *Epistolario (1790–1817)*, ed. Domenico Conte and Maurizio Martirano (Rome-Bari: Laterza, 2007), p. 348.

8. See Fulvio Tessitore, "Cuoco lungo due secoli," in *Vincenzo Cuoco nella cultura di due secoli*, ed. Luigi Biscardi and Antonino De Francesco (Rome-Bari: Laterza, 2002), pp. 7–8.

This is the theme we saw in Machiavelli of the reemergence of the origin—at once energetic and violent—into a time that seeks to remove all memory of it. Cuoco's work must be recognized as belonging to this current of Italian thought—which, in some ways, he brings to its culmination: if the historical process harbors its opposite, if it is in constant tension with its own internal limit, then our thought must comprehend the dramatic possibility of its standstill, and also its reversal. From this point on, reflection on history will start to become indistinguishable from thought about its crisis.

2. The experience of revolution constitutes both the tangible evidence and the testing ground of this inevitable coimplication between history and crisis. It represents the sharp, dramatic point at which history begins to contradict itself—splitting its linear motion into two discontinuous layers that do not correspond to each other and even tend to diverge. Under its force of collision, the line of temporality breaks up and then violently folds over on itself, with an outcome whose modalities and effects remain highly indeterminate. It is in this regard, in relation to this complex dynamic forming part of the revolutionary phenomenon, that Cuoco's text goes well beyond the boundaries of contemporary historiography to come under the realm of speculative thought. But, as we were saying, this thought is in itself alien to the various philosophies of history, whether progressive or regressive, that extended out of the late eighteenth century and into the next. From this perspective, the protracted controversy on the ideological position of the author, yet to be definitively resolved, is no longer relevant; or, at the very least, its significance as a whole is changed. As is clear from recent studies, starting with the excellent new edition of the *Historical Essay on the Neapolitan Revolution,* by Antonino De Francesco,[9] the various images of Cuoco—as a democratic or a moderate, as a radical or a conservative, as a Jacobin or a nationalist—that have followed or even overlapped on one another turn out to be projections, and ideological ones at that, in the debate on Italian unification which began during the Risorgimento and which has lasted with varying success until now.[10] Compared to projections

9. In addition to the fundamental, new edition of the *Saggio* by Antonino De Francesco (*Saggio storico sulla Rivoluzione napoletana del 1799* [Manduria: Lacaita, 1998]), see also his *Vincenzo Cuoco: Una vita politica* (Rome-Bari: Laterza, 1997).

10. On this topic, see the introduction to the previous edition of Cuoco's *Saggio storico sulla Rivoluzione napoletana del 1799* (Turin: UTET, 1975), by Anna Bravo.

of this sort, it seems like a healthy tendency to situate Cuoco in the context to which he effectively belonged: namely that of the democratic exiles gathered in Milan after the failure of the revolution of 1799.[11]

But this historical backdrop—necessary, of course, to reconstruct the different political and cultural attitudes Cuoco assumed over time—does not suffice to exhaust the question of his philosophical thought, which is what we are primarily interested in here. Nor does it help us particularly to understand what in his thought went beyond the competing philosophical cultures of the time that sought to assess the revolutionary event. If his specific contribution is difficult to fit into the reassuring framework of post-Enlightenment- or Neoromantic-inspired theories of progress, it hardly fits with reactionary or counterrevolutionary ones either. The most perspicacious critics have rightly stressed Cuoco's distance from the latter: he ideally enters into dialogue with Humboldt, Constant, and Tocqueville more than with Maistre, Bonald, or Haller.[12] But this is not the point, or not the only one. Rather than fleshing out his biographical or ideological profile, what we seek to identify is the theoretical dispositif that distances him from these thinkers at the same time as it distances him from their progressive opponents. Although starting from opposite assumptions and intentions, while both camps remain within a philosophy of history (the former progressive and the latter regressive) Cuoco stands dramatically outside it, because he situates the point of conflict—the contradiction, in other words—within the same historical movement. This is why he remains sheltered from both camps—from whoever, "following in the footsteps of Condorcet, believes in the infinite perfectability of a finite being like man,"[13] as well as from those who, in their restoration fury fail to realize that "just as nature does not suffer forward leaps, nor does it allow one to go backward,"[14] What escapes both schools is that taking sides for or against revolution is not possible, since the distinction between positive and negative, possible and impossible, passes right through it. In revolu-

---

11. On the Milan exiles, see Anna M. Rao, *Esuli: L'emigrazione politica italiana in Francia (1792–1802)* (Naples: Guida, 1992).

12. See especially Fulvio Tessitore's "Vincenzo Cuoco tra illuminismo e storicismo," in *Contributi alla storia e alla teoria dello storicismo* (Rome: Edizioni di Storia e Letteratura, 1995), pp. 247–89.

13. Cuoco, "Frammenti," p. 517.

14. Ibid., p. 523.

tion, the two contrasting elements of the historical and the unhistorical, articulated differently over the long term, are dizzyingly concentrated into a very brief period of time, with potentially self-destructive results.

It is to this contradictory encounter that we owe the concept made famous by Antonio Gramsci's reexamination of it, that of "passive revolution"—which was itself borrowed in inverted form from Francesco Lomonaco's "active revolution," coined only slightly earlier in the second edition of his *Report to Citizen Carnot*.[15] While "active revolution" simply referred to the autonomy of the struggle for national independence, the category of "passive revolution" that Cuoco relaunched referred to an event, in itself positive, that bears its opposite within it. Unlike the revolutionaries, who compare revolution only to itself, and unlike the counterrevolutionaries, who oppose it to an affirmative polarity external and contrary to it—namely the metaphysical stability of order—Cuoco thinks in terms of revolution and counterrevolution, action and reaction. What he does is introduce the *counter-* or the *re-* within the movement that they oppose, thereby exposing them to the possibility of a catastrophic reversal. Not surprisingly, in confirmation of this constitutive contradiction, when it came to the subject of passive revolution, Gramsci himself would talk about "revolution without revolution" or even "revolution-restoration." While the French Revolution, triggered by popular initiative, came into being as an active revolution and only degenerated into extremism after an initial emancipatory phase; the Neapolitan Revolution, precisely because it was passive from the beginning, contained within itself from the outset that which would rapidly lead to its own negation. That is why, in his interpretation, the "before" cannot be separated from the "after": the one—what would happen—has to be read within the other, in the atrophied context in which the revolution was inscribed from its origin: "I follow the course of my ideas," warns Cuoco, "rather than the course of time. So many events were piled up in such a short time, practically massed together, that instead of following upon one another, they crisscrossed each other; nor can a proper opinion be arrived at without observing their relations."[16] In short, unlike the French Revolution, the Neapolitan Revolution is a unique event

---

15. On Francesco Lomonaco, see the version of the *Rapporto al cittadino Carnot receduto dalla traduzione dei "Droits et devoirs du citoyen" di Gabriel Bonnot de Mably*, ed. Antonino De Francesco (Manduria-Bari-Rome: Lacaita, 1999).

16. Cuoco, *Saggio storico*, p. 369.

in which positive and negative, transformation and stasis, history and nature intersect in the same block of time, causing it to explode.

A confirmation that this is the point he is making—regarding the combination of the historical and the unhistorical (in other words, the historical and the natural) in one event—is explicitly provided by the author from the very first page of his masterpiece, when he observes by way of introduction that "great political revolutions occupy the same place in human history that extraordinary phenomena have in natural history,"[17] except that "in most cases a physical catastrophe is observed more carefully and described more accurately than a political catastrophe."[18] The fact that history and nature correspond, or to be more precise, intersect with each other in a contradictory fashion in the figure of the catastrophe is not without influence on the entire order of Cuoco's argumentation. It is proof of the correspondence—both epistemological and real—between history and crisis with which we started. This is partly because catastrophe is the most propitious lens for seeing deep into the heart of an event and for unraveling its tangled threads, since "an extraordinary event seems to give us new life, new objects are presented to our eyes; and only in the midst of the general disorder, seemingly aimed at destroying a nation, do we glimpse the character, customs, and laws of an order of which, previously, we had only viewed its effects."[19] But also because in order for history, the sequence of events, to regenerate itself—to regain new life—it must go through that abrupt interruption of time, through that bottleneck in which an entire civilization appears to plunge into an abyss: "Only through extreme evil and wrongdoings [mali] does the human species pass into a new order of goodness and right acts [beni]."[20] The voice of Vico resounds again: when ideas become too radically separate from things, and life appears to be losing strength beyond measure—in other words, when human history fails to recognize its own unhistorical limit, imagining that this can be decreed out of existence—then the only option left is a relapse into barbarism. This is both the lowest point of the historical trajectory and the point at which history begins to generate new life: "The periods we call barbarism are indispensable to every living creature whose life is

17. Ibid., p. 221.
18. Ibid., p. 222.
19. Ibid.
20. Ibid., p. 509.

not limitless—providing new strength or renewing waning forces. . . . Just as a greater civilization always rises again out of barbarism, in the same way, a better species will rise again out of a big natural crisis—even if all previous memories are destroyed by a massive natural disaster."[21]

3. The last passage we cited is taken from a work, unique for its inspiration and structure, that goes by the name of *Plato in Italy*. It recounts the journey of Plato and a young Athenian called Cleobulus in their search for the ancient Italic civilization. The narrative of how the early Italians were soon stifled and made to conform to their foreign rulers, first by Greek colonialism and then by Roman imperialism, is told in a form that symbolically alludes to the establishment of Napoleonic rule from 1800 to 1815. On these lines, despite his realistic acceptance of the existing regime, *Plato in Italy* reveals Cuoco's obvious political intention to lay the cultural foundations for future independence. But the most significant aspect for our purposes is his development of an interpretative theme, one destined for remarkable success, that views Italian philosophy as the locus for the formation of a national consciousness. As is also apparent from newspaper articles written in the same year,[22] Cuoco identifies the distinguishing trait of Italian thought as its civic and political vocation. This is what he sees as uniting under the same genealogy the powerful vision of Dante with the engagement of the southern Enlightenment thinkers, in spite of the obvious distance between them, passing through the work of Machiavelli,[23] Campanella, and Vico. In order to create awareness of a liberation movement that would otherwise be deprived of intellectual roots and remain subordinate to other interests, we must look to Italian philosophy rather than to foreign traditions, no matter how illustrious they may be: "We, who are not Kantists, wish for Italy its own Italian philosophy. These philosophical schools are closely related to the political state of societies, and it is more important than generally believed whether a nation possesses or does not possess a philosophy of its own. For a long time now we have received

21. Vincenzo Cuoco, *Platone in Italia*, ed. Antonino De Francesco and Annalisa Andreoni (Rome-Bari: Laterza, 2006), p. 509.

22. See the introductions by Maurizio Martirano and Domenico Conte to the *Scritti giornalistici*, by Vincenzo Cuoco, 2 vols. (Naples: Fridericiana Editrice Universitaria, 1999).

23. On Cuoco and Machiavelli, see Nunzia Di Maso, *Il repubblicanesimo di Vincenzo Cuoco a partire da Machiavelli* (Florence: Centro Editoriale Toscano, 2005).

it from France through the work of Descartes, then later from England through Locke: up to the fifteenth century, we were the ones who gave it to other peoples. Survey the periods of political greatness of all nations: they are the same as those of their philosophical greatness. The greatest strength lies in the brain; the brawn of those who do not have a philosophy, or who believe themselves to be lacking in one, is always weak."[24]

These words, too, which conclude by referring to when the mind is immersed "in the general order of things,"[25] contain a clear reference to Vico's teachings. After all, was it not Vico who initiated a genealogical reflection on the ancient wisdom of the Italians, now given a central role in Cuoco's "novel"? And yet he had criticized his revered predecessor for being "overly metaphysical." This brings into play more than a simple methodological difference, calling into question that aporetic relationship between the historical and the unhistorical that we brought up earlier. As part of his critique, Cuoco objects that Vico "did not analyze the nations, he considered them en masse: he showed that they all have a cycle, a 'course' through which they pass from culture to barbarism and from there return to culture. But, besides this great truth, he says almost nothing else."[26] In reality, however, Cuoco is asserting the importance of what escapes from the verticality of the historical process because it cuts diagonally across it along a plane that is not coextensive with it. What he is referring to is a difference between nations and peoples that does not have to do exclusively with their different histories, but additionally, with a sphere closer to geography, or even geology. We thus return to that sideways shift of the gaze that, while not negating the importance of the temporal axis, makes it intersect productively with a more profound perspective, because it is rooted in a layer that apparently precedes, or at least exceeds, that of history proper. This originary layer, hidden by subsequent sedimentations, is the archeological, or to be more exact, the genealogical object of *Plato in Italy*, which, not by chance, undergoes a subtle but symptomatic modification by Cuoco with respect to Vico's archeology. While both authors argue the originarity of the Italian philosophical tradition with regard to the knowledges or powers that overlie it—starting from the universalizing claim of Greek thought—their excavation procedures, so to speak, are

24. Cuoco, *Scritti giornalistici*, vol. 1, p. 249.
25. Ibid., p. 312.
26. Ibid., vol. 1, p. 343.

marked by a significant difference. While Vico takes the language spoken by different civilizations as the criterion of precedence among them—and therefore a factor that is in its turn historical—Cuoco shifts his study to the natural sphere of the land.[27] The most ancient people is the one that inhabits the most ancient land. Not that language formation does not count, but it comes later, and is thus derivative compared to an even more originary layer that consists of the physical place of settlement and that is destined to indelibly mark the character of different peoples. It is true that the current shape of their inhabited land is the momentary outcome of landslides and earthquakes, which, along with the landscape, have changed the life of the populations settled there. But even the ruin cyclically caused by natural disasters can be traced to the telluric substance that precedes the historical times during which historical civilizations have developed from one time to the next. The most ancient civilization is the one rising out of the most ancient ruins, from an earlier destruction—which is the only thing that gradually creates the conditions for a new rebirth.

Like a fact of destiny that defies human will, there is a dramatic tone to this conception that goes far beyond the conclusions Cuoco draws regarding the supposed primacy of the Italic civilization, and which is somehow also projected onto the tragic outcome of the Neapolitan Revolution. This was caused not only by contingent circumstances or strategic errors but also, and above all, by a fatal inability to dig down to the anthropological, ethnological, and even earlier geological strata on which the Neapolitan people had always—from the beginning of their history, in other words—been settled. True, Cuoco never flattens human history into natural history: for him, the ethnic component always enters into a dialectical relationship with external events and subjective choices overlaying the originary structure. But the point he insists on is that when we aim too high, in an attempt to go beyond the bioanthropic limit that nature places on history, then the consequences are likely to be fatal: "Nature had divided up the land of our republic"[28] explains the author. Mountains, seas, and rivers followed natural boundaries within which, for centuries or millennia, the life of the peoples in the south had always been the same.

27. On this subject, see the incisive comments by Rosario Diana in "Vincenzo Cuoco pensatore storico," in Cuoco, *"Platone in Italia": Sette itinerari*, ed. Rosario Diana (Naples, 2004), pp. vii–xxvii.

28. Cuoco, *Saggio storico*, p. 400.

"Instead of this, there appeared districts that cut across each other,"[29] artificially changing what geography had brought into being, until, when it was already too late, the new government had to resort to "means with which they should have begun, namely, to commission a geographic work from our geographers."[30] They wanted to divide what nature had joined together and join together what nature had divided, without taking into consideration that "there is more difference between one land and another than between two people from the same land."[31] Thus a single population was understood to be the sum of human aggregates who, living on lands with different geographical conformations, were in fact different populations— as are those ranging from the "idle shirkers of Naples, the fierce Calabresi, the lightweights of Lecce, to the phoney Samnites."[32] This insurmountable diversity ensured that in one same revolution "there were many populations in open counterrevolution."[33]

Not only that, but within each population there are different and often conflicting layers, natures, and characters: seeking to ignore them is both naive and fatal. It must also be said that Cuoco was one of the first authors to take as an object of study the category of "population,"[34] lending it a complex meaning corresponding neither to the classic, undifferentiated mass of subjects under the sovereign will nor to the democratic idea of a people as the bearer of the national will. This distance from the dominant legal paradigms explains his explicit rejection of the contractual model: "It is easy to go back to the origin, analyze the nature of the social contract, and draw up the declaration of the rights of man and the citizen; but to ensure that human beings, who are not always wise, and rarely just, do not abuse their rights, or make use of them only to the extent they lead to the common well-being, *hoc opus hic labor es* [what work, what labor it is]."[35] This brings into view another fixed trait of Italian philosophy in contrast to the majority view of modern political philosophy—as it ex-

29. Ibid., p. 401.

30. Ibid., p. 402.

31. Cuoco, "Frammenti," p. 530.

32. Ibid., p. 518.

33. Cuoco, *Saggio*, p. 324.

34. On the notion of the people, see P. Girard, "Peuple et politique dans la pensée de Vincenzo Cuoco," in *Laboratoire Italien* 1 (2001): pp. 53–63.

35. Cuoco, "Frammenti," p. 546.

tended along the axis running from Hobbes through Rousseau and arriving at Kant. The population is not a unitary whole of individuals, subjects, or citizens, made equal by their obedience to a law that they have given to themselves; rather, it is an inhomogeneous body, cut through by internal fractures that render difficult any unambiguous interpretation—as proved by the convulsive, disastrous experience of the 1799 revolution. Not only did this see different populations, from the capital and the provinces, diverging from each other, the Neapolitan nation itself was "for two centuries divided into two nations, and by two degrees of climate"—meaning, not only by historical factors, but also by geophysical characteristics.[36] It is as if a dull conflict were to break out between two components of the same people, a subjective one aimed at historical development, and a natural one, not completely subjective but much more deeply rooted in the land, from which it absorbs a force of resistance destructive to anyone who seeks to tear away its land. The only way to not be trampled by it—which is what happened to the revolutionaries—is to adhere to this deep stratum of the population, permeating it from inside, avoiding shocks and forced moves: not giving up on providing these people with a constitution, but adapting it to them, like a garment that you cut out based on the features of the body, without expecting to change the body to suit the clothing. When this does not happen, when ideas separate radically from things and history seeks to liberate itself from nature, imagining that it can pass beyond the limit it bears inside itself in the form of its own "un-", then its fate is sealed. Then the subterranean crack running through life splits open like a land shaken by an earthquake, swallowing up those who failed to recognize the signs and driving the entire civilization to its ruin.[37]

Nothing in Common

1. In the work of Giacomo Leopardi, the relationship between philosophy and life is even more complex and torn than in other authors. So much so that his poetry can be interpreted as the place way up on high

36. Cuoco, *Saggio storico*, p. 326.

37. On the semantics of ruin, see Emma Giammattei, "Alle origini della scrittura laica: Modelli letterari e storiografici nell'opera di Vincenzo Cuoco," in *Vincenzo Cuoco nella cultura di due secoli*, pp. 227–53.

where his thought regains its impact force in its frontal break with modern philosophical language. To begin with, contrary to a mannered image flattened into a semantics of death, it must be said that the poet's gaze is focused from the beginning on the dimension of life as the natural form of existence: "Nature is life," he writes in a fragment dating from 1823. "She is existence. She, too, loves life, and provides for life in every way, and tends to life in all her actions. This is why she exists and lives. If nature were dead, life would not be. To be dead: these are contradictory expressions. If nature tended to death in any way, if she provided for it in any way, she would do so against herself."[38] Both happiness, which constitutes its absolute fulfillment, and pleasure, to which it tends unceasingly, are the expression of an unstoppable impulse of life toward its unlimited expansion: "Pleasure is nothing but life. And life is pleasure necessarily, and the greater and more lively is life, the greater the pleasure. Life is generally all one with nature, life divided into particulars is all one with its respective existent subjects. Therefore, each being, loving life, loves itself" (*Z*, 3814). However, although love of self responds to a natural urge, projecting the desire for existence toward a point beyond the reach of the finite forces of individual living beings, it ends up gradually leading human beings out of the order of nature—into that historical dimension that corrodes it from inside. As we saw with Cuoco, the critical point where life seems to twist around on itself is constituted by the conflict that is generated in it between nature and history. But now, in Leopardi, the proportions between the two spheres are changed to the point of overturning their relationship. The clash between the historical and the unhistorical no longer lies in the framework of history, but in nature, which, as we have just seen, coincides with the very substance of life. It is as if a crevice had opened up in the naturalness of *bios* into which the living being is gradually sucked. History—especially modern history—marks the pulse of this current. The farther it advances, freeing itself from its natural limit, the more its vital substance dries up to the point of atrophying altogether.

Philosophy is the modality through which this devitalization is expressed. It is one particular language that is part of knowledge, but it is also something more intrinsic to the chain of events that, starting from late antiquity, took the name of civilization. Of course, not all philosophers,

38. Giacomo Leopardi, *Zibaldone di pensieri*, ed. Francesco Flora, 2 vols. (Milan: Mondadori, 1937–38), p. 3813; henceforth *Z*. All quotes are translated from the Italian by the translator of the present volume.

or philosophies, are equal in quality and inspiration. Leopardi is careful to distinguish between them, but not without noting the direction they take as a whole, whose dissipative effects are obvious to him. The deciding match is played out in the inversely proportionate relationship between matter and spirit, body and reason, action and inaction. In the ancient world, the natural energy of life extended itself through the primacy of corporeality, in the greatest use of the senses and in the free development of the imagination. Modern civilization—anticipated in this respect by both Platonism and Christianity—is instead internally traversed and even constituted by a movement of spiritualization: although the bodily sphere isn't entirely eliminated, it is destabilized by being made subordinate to a power transcendent to it. In reality, this process of idealization arises from the dual need to reduce reciprocal violence in the community and to free up the higher human functions, sharpening the senses and enhancing the faculty of reason. But the final outcome appears largely counterproductive to Leopardi, because by tearing life away from its natural roots, exactly what was intended to be nurtured is weakened.[39] From this point of view, as will be more fully theorized by Nietzsche, one of the early admirers of Leopardi, it comes as no surprise that modern rationalization has a frankly immunitary character, in the sense described earlier: it claims to heal people by inoculating them with a poison that, in the long run, is lethal to them. On these lines, it can well be said that modern rationalization protects life by negating its primal force. Moreover, the very notion of spirit is negative in itself—defined by what it is not, namely matter, and for this reason capable of turning its power of annihilation against matter: "It is well-known and clear," observes Leopardi, "that the word and the idea of *spirit* cannot be defined in sum and in conclusion other than as a *substance that is not matter*, because we cannot know or name any of its positive qualities" (*Z*, 4205). On the other hand, as is characteristic of all immunization procedures, its consequences wind up being the reverse of the intended effect: the pursuit of health causes a more severe disease; in other words, it brings about the withering away of the very sensibility it was supposed to enhance. Similarly, with the same counterfactual outcome, in seeking to bring about absolute equality, the moderns have transformed

39. On the intrinsic relation between life and illness, see Bruno Moroncini, *L'autobiografia della vita malata: Benjamin, Blanchot, Dostojevkij, Leopardi, Nietzsche* (Bergamo: Moretti & Vitali, 2008), especially pp. 9–32.

ancient difference into a new and more marked inequality: the fight with foreign enemies into civil war and the heroism of the ancients into the ordinary insipidness of equally self-seeking individuals.

The culminating point of this contradictory route is represented by the French Revolution—not so much because of its specific content, but because that tangential point between history and philosophy that was destined to lead modernity down an irreversible path appears to be condensed inside it. Although the French Revolution was only prepared and certainly not carried out by philosophy—since philosophy is incapable of producing action—by attempting to "geometrize all life" (*Z*, 160), it lost sight of the fact that "reason and life are two incompatible things" (*Z*, 358), seeing as "a people composed of philosophers would be the smallest and most cowardly in the world" (*Z*, 115). The still cautious and moderate views expressed by Cuoco have clearly been taken to a whole new level as well as being sharply radicalized. The failure of the revolution, for Leopardi, was not due to subjective errors or factual circumstances that forced it out of its natural course, but the result of a long-term process of abstraction by which human life is at the same time protected and undermined. By stripping nature of its veil—by removing it from its latency in the furious search for a naked truth—the Enlightenment, which was a direct progenitor of the revolution, deprived humankind of its material roots. In this way, and in contrast with its own sensist ideology, it brought to completion that process of idealization initially set into motion by the Platonic and then Christian traditions, which view spirit as "more perfect than matter" (*Z*, 1615). But to define a part—and only one part—of the living being as perfect means at the same time to take value away from the other part, making it subordinate to the first. It literally snaps human life into two, placing one of its dimensions, the biological one of the body, under the dominion of the other, defined as personal, spiritual, and rational:

It is not possible—especially in the same individual, in the same class of beings, and of the highest beings in the natural order, as is man—that the perfection of a highly important, principal part of it, intended and ordered by nature, should cause harm to that of another, similarly principal part. Now if what we call the perfection of our spirit, if the present civilization was willed and ordered by nature, and if it was in sum our perfection, then the absurd contradiction that I expressed would occur, since it is incontestable that this alleged perfection of the soul is harmful to the body. (*Z*, 1597)

This is the precipitating point in the process of internalization that at the same time puts human beings at the center of the world and places consciousness over the body.

Against this anthropocentric inflection, Leopardi launches a vector of meaning that leads back not only to the indissoluble bond between body and life sealed by Machiavelli and Vico, but also and especially to the radical critique of personalist humanism initiated by Bruno along two directions: the infinity of the universe and the centrality of the animal world. As regards the first, just reread in sequence the dialogues between *A Goblin and a Gnome*, *The Earth and the Moon*, and *Copernicus* to understand how shattering it was to all humanistic teleologies to reduce the Earth to just one of an infinite number of planets, rotating anonymously in a sky that is remote and indifferent to the fate of human beings.[40] One in which the personification of the Moon ("My dear Moon, I know you can talk, and answer questions, since you are a person, as I have often heard from the poets")[41]—the only interlocutor to speak to the shepherd wandering in the desert in canto 23—is matched by the obvious impersonality of the human, made equal to all others by the same condition of finitude and suffering. As for the second aspect, from the "Dissertazione sopra l'anima delle bestie" (Dissertation on the soul of animals) to the "Canto del gallo silvestre" (The song of the wild cock), from "Paralipomeni della batracomiomachia" (The war of the mice and the crabs) to the *Zibaldone*, the powerful, varied, and moving references to the animal world in Leopardi's work make it part of a line running from Bruno to Nietzsche that opens up a hitherto unknown or emarginated possibility in modern philosophy. On the one hand, in their biological destiny and in their adaptability to external stresses, the animal species are quite close to the human, so that "one might think that the difference of life between animals and humankind is

40. On the scientific and cosmological aspects of Leopardi's thought, see Gaspare Polizzi, *Leopardi e "le ragioni della verità": Scienza e filosofia della natura negli scritti leopardiani* (Rome: Carocci, 2003), with an introduction by Remo Bodei.

41. Giacomo Leopardi, "Dialogo della terra e della luna," in *Operette morali* (Milan, 2008), p. 193; there are a number of English versions, among which: "Dialogue Between the Earth and the Moon," in *The World's Wit and Humor*, vol. 13 (New York: Review of Reviews, 1906); p. 82; canto 23: "Night Song of a Wandering Shepherd of Asia," in *Giacomo Leopardi: Canti with a Selection of His Prose*, trans. and ed. J. G. Nichols (New York: Routledge, 2003), pp. 94–97.

born from accidental circumstances, and from the different arrangement of the human body which is more suited to society" (*Z*, 56). On the other hand, in some ways animals are even superior, for their ecstatic vitality and intraspecies compassion which humans have lost. In this sense, the animal is nothing but the part of ourselves that we have repressed in our mad pretension to rise above our own natural component. The idea, profoundly innervated in our tradition, that the animal should be a simple tool in the hands of a superior being allowed to use it, kill it, and eat it at will is, for Leopardi, the proof of the complete lack of distinction between civilization and barbarism that runs beneath the entire history of humankind.

2. But this positive attitude toward the animal world should not be limited to his criticism of anthropocentrism. The animal is not only humans' neglected and marginalized other. It is also our "before." The animal is what infinitely precedes the human, because it is still rooted in the natural dimension from which the human species detached itself when it entered into the alienating regime of history. Not by chance, in the emotional tonality of the poet, the animal is associated with the primordial figures of the child, the savage, and the ancient world, united by their constitutive relationship with the origin. If modern history—in its intrinsically philosophical timbre—has resulted in a progressive devitalization of the world, only the reestablishment of an originary condition can reinstate a direct, positive relationship with life. From this point of view, Leopardi sees himself precisely in that stretch of Italian thinkers—between Machiavelli and Vico—who viewed the return to the origin as the ultimate remedy to cure the crisis of civilizations that are too feeble to survive.

Things are not that simple, though, for several reasons. The possibility of reversing the timeline is utterly precluded. Leopardi returns to this preclusion with such insistence and conviction that no room for doubt remains. Once human beings have entered into the stream of history, there is no way for them to get out of it. Likewise, once we have put the analytical resource of reason into action we can't do without it, since in the final analysis even to reject it requires reasoning. Any attempt to remythologize the *logos*—or to reenchant a world already exposed to the winds of disenchantment—remains caught in the circle it seeks to break out of. This point of view alone is enough to separate Leopardi's position, including his ideological stance, from the perspective of reactionary authors, who receive no less scathing criticism from him than what he directs toward the advocates of limitless progress. But there is another, even more compelling reason why humankind cannot leave history: the fact that there is no other unhistorical—or natural—dimension for us to return to. From this angle, Leopardi's distance from Rousseau, to whom he feels united in their common rejection of the myth of progress, is insurmountable. For the poet there is no state of nature accessible to human beings. Nature has never yielded itself, in its transparency, to our gaze. Even in the society of the ancient world, when human beings were not yet separated from themselves and nature was their horizon of meaning, it appeared covered by a veil that allowed it to shine through only by removing it from plain sight. It was modern thought, culminating in the presumption of the Enlightenment, that imagined being able to rip it open, unaware that by doing so, by taking nature as the object of its own representation, nature would lose its symbolic potential, its originary energy. From then on, precisely because it is fully exposed, it has remained unknown and hostile to us in its enigmatic indifference. If what was natural was its latency, rather than its complete vision, the attempt to bring nature to light has in some way made it unnatural.[42] Hence, the closer we try to come to it, the more blurry its contours become, just like when a shadowy stain is so close to us that we are enveloped in its darkness.

This tragic dialectic—which precludes us from the natural principle of our lives—does not entirely exhaust the question, however. Before surrendering to its inevitability by recognizing it as the specific bond that ties all human beings to the same fate, Leopardi works out another, less radical response, aimed at carving a space, however small, for a possible defense against the unhappiness that looms over us. It is a matter of an attitude, which is also immunitary in character—in other words, self-preservational in a negative way—no different in this sense from the one we have already recognized in the process of rationalization, but now organized around the category of illusion. Its premise is that not even the most incontrovertible reality entirely fills the scene, thereby excluding a different perspective through which to filter it. There is always a little opening, something left over, a line of flight along which the vision of things can appear differently from what is there. This opening can be accessed through various paths

---

42. See Alberto Folin, *Leopardi e l'imperfetto nulla* (Venice: Marsilio, 2001), especially pp. 29 ff.

that converge in the same direction. The first is action, which, through its excitement, distracts us from the task of what makes us suffer: to combat unhappiness, says Leopardi, "only one remedy remains: distraction. This consists in the greatest amount of activities, of action, which occupies and fills the developed faculties and the life of the soul" (Z, 4187). Unfortunately, for this remedy to work—for us to be able to act without stopping to reflect on the meaning of this action—requires a vitality that we do not always possess and, indeed, according to Leopardi's own analysis, that decreases steadily. To not think about the ebbing of life that brings us closer to death, we must act without stopping; but, to do so, requires a surplus of the same life force that is fading away. Here, the immunitary procedure described by Leopardi already brings into view an aporia that is difficult to resolve. A second route remains open, however: that of the imagination, which, despite the increasing expansion of reason, can still be put into action at its outer boundaries and inside its internal fractures. This second immunitary device also requires a kind of forgetfulness of the real, a lack of consciousness in which the reality of things seems to fade away—or to be transfigured through a metaphorical transposition that reshapes its features. This result is achieved not through action but through poetry, which, at least at this stage—or, to be more precise, in this layer of his thought— Leopardi opposes to philosophy as regards intentions and results.

However, contradictions abound in this case as well. While the bodily, material, fantastical poetry of the ancients was reflected in the still intact mirror of nature, the romantic, melancholy poetry of the moderns is inscribed in the world of reason—it is continually contradicted by a philosophy that is in principle hostile to any illusion. The only possibility that remains to the poet under these conditions is to superimpose illusion and reason—in other words, to delude oneself while being aware of it; to recognize the illusory nature of illusion by turning a once spontaneous activity into a conscious fiction. It is a matter of pretending not to know, and knowing that one is pretending at the same time. Leopardi is aware of the narrowness of the path he embarks upon—of its unresolvable antinomy. Since distraction—to which both action and poetry lead in the end—resides in a temporary withdrawal of reason, it is both irrational and rational; indeed, it is more reasonable than the reason which intentionally calls it into being: "And yet it is quite certain that everything we do is done under the power of a distraction and a forgetting, which is directly contrary to reason. Though this be utter madness, it is the most reasonable madness in the world; indeed, the only reasonable thing, and the only thorough and *continuous* wisdom, while the others are not, except for brief spells" (*Z*, 104). Conscious illusion, or artificial fiction, is thus not only internal to the reason it seeks to surpass, it constitutes its extreme intensification— a reason so rational that it can interrupt itself without ever losing technical control of the operation, and, indeed, it thereby gains even more mastery of its own game. Rather than recover a relationship with nature—as the ancients believed they were doing—the only thing left for the moderns is to feign "a second nature" that is entirely artificial and therefore even less natural. The result appears to be increasingly far from the objective: the more nature is sought, the more technique is enhanced; the more reason is opposed, the more it is strengthened, with the contrary-to-life consequence to which this inevitably leads. Superimposed upon the immunitary dispositif of rationalization, stuck inside it, the dispositif of illusion ushers in an even more intractable contradiction. It is as if, in this case, the two defensive procedures—the two protective remedies—were screwed into a short circuit that multiplied their negative charge. Rather than reason and illusion being reconciled, they do nothing but destroy each other, emptying one another of substance for something that is neither one nor the other but the negation of both: "Reason needs the imagination and illusions it destroys" (*Z*, 1839). In the background of the scene, where the useless attempts at conservation collide with one another, looms the ghostly silhouette of pure nothingness.

3. On top of this first layer of his discourse—still within the immunitary logic of "remedy," "shelter," and "defense" against the overwhelming fury of nothingness—a second layer expressing a slightly different attitude is added, or to be more precise, is overlaid. However, we need to avoid a misunderstanding about the meaning of this distinction. It should not be attributed entirely to the sequence of two different phases—before and after 1824, the date to which a negative change in Leopardi's concept of nature is usually traced—but neither should it be exaggerated in the form of a clash between different conceptions. It is better understood as two layers of one thought—concerning the relationship between reality and illusion—that sometimes merge and at other times diverge, even on the same page. What distinguishes them is an often imperceptible shift in per-

spective, large enough however to shift the emphasis from one pole to the other of a single conceptual chunk. To talk about an illusory reality is not the same as talking about a real illusion, of course. Just as pretending that something is true is not the same as the truth of a fiction.[43] The complex relationship between philosophy and poetry is played out on the crest of this narrow ridge. While up to a certain point Leopardi opposes one to the other—assigning to the first a negative significance for life and to the second a positive one—later, or elsewhere, he tends to reunite them at a higher level into the same attitude, which, quite aptly, has been given the name of "poetizing thought."[44] From this second standpoint, he comes to define the great poets like Homer, Dante, and Shakespeare as thinkers, and some of the great philosophers, starting with Plato, as poets. According to a recurrent topos in Italian thought running between Bruno and Vico, the imaginative faculty is anything but separate from the reflective one; instead, the imagination is an indispensable, internal structure of reason. Humans are beings who, by nature, imagine even when they think—both in the sense that the image always contains a conceptual element, and in the sense that we also think through images. But if this is true—following a conception traceable back to Leonardo and Vico—if the mind itself is what is imagining, in its own way and according to its own particular rhythm, how are we to interpret Leopardi's oft-repeated opposition between poetry and philosophy? And why, at a certain point, does this distinction seem to fade away?

This semantic and categorial slippage, in its turn, concerns an inhomogeneous judgment—one punctuated by temporal and qualitative thresholds—of philosophy itself. We are familiar with the general difference that Leopardi traced out between ancient and modern thought. While the thought of the ancients did not violate nature and thus safeguarded its secret, the thought of the moderns, by taking nature as its object of representation, illuminated it to the point of scorching it. This first division between ancient and modern is joined by a second one, between the philosophy of the early modern period—aimed at the formulation of an abstract truth, and therefore separate from life—and the philosophy

43. On the reality of fiction, see Arturo Mazzarella, *I dolci inganni* (Naples: Liguori, 1996); also by Mazzarella, *La potenza del falso: Illusione, favola e sogno nella modernità letteraria* (Rome: Donzelli, 2004), pp. 19 ff.

44. See Antonio Prete, *Il pensiero poetante* (Milan: Feltrinelli, 1980).

of Leopardi's contemporaries, which is a weakened, filtered version of the first, although not completely lacking in a driving force. Dubbed a "half philosophy" by the poet, it, too, is in itself erroneous and contrary to life, but in a form aimed at immunizing against (treating homeopathically, that is) the lethal effects of the first philosophy: "So the errors of the half philosophy can serve as medicine for errors that are more contrary to life; although these, too, ultimately stem from philosophy, from the corruption caused by an excess of civilization, which is never unrelated to the relative excess of the Enlightenment from which it largely derives. What little life and popular movement there is today actually springs from the half philosophy" (*Z*, 521). Leopardi's attitude toward this halved philosophy vacillates. On the one hand he appreciates its capacity to leave a residual space open for imagination and action; on the other hand, he condemns it as cowardly and regressive compared to the cognitive force of the previous form of knowledge. To go back to the dialectic mentioned earlier, one could say that, unlike true philosophy, it relates more to the illusion of fiction than to the reality of fiction. The "half philosophy" is concerned with protecting people from the brutal impact with the truth that early modern thought confronted without caring about the consequences. Because of its crepuscular character, Leopardi envisages that it will go rapidly extinct, to be replaced by a new form of reflection that he calls "ultraphilosophical." This is destined to carry on the analysis of the truth started by great modern philosophy, but without deluding itself that illusion can be dispensed with, and thus recognizing a primary role for poetry.

An understanding of Leopardi's complex relationship with nihilism—reconstructed with exceptional exegetical rigor by Emanuele Severino—must take its start from this internal difference.[45] Severino's thesis, which I largely share, is that the Italian poet should take his place at the height of the great philosophy of his time—from Hegel to Nietzsche—which he surpasses, however, because he penetrates more deeply into the aporetic implication between being and nothingness. I would say that this happens, in the end, when what we have called the second layer of his thought prevails

45. See Emanuele Severino, *Il nulla e la poesia: Alla fine dell'età della tecnica; Leopardi* (Milan: Rizzoli, 1990); and his *Cosa arcana e stupenda: L'Occidente e Leopardi* (Milan: Rizzoli, 1997). Severino's reading of Leopardi's nihilism should be compared and critically contrasted with Sergio Givone's in *Storia del nulla*, pp. 135–54, which takes a different direction, slanted toward the tragic.

over the first. We have seen that the latter expresses or bears within itself an immunitary tendency aimed at constructing a protective shield against the contrary-to-life current of the Modern. From this angle, the fury of nothingness has not yet covered the entire surface of reality, in the sense that it seems to leave open a residual space, a "rest of nothing" that is taken up from time to time, or all at the same time, by the various remedies of distraction: action and imagination. In this phase, or fold, of Leopardi's discourse, poetry, in its ability to soothe our existential wounds, seems to be the last *katechon* still standing in our defense against the annihilating violence of nothingness. In reaction to this first expressive mode of Leopardi's thought, however, there comes another, more extreme impulse: according to this, nothing can be opposed to nothingness except nothingness itself—transposed from its destructive meaning, however, to the affirmative significance of "nothing-in-common." The texts that push the poet's perspective in this direction, the truly definitive one—from the *Dialogue Between Plotinus and Porphyrius* to the *Ginestra* (Broom plant)—are well known. Having now entirely occupied all reality—not only as its fateful outcome, but as its originary premise—the power of nothingness not only cannot be stopped or mitigated by any protective shield, it must be assumed in its unmovable fatality.

From this point of view, the only philosopher who really "corresponds" to the poetizing thought of Leopardi is Nietzsche. For him, too, the only non-nihilistic way to deal with nihilism is not to fight it in vain, but to push it so far to the bottom that it sinks down into its own maelstrom. Only in this way, like a ricochet movement, will it produce a recoil capable of keeping its head, recognizing in the sovereign power of death the pulsing of a life that it cannot entirely eliminate because it constitutes the matter, so to speak, without which death would not be what it is: it would go around in circles, with no object for its horrendous work: "Besides this, the feeling of nothingness is the feeling of something dead and deadly. But if this feeling is alive, as it is in the case under discussion, its liveliness prevails in the soul of the reader over the nothingness of the thing that makes itself felt, and the soul receives life (momentary, at least) from the same force with which it feels the perpetual death of things, and its own death" (*Z*, 261). We are at the turning point, the last tear from which all the folds of Leopardi's thought seem to unfold along a path that is extreme in all senses, with no return or safety nets. Once all the immunitary *dispositifs* used so far have been dismantled, the life force that poetry communicates to us is no longer sought by him in the poetic content, but in the simple fact of being poetry. We no longer require it to delude us, or distract us, because the consolation it brings no longer resides in what it says—but only in its saying what can no longer be concealed. On these lines, poetry can be united with a thought that is capable, in its turn, of giving up on its mad pretensions, in order to reflect itself in poetry in the name of the common truth—of the bond, whether conscious or unconscious, that it establishes between all those it addresses. That its content is death, the inevitable death of humans, animals, species, genera, worlds—as the broom plant that bloomed for an instant on the edge of the volcano knew well—does not cancel out its significance: on the contrary, this makes it even more powerful than the hurricane destined to eventually ravage it. Only if the flower knows that there is no escape from the desert that stretches all around it can it sing out its song of truth. Similarly, only if we give up all will to power, feeling ourselves as part of everything that encompasses us, expropriating ourselves of all properties, will we be able to recognize the contours of that *communitas* that our immunitary procedures have attempted to restore, ending up instead by negating it altogether.[46] Of course, a community of this sort will have none of the identity or identification that we foolishly seek in it. It will not bring us closer in the name of proximity and belonging. It can only be a community of the distant and the estranged, the loners and the dispersed: those who have nothing in common other than their nothingness. But it is a nothingness cut through for a brief instant by the flash of light that reveals it.

Science and Life

1. The third author whose work focuses on the unresolved tension between knowledge and life—although in a very different way from Cuoco and Leopardi—is Francesco de Sanctis. The fact that, professionally, he was a literary critic—the greatest Italy has ever produced—does not conflict with what has been said thus far. On the contrary, this provides further confirmation of the need for Italian thought to use a differ-

46. On this line of interpretation, see Antonio Negri, *Lenta ginestra: Saggio sull'ontologia di G. Leopardi* (Milan: Sugarco, 1987).

ent language from the technically philosophical one in order to open up a perspective that is somehow heterogeneous to the European reflection of its time. This conceptual and semantic difference is all the more symptomatic when the author in question, far from rejecting a relationship with philosophy, takes it as the privileged reference for his own discourse. This is what de Sanctis did with respect to the Hegelian tradition. The leading role he played in Neapolitan Hegelianism is so well known that there is no need to return to it in detail.[47] For de Sanctis, as for a whole generation of intellectuals, Hegel was the best alternative from the 1840s on—both philosophically and politically—to the stalemate of a culture that still vacillated between the eclecticism of Victor Cousin, the formalism of Kant, and the spiritualism of Gioberti. Although he was initially influenced by Gioberti—appreciated for the breakup of the reactionary front provoked by his neo-Guelphian initiative—de Sanctis had never shared his narrow notion of Italian supremacy built on the rejection of the Lutheran and Cartesian origins of modern philosophy. Much more sensitive to Cuoco's more enlightened, open conception, he was convinced that an Italian identity could only arise out of an encounter and dialogue with the great European culture. On these lines, he soon recognized that the conceptual *dispositif* best suited to the future constitution of the national state was to be found in the Hegelian philosophy. Nobody had learned and theorized better than Hegel how to marry individual interests with collective goals, real needs with ideal values—something that de Sanctis saw, from his vantage point, as the task and the goal of the new Italian ruling class.

And yet the increasing difficulties this project encountered must have been exactly what convinced him of the practical, but also philosophical, inadequacy of the Hegelian model. This distrust, even though it never led him to completely abandon what still struck him as the cutting edge of modern knowledge, did not come to maturity all at once. It initially grew around the borders of the Hegelian system, particularly regarding the apodictic assumption of the death of art, which de Sanctis rejected as an unwarranted extension to the complex historical devel-

47. Guido Oldrini, *La cultura filosofica napoletana dell'Ottocento* (Rome-Bari: Laterza, 1973), is still a useful source on Neapolitan Hegelianism. From a different, more critical perspective, see Alberto Asor Rosa, "La cultura," in *Storia d'Italia*, vol. 4, *Dall'Unità a oggi* (Turin, 1975), pp. 850–78; as well as Fulvio Tessitore, *Da Cuoco a de Sanctis: Studi sulla filosofia napoletana del primo Ottocento* (Naples: Malusa, 1988).

opment of an experience that was limited to a specific phase. But in this way, what was introduced as a specific objection limited to aesthetics ended up by force of circumstances bringing down the entire framework of the Hegelian edifice, starting from the philosophy of history that was its foundation.[48] Even the triadic rhythm of the Hegelian dialectic appeared to the Italian critic as a sort of secularized transposition of Trinitarian theology, in which the concreteness and the accidental nature of the real were sacrificed to an ideal paradigm that was superimposed on top of them, and therefore unable to account for them. From this point of view, the attitude toward Hegelianism that de Sanctis matured over time, though never resulting in a complete rejection, had a number of affinities in its basic inspiration with the antimetaphysical and even anti-philosophical attitude we met up with earlier in Cuoco, and later, in a much more radical form, in Leopardi. Two letters by the critic, written a few days apart in 1857, one to De Meis and the other to Villari, convey the sense of this gradual detachment. While in the first, de Sanctis limits himself to indicating a growing uneasiness with Hegelian apriorism, going so far as to state that Hegel had "dried up his soul" and that reading him had become "unbearable,"[49] in the second he identifies the point of disagreement that by then had clearly distanced him from the German philosopher. Affirming that "Hegel's primary mistake is to take as the evolution of humanity something that is nothing but an evolution of one of its periods,"[50] de Sanctis opposes the Hegelian philosophy of history, oriented toward a necessary fulfillment, with a differently structured conception of historicity divided into two superimposed layers, one of which proceeds without interruption, while the other tends to get stuck and even go backward periodically. It is not difficult to recognize, behind this irregular pattern, the name of the person who gradually began to take the place of Hegel in de Sanctis's formation: "The content does not come

---

48. On de Sanctis's complex relationship and gradual distancing from Hegel, see M. T. Lanza, "De Sanctis e Hegel," in *Francesco De Sanctis nella storia della cultura*, vol. 1, ed. Carlo Muscetta (Rome-Bari: Laterza, 1984), pp. 155–84. A different and more intrinsic relationship to the Hegelian philosophy of history is identified instead by Giorgio Ficara, in *Stile Novecento* (Venice: Marsilio, 2007), pp. 53–72.

49. Francesco de Sanctis, *Epistolario (1856–1858)*, in *Opere* (Turin: Einaudi, 1965), vol. 19, p. 403.

50. Ibid., p. 406.

back, it always progresses; the forms are subject to Vico's law of return. Hegel confuses the two things and makes humanity end with him. . . . He is thus wrong both in general and in particular."[51]

What is the significance of Vico's presence—located along the line of realism connecting Machiavelli to Leopardi—within a cultural horizon still marked by Hegel? How does it work? First of all, it expresses an explicit distancing, typical of all Italian thought, from an abstract, deductive [...]noved from the density of bodies and passions, [...] this point of view, and in contrast to the cat[...]n logic, the reference to Vico recalls the inex[...]erience. But on the other hand, it points to a [...]om the linear fluidity of time and always chal[...]ts own internal limit. This is what we have de[...]us of history that is unhistorical, or not fully [...]int, inside history, beyond which it seems un[...]it proceeds with difficulty and effort, along a [...]s that diverge and will eventually collide with [...]hile Cuoco recognized a geoanthropic element [...]ot always accessible and, indeed, was often re[...]Leopardi brought it back to a concept of na[...]ucible, if not hostile, to the historical plans of [...]mpts to translate the same crux of problems [...] the basis of a lexicon that recurs in his most important essays, this unhistorical residue of history is defined as a "limit" which, arising as an "obstacle," if recognized as such, can become a "stimulus." But this transposition into Hegelian terms is precisely what highlights a profound dissonance with the German philosopher. As we know, for Hegel, the limit against which something hits up is what gives it meaning; but we also know that the consciousness of limit also contains its going beyond [*oltrepassamento*].[52] This is the exact point of divergence from de Sanctis. Of course, for him, too, the limit is a point of negative contrast necessary for further development. But in a form that is not necessarily compatible with a new synthesis, not always destined to be reassembled. The reason for this is not only because, just as an obstacle can become a

---

51. Ibid., 406–7.

52. See the introduction by M. T. Lanza to Francesco de Sanctis, *L'arte, la scienza e la vita* (Turin: Einaudi, 1972), pp. xxxix ff.

stimulus, similarly a stimulus can go back to being an obstacle. But also because the limit is not only what detains history momentarily with a view to further progress, the limit is also the very content of history, its constitutive material, its effective reality.

To this reality, de Sanctis assigns the name of "life," with a frequency and intensity rarely matched in other authors. On the one hand, life is what the limit acts on in determining its boundaries; on the other hand, it is the limit itself for any abstract design that expects to realize itself without being in harmony with its own content. That is what happened to the French Revolution and what is likely to happen every time one loses sight of the profound interest of peoples and individuals, as he writes with the unmistakable overtones of Cuoco: "That history [of the French Revolution] is a lesson, especially for us who also live by absolute concepts, and whose institutions are borrowed from outside, very remote from life and customs. We have a long novitiate to undergo, until our life meets up with our institutions."[53] One can say that de Sanctis's entire intellectual and political project is marked by this need, repeated with pounding regularity: to give life to ideas, and to root ideas in life. The concept of realism itself, around which his entire historical and critical perspective revolves, refers to the union—one that is necessary but far from obvious or definitively attained—between form and content, where the content is nothing but life itself in its concrete effectiveness: "Realism, investigating not a series of preconceived ideas, but a series of social facts, and acquiring an adequate knowledge of the effective life of nations, places the limit on ideas. When they overlap onto life, life rejects them."[54] Never as in de Sanctis has politics sought its source of legitimacy in its originary and intrinsic relationship with life, outside of which even the modern categories—of sovereignty, power, liberty—lose their significance and are emptied of substance: "Nowadays it isn't enough to call oneself liberal. Liberty is a tool, not an end; it is an empty form, unless we fill it with some content, which is the life of our nation and our ideals. And this content is the limit in liberty, what makes it not an abstract idea but a living thing."[55]

53. Francesco de Sanctis, "Il limite," in *I partiti e l'educazione della nuova Italia*, in *Opere*, vol. 16, p. 171.

54. Ibid., p. 172.

55. Ibid., p. 173.

2. The relationship with life—as a dense and profound reality that gives meaning to the common action of human beings—is central to de Sanctis's greatest work. In it, Italian literature is interpreted and judged based on whether or not a living content is given form, which varies from one instance to the next. It is striking that, on balance, shadow prevails largely over light—that in the history of Italian literature, life is captured much more in its contraction than in its expansion. Early on, the current of Sicilian culture "remained alien to the soul and to real life,"[56] "to the seriousness and intimacy of life,"[57] while Petrarch failed to have "the possession and enjoyment and seriousness and force of real life," because his art was "shadow and simulacrum, not a living thing."[58] Differently, but with similar effects, Boccaccio "lacked all the high sentiments of public and religious life," so that "there remains no other poetry than that of private life. Which is vile prose, when the purpose of life is only gain."[59] This is also the reason behind the lack of inspiration in the humanistic culture, since "with an empty conscience and life all external and superficial, drama was no more possible than tragedy."[60] Not to mention the next two centuries, when "the circle of life shrank,"[61] and "literature became an increasingly conventional form that was separated from life."[62] From the Mannerism of the seventeenth century to the Arcadia movement in the eighteenth, the Italian literary world was apparently devoid of ideals and reality, "which is to say, not practiced in life, and with no purpose or tendency of life."[63] A void, of sense and substance, which extends, with varying fortunes, until de Sanctis's time, in which "the grandiloquence and rhetoric continues, a subject scarcely serious enough for study or life. We live greatly on our past and on the work of others. Our life and our work is not to be found there."[64]

True, in the face of this aesthetizing or privatist current—although they were never able to put a stop to it—stand the great figures, "the

56. De Sanctis, *Storia della letteratura italiana* (Turin: Einaudi, 1958), vol. 1, p. 14.
57. Ibid., p. 19.
58. Ibid., p. 303.
59. Ibid., p. 336.
60. Ibid., p. 404.
61. Ibid., p. 471.
62. Ibid., p. 692.
63. Ibid., p. 718.
64. Ibid., p. 975.

greatest stars, around whom move the ranks of free men, animated by the same spirit,"[65] bearers of life and immersed in life—starting from Dante, "a man who considers life seriously. Life is philosophy, truth realized,"[66] to Machiavelli, Bruno, Campanella, Galileo, Vico, and Leopardi. That these authors are, to a large extent, also the protagonists of our genealogy is an integral part of the basic antinomy that underlies de Sanctis's position. Despite having staked out the terrain of his—clearly philosophical—reflection in the discipline of literary criticism, he identifies the high points of Italian literature (with the sole exception, perhaps, of Manzoni) in texts and authors who lie on the margins of literary language, and indeed in a horizon that for various reasons can be said to be philosophical. In this, the absolute specificity of de Sanctis's work comes to the fore compared to all previous and subsequent histories of literature, whether Italian or otherwise. The objective toward which his hermeneutic path leads would appear to be an empty ground; specifically in the sense that its object seems to be largely absent. Once the truth of a given literature, namely, its force and authenticity, has been tied to its ability to form a character—to the moral, political, and civic life that it is able to express and stimulate—the result is that, with rare exceptions, its highest moments are represented by the authors who make up only a marginal part of it, since what they specifically provide belongs more properly to the sphere of philosophical, political, or scientific thought. So much so that, in the case of the two great poets who respectively open and close this series—Dante and Leopardi—the most meaningful sense of Italian literature is created precisely on the shifting boundary where poetry meets up with philosophy, in a dramatic tension with the meaning of life.

The source of this imbalance in de Sanctis's text is a perspectival split between two copresent, but mutually incompatible, interpretive axes: one, cast in Enlightenment but also Hegelian hues, which sees in Renaissance literature the successful launching of the modern era; and the other, descending from Rousseau, which instead views the journey from Dante to Metastasio as a gradual process of decline.[67] From this latter standpoint—

65. Ibid., vol. 2, p. 797.
66. Ibid., vol. 1, p. 72.
67. See the still indispensable monograph by Sergio Landucci, *Cultura e ideologia in Francesco De Sanctis* (Milan: Feltrinelli, 1963).

which de Sanctis received through the mediation of Sismondi, but which is also expressive of an "Italian ideology" recognizable in its most symptomatic form in the work of Alfredo Oriani[68]—not only did the Renaissance culture fail to bridge the ethical-political fracture that occurred at the end of the city-state civilization, it deepened the chasm through a more pronounced gap between form and content, art and society, intellectuals and the common people. This initial hermeneutic indecision is overlapped by another, no less significant one regarding the lack of a national character in Italian literature. This is the question—part of the internal dialectic we introduced earlier between territory and deterritorialization—of the cosmopolitanism of the Italian literary tradition. Again de Sanctis is divided between two different, and even opposing, critical attitudes. On the one hand, he emphasizes the ability of Italian culture to absorb external elements, but also to export its artistic and philosophical experience, as occurred with the "new science" between Bruno and Vico, in relation to the philosophy of Bacon and Locke, Spinoza and Leibniz: "Nations die," he writes in line with Spaventa's theory of the circulation of European thought. "But the human spirit never dies. Eternally young, it passes from one nation to another, and continues the history of humankind according to its organic laws."[69] On the other hand, at the same time, he identifies in this passage to the outside a sort of estrangement of the originary Italian traits and, thus, an objective impediment to the development of the very national identity that Italians lack. Looked at from the first angle, Italian cosmopolitanism turns out to be part—indeed, the origin—of that process of the universalization of ideas that was destined to lead to the French Revolution. The other perspective, strongly marked by Quinet's book on the Italian revolutions,[70] inaugurates instead the regressive rejection of national identity that ended up promoting Catholic hegemony. What results from the intersection of these internally clashing perspectives is a figure that is literally overturned. The irregular, disproportionate, excessive traits of de Sanctis's *History* have been repeatedly stressed: the structural imbalance between its parts, which are hugely expanded in some cases and incompre-

68. On the role of Oriani, and on the characteristics of the "Italian ideology," I refer to the particularly lucid essay by Ernesto Galli della Loggia, "Alle origini della ideologia italiana: Alfredo Oriani e *La rivolta ideale*," *I Quaderni del "Cardello,"* 10 (Ravenna, 2000): 11–29.

69. De Sanctis, *Storia*, vol. 2, p. 572.

70. Edgar Quinet, *Les Révolutions d'Italie* (Paris, 1848).

hensibly small in others; the overblown presence of some authors and the unjustified absence of others.

This is true, but it is not the whole story. It is not only about an internal disharmony, due to the labored and discontinuous development of the work. There is a more apparent lack that, as we've said, even prior to any particular author or literary movement, has to do with its own object, the very existence of something like an Italian literature. It is remarkable, and also symptomatic, that a work created with the stated intent to define or construct a national identity identifies this precisely in its continuous modification or moving away from what should be proper to it, in an unstoppable slide into a constitutive "improperty [improprietà]." But in addition to putting its absent—or at least elusive—object into question, the *History of Italian Literature* also questions its own historical dimension. We have seen how this is undermined, and almost prevented, by an irresolvable crisis—the divergence between form and content, between representation and life—that threatens almost everything along its path. The *History* ends with the despairing symbol of an ultimate formlessness that is all the more crushing when compared to the successfully concluded process of political unification: "You could say that the intellectual and political world out of which the nation arose lost its form precisely when Italy took form."[71] But this final dissonance is practically a preordained outcome of a wound that is even more incurable, because it is originary—and even identical with the origin, seeing as "Dante, who was supposed to be the beginning of a whole literature, was its end."[72] This coinciding of beginning and crisis, summit and abyss, will be cyclically reproduced in subsequent eras, like in Machiavelli's time, when "just at that point, when Italy had all the appearance of youthful vigor, it disappeared from the roster of nations,"[73] since the "period referred to as our Risorgimento, or resurgence . . . was also that of our decadence or decay."[74] For this reason, in de Sanctis crisis appears no more internal to history than history appears entirely projected onto crisis. A history of uninterrupted crises, according to the Viconian conception which, once again, seems to call into question and knock the bottom out of every utopian model, every abstractly phil-

---

71. De Sanctis, *Storia*, vol. 2, p. 974.
72. Ibid., vol. 1, p. 310.
73. De Sanctis, "Conferenze su Nicolò Machiavelli," in *L'arte, la scienza e la vita*, p. 43.
74. De Sanctis, "L'uomo del Guicciardini," in *L'arte, la scienza e la vita*, p. 94.

osophical system: the more science progresses and evolves, the more it is separated from the material needs of life, and hence, the more civilization starts to falter and wither away.

3. This is the underlying theme that runs throughout the extraordinary opening lecture to the course de Sanctis gave in Naples in 1872, entitled "Science and Life." In these powerful, dazzling pages, the tension of the dialectic between life and philosophy reaches its apex. It is as if the slash mark in the authors we have examined so far that joins life and philosophy by disjoining them had become his central and almost exclusive object. The moment that knowledge—whether scientific or philosophical—loses its relation with its living content, it eventually dries up and withers away. By uselessly trying to force the irregularity of life into its abstract patterns, knowledge is overwhelmed by its violent reaction. This is why younger, still barbaric peoples prevail over those enfeebled by an excess of civilization, to replace them on the stage of history. Behind the crepuscular metaphor of the Hegelian owl, there appears the far more dramatic theory of Vico's *ricorsi*. Philosophical abstraction is not limited to only completing a historical cycle, it can also drive the cycle toward its dissolution. France's recent defeat by Germany— which appeared to bring the cycle begun by the "philosophical" revolution of 1789 to a close—provides the ultimate proof of this:

Science is the product of the mature age, and lacks the strength to undo the course of the years, to bring back youthfulness. Maturity is certainly the most splendid age of life, not the beginning, but the result, the noble crown of history, rather, which stimulates and begins a new history. After her comes old age and dissolution: and new, younger peoples take her place, the eternal law of nature: the dissolution of one is the generation of the other.[75]

From ancient Greece, which was defeated by the uncivilized Romans, who, once civilized, were beaten by the barbarians; to the enfeebled Italian cities of the sixteenth century, who were invaded and conquered by foreign armies; to France, now defeated by the Germans, history has always reproduced the same dialectic that, after Vico, was recognized by Cuoco, and in a more radical form, by Leopardi as well: when life is overwhelmed and violated by a philosophy that forgets its own limits, then life vanquishes history with its primordial force. "Thus vanished the realm of philosophy;

75. De Sanctis, "La scienza e la vita," in *L'arte, la scienza e la vita*, p. 318.

life revenged itself and out of contempt called it ideology; people believed a little less in ideas and a little more in things. The more profound their faith in science, the more bitter their disillusionment. From whence they drew this harsh truth: Science is not Life."[76]

A lot has been said about de Sanctis's inaugural lecture, but not always in an appropriate way. Dismissed by Spaventa as a tirade with an effect comparable to "Christmas Eve, when they shoot off fireworks and light up Bengal flares,"[77] it could not, of course, inspire Croce's enthusiasm, because, in terms of merit and tone, it was too distant from his perspective.[78] Gentile had more appreciation for it, but he also forced it into a more activist direction.[79] The person who gave it its rightful place in de Sanctis's oeuvre—but, more generally, in the Hegelianism of southern Italy—was Luigi Russo on the basis of an opinion also shared implicitly by Gramsci.[80] Far from being an expression of vitalistic irrationalism, de Sanctis's text does not mechanically oppose science to life, but, if anything, tends to integrate science into life as "an active, continuous production of that collective brain, called a people, a production imbued with all the elements and forces and interests of life. . . . The more one delves into life, the more it imitates history in its processes, the more it conceals itself in those forces and in those interests, and the more effective and expansive its action will be."[81] Only to the extent that it serves life rather than attempting pointlessly to free itself of it, or even to control it from on high through its principles, does science find its measure and its role. Vico's appearance in these pages, a typical feature of Italian thought in the first half of the nineteenth century, has been commented on. But a more elective affinity to another author cannot be overlooked.[82] Although this affinity is less amenable to philological evidence, it appears to push these pages beyond their space

76. Ibid., p. 321.

77. Bertrando Spaventa, letter to Camillo De Meis of December 14, 1872, in *Ricerche e documenti desanctisiani* (Naples: Giannini, 1915), vol. 9, ed. Benedetto Croce.

78. Benedetto Croce, *Cultura e vita morale* (Bari: Laterza, 1955), pp. 272–76.

79. Giovanni Gentile, *Che cosa è il fascismo* (Florence: Vallecchi, 1924), pp. 157–58.

80. See Luigi Russo, *Francesco de Sanctis e la cultura napoletana* (Florence, 1959; repr., ed. Umberto Carpi (Rome: Editori Riuniti, 1983), pp. 324 ff; and see Antonio Gramsci, *Letteratura e vita nazionale* (Turin: Einaudi, 1950), pp. 5 ff.

81. De Sanctis, *L'arte, la scienza e la vita*, p. 331.

82. Gennaro Barbuto has aptly pointed out this symmetry in *Ambivalenze del Moderno: De Sanctis e le tradizioni politiche italiane* (Naples: Liguori, 2000), pp. 95 ff.

and their time, into a different, more distant horizon. Two years after de Sanctis's lecture, the second of Nietzsche's *Untimely Meditations* seems to unknowingly retrace his reasoning process. If we reproduce what Nietzsche writes on history—which should largely be understood as a historical science—to what the Italian critic says about science, the parallel is almost perfect. Of course, in a different framework—or even an opposing one, for example, regarding his opinion on the Italian Renaissance or the role of Germany—this time sharply reversing Hegel's point of view, Nietzsche also makes the value of history, acted and thought, dependent on its respect for an internal limit that is one and the same as its vital content. The correspondence with de Sanctis's text is striking when Nietzsche writes, "Insofar as it stands in the service of life, history also stands in the service of an unhistorical power, and because of this subordinate position, it neither could nor should become a pure science. . . . For at the point of a certain excess of history, life crumbles and degenerates—as does, ultimately, as a result of this degeneration, history itself, as well."[83]

We know that when he uses the term *unhistorical* Nietzsche refers to something more than a generically vital content. Unhistorical, for him and in this context, means also and essentially "biological," not only in relation to the human species. His whole text—not by chance, beginning with a specific reference to Leopardi—focuses on the animal ground of life that historical knowledge must not violate, if what it wants is to avoid self-destruction. All this, at least in the literal sense, is missing from de Sanctis's inaugural lecture. But—here is the element that justifies the juxtaposition—it is part of the critical and biographical experience of the Italian critic, in forms peculiar to de Sanctis, of course, that cannot be superimposed onto Nietzsche's semantics. The point of connection between their two lexicons is not the traditional positivist culture but the influence of Darwin. Without going into the complex question of Nietzsche's Darwinism, it can be stated that de Sanctis's version is based more on an emotional involvement than on a reasoned adherence. And yet, if one reads his essay on Zola, followed by those on Darwinism in art, his reference to the biological given as an invariant element of human history—as an un-

83. Friedrich Nietzsche, *Unzeitgemässe Betrachtungen: Zweites Stück; Vom Nutzen und Nachteil der Historie für das Leben.* English version: "On the Utility and Liability of History (1874)," trans. Richard T. Gray, in *Complete Works: Unfashionable Observations* (Stanford, CA: Stanford University Press, 1995), p. 95.

historical element, in other words—but also his mention of the originary and never fully superable animal dimension of the human being, strike the reader as anything but a rhetorical turn of phrase. This does not mean that de Sanctis unquestioningly accepted everything Zola produced, or more generally, everything that was circulating in a time indelibly marked by Darwin's influence. Indeed, it is as if he tried in his essays to divert the Darwinian tendency into channels with easily controllable embankments, seeking, by means of the concept of realism, a balance between the idealistic tradition and the positivistic conception. Or, to return to the dichotomy with which we began: between the historical and the unhistorical, culture and nature, *logos* and *bios*. But without ever relinquishing a sharp critique of the anthropocentric view.

While de Sanctis rejected any kind of biologistic determinism—aimed at flattening the identity of human beings into their genetic component—he located himself at an equal and even greater distance from any sort of humanistic spiritualism that lacked the capacity to see through the reality of people and things. Of course, he moved with great caution in a field like art and literature, in which the threshold of difference between human beings and other forms of living species is obviously more pronounced. But—once this insuperable boundary was established—the target of the critic's polemic became the opposite tendency to isolate the rational and spiritual attributes of the person from the bodily world, and in this animal sense, in which they are naturally embodied. In this case, his continued reference to Vico, which never slackened over time—directed against the idealistic tradition that claimed to continue it, but without fully understanding it—comes across as a choosing of sides: "The precursor is Vico, the true father of this new art, whose world is not so much a logical ideal, as maintained by German philosophy, which vaunted itself as the continuer of Vico; his world is philological, historical, psychological, positive, concrete, opposed to innate ideas, and to the abstract ideas of Cartesianism. The continuation of Vico is the science based on observation and on the real."[84] As a confirmation of the genealogy we have reconstructed so far, in the same overture made to the naturalness of the human being, overlying the references to Vico throughout de Sanctis's work there is an equally active and effective appeal to Machiavelli. If Vico represents

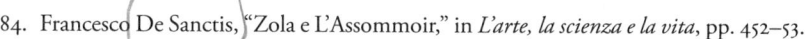

84. Francesco De Sanctis, "Zola e L'Assommoir," in *L'arte, la scienza e la vita*, pp. 452–53.

the indissoluble unity of the living body, in opposition to the abstract isolation of the subject and the rational absoluteness of the person, Machiavelli stands for the primacy of force over form: "The idea is not enough for
us; we want see the force in it, to what extent it is feasible and opportune,
and as for the unarmed apostles and cowardly ideas that have pretensions
of ruling the world, we regard them with the same amusement as Machiavelli did. The old maxim:—Ideas rule the world—has given way to this
one:—Where there is no force, there is no life, neither real nor ideal."[85]
Without going so far as to misunderstand and distort this dynamic of life
into the conclusion drawn by others, that "force defeats right,"[86] de Sanctis
is not afraid to take his place, with all his originality, in that line of Italian
thought running from Machiavelli to Bruno and from Vico to Leopardi
that links the development of the human animal to its ability to understand its membership in the great chain of living beings.

85. De Sanctis, "Il darwinismo nell'arte," in *L'arte, la scienza e la vita*, p. 461.
86. Ibid.

PASSAGE III: *INFERNO*

According to the dialectic between territory and deterritorialization that we discussed in Chapter 1, if the quality of Italian thought is also to be measured by its expansive capacity, few texts are entitled to represent it with the same authority as Cesare Beccaria's *On Crimes and Punishments*. Triumphantly welcomed by the French Enlightenment, particularly by Voltaire, it brought a profound renewal to the whole European debate on justice, even directly influencing Catherine the Great's prison reform in Russia. This extraordinary success, however, has never been separated from a sort of interpretive *décalage* which had the effect of dampening its purely philosophical impact, harnessing it to a more technically juridical sphere. The first translation, by the French Abbé André Morellet, to which Beccaria's essay owes its widespread diffusion outside Italy, bears the traces of this shift in the different arrangement of the arguments, changed from the original to present it as the possible basis for a new codification. But this revised presentation ends up obfuscating its more substantial theoretical character. Moreover, even in Italian Enlightenment circles, where the essay was conceived, there was no lack of reservations and misunderstandings about it—as if it were prudent "to praise the work while pulling a veil down over its principles,"[87] as Gianrinaldo Carli wrote to Paolo Frisi. Not to mention the explicit doubts expressed about it in Naples, by both Francesco Mario Pagano and Gaetano Filangieri, regarding its sharpest point: the proposed abolition of the death penalty.[88] All these hesitations and even steps backward regarding the explosive novelty of the essay have been traced by the critical literature to its Rousseauian slant—namely the egalitarian premise that drives it, which was judged excessive for the moderatism of the Milan group and somehow unpopular even among the French Encyclopedists, who by then had broken off personal relations with Rousseau. And yet it was precisely on this more controversial issue of the death penalty that, rather than anticipating Beccaria's firm abolitionist stance,

87. The citations come from the edition by Franco Venturi of Cesare Beccaria, *Dei delitti e delle pene* (Turin: Einaudi, 1965), with a collection of letters and documents chronicling the essay's reception, p. 187.

88. On the complex relationship between Beccaria and the Neapolitan intellectuals, see A. M. Rao, "'Delle virtù e de' premi': La fortuna di Beccaria nel Regno di Napoli," in *Cesare Beccaria tra Milano e l'Europa* (Rome-Bari: Laterza, 1990), pp. 535–86.

Rousseau pronounced the criticism that would later be directed toward the Italian thinker, using different arguments, first by Kant and then by Hegel.[89] So from this angle, too, we see the semantic overstepping of an Italian text—its lexical heterogeneity—relative to the horizon in which it inscribed itself: with a modality that made it irreducible to the dichotomy between the old antimodern front—soon to viciously attack it—and that of the moderns, represented mainly by Kant, who were to target it with an equally rancorous critique.

What threshold did this particular overstepping trangress? What in Beccaria's essay did contemporary culture fail to understand or frankly reject? What is the message that had to be nuanced or veiled, if not censored, because it was unrepresentable in the dominant theoretical paradigms? To approach this message—which was implicit but not reducible to the call for the abolition of the death penalty—it may be useful to start from the rejection on the part of Rousseau and Kant. Rousseau rejected the argument used by Beccaria of the inalienable right to life in favor of those who should ensure its safety. Kant, transferring the discussion from the utilitarian plane of the *conservatio vitae* to the ethical plane of conformity to the categorical imperative, identified in the law of retaliation—and therefore also in the death penalty—the only moral criterion for the implementation of justice. In both cases, then, whether the sphere of politics or that of law is involved, human life is not considered to be the primary good after which all the others should be placed. On the contrary, the ultimate guarantee of order—both political and moral—is still sought in death: "In accordance with the pharisaical saying, "It is better for one man to die than for an entire people to perish," writes Kant. "For if justice goes there is no longer any value in human beings' living on the earth."[90] Rousseau echoes him by saying, "When the prince says to [the subject]: 'It is expedient for the State that you should die,' he ought to die, because it is only on that condition that he has been living in security up to the present, and because his life is no longer a mere bounty of nature, but a gift made conditionally by the State."[91] It is this thread of reasoning—the cogent nexus

---

89. On this topic, see Norberto Bobbio, *L'età dei diritti* (Turin: Einaudi, 1990), pp. 181 ff.

90. Immanuel Kant, *Grundlegung der Metaphysik der Sitten*, in *Gesammelte Schriften* (Berlin, 1902–), vol. 4; English version: *The Metaphysics of Morals*, pt. 1, ed. Mary Gregor (Cambridge: Cambridge University Press, 1996), p. 105.

91. Jean-Jacques Rousseau, *Le contrat social*, in *Oeuvres complètes* (Paris, 1959–69), vol. 3;

between politics and death, namely the conditioned character of life, dependent on the will of those who are its rightful owner—that Beccaria breaks with by deploying a philosophical option that, at least in this form, was unprecedented. Not because it sought to oppose the unconditionality of life to the necessity of politics or to the force of the law, but because it recognized prematurely that politics and law only find their ultimate criterion of legitimacy in life. From this point of view, once the utilitarianistic framework of his cultural background is established, the question that critics have long debated about Beccaria's exact position along the oscillating line between hedonistic individualism and social humanitarianism loses its relevance.[92] What matters—pushing it into a theoretical orbit that is no longer Locke's or Helvetius's, or Rousseau's and Kant's either—is his early intuition of a transition between eras that places reflection on justice also into a different economy of the living. Michele Foucault, who was the first to identify the underlying premise, wrote: "Here the principle takes root that one should never apply 'inhumane' punishments to a criminal who, nevertheless, may well be a traitor and a monster. If the law must now treat in a 'humane' way an individual who is 'outside nature' (whereas the old justice treated the 'outlaw' inhumanely), it is not on account of some profound humanity that the criminal conceals within him, but because of necessary regulation of the effects of power. It is this 'economic' rationality that must calculate the penalty and prescribe the appropriate techniques. 'Humanity' is the respectable name given to this economy and to its meticulous calculations."[93]

If this is true, then what comes to light is also that intractable element which, much more than Rousseauian egalitarianism, distances Beccaria not only from his reactionary adversaries but also from the modern thinkers: it is the attack on the theological-political category of sovereignty that serves as the common background of markedly different authors like Hobbes, Rousseau, and Kant—as well as Hegel, although in a framework

English version: *The Social Contract, A Discourse on the Origin of Inequality, and A Discourse on Political Economy*, trans. G. D. H. Cole (Stilwell, KS: Digireads, 2006), p. 16.

92. This is the main theme of the monograph by Giuseppe Zarone, *Etica e politica nell'utilitarismo di Cesare Beccaria* (Naples: Istituto Italiano di Studi Storici, 1971).

93. Michel Foucault, *Surveiller et punir: Naissance de la prison* (Paris: Gallimard, 1975). English version: *Discipline and Punish: The Birth of the Prison*, trans. Alan Sheridan (New York: Random House, 1995), p. 92.

that was no longer contractualist. It is on this threshold—of distinction, and also of opposition, between the new biopolitical regime and the preexisting sovereign regime—that the otherwise elusive philosophical meaning of a work like *On Crimes and Punishments* is to be grasped. When Beccaria writes that sovereignty and laws "are nothing but the sum of all the smallest portions of the personal liberty of each individual," and asks the question how "is it possible that, in the smallest portions of the liberty of each, sacrificed to the good of the public, can be contained the greatest of all good, life?"[94] he is removing the sphere of human life from the sovereign person. First, in denying that the sovereign—even if embodied in a human being—is to be considered a "Person," since he is merely a "depositary and custodian" of those "minimal" sacrifices that the subjects make of their liberty, which certainly do not include the right to life, since it is inalienable: "Hence, it is certain that each man wanted to put into the public depositary the smallest portion of his liberty possible, only enough to induce others to defend it."[95] What counts here—in order to deconstruct the theological-political knot that tied the sovereign person to the supreme power of an irrevocable decision on life and death—is to preserve the impersonal character of justice, being careful "not to attach to this word 'justice' the idea that it is something real, like a physical force or something that actually exists." "Of course, I do not speak of the kind of justice that emanates from God and that is directly linked to the punishments and rewards of the afterlife."[96] This antitheological—and thus also antisovereign—option is made even more evident at the end of the essay, in his rejection of "this virtue that was at times a substitute for all the duties of the throne . . . , a very desirable attribute of the sovereign,"[97] to wit, the power of clemency. It—perhaps even more than the right to put to death—is the divine emblem of sovereignty, namely, the possibility of giving life back after the death sentence by going backward through that zone of indistinguishability between life and death that is precisely the last ground of the

---

94. Beccaria, *Dei delitti e delle pene*, p. 62. Citations are translated directly from the Italian, although two English versions were consulted: *On Crimes and Punishments*, trans. Graeme R. Newman and Pietro Marongiu, 5th ed. (New Brunswick, NJ: Transaction, 2009); trans. Aron Thomas (n.p.: Seven Treasures, 2009).

95. Ibid., p. 13.

96. Ibid.

97. Ibid., pp. 102–3.

sovereign decision.[98] This—the attribution of clemency not to the objective system of laws, but to the subjective will of the monarch—was linked to the originary superimposition between crime and punishment through the common identification with the crime against a power that was originally divine.

Beccaria's entire essay strikes out against just this notion. To restate that he speaks "only of crimes that emanate from human nature or the social contract, and not of sins, of which even temporal punishments must be regulated through other principles than those of a limited philosophy,"[99] means not only to affirm the secular character of his discourse, but also, implicitly, to criticize, in its theological-political foundation, the very form of sovereign punishment. To it is intimately linked the figure of excess that, in the public ritual of execution, leads the punishment well beyond its necessary role of correcting the offender and acting as a deterrent to anyone wanting to follow his example. Because, unlike what is always proclaimed, the principle that governs royal torture, of which the death penalty is but the latest inheritor, is not that of just retribution but that of the exhibited disproportion between crime and punishment. Only this—the surplus of meaning that is publicly discharged on the body of the offender—can restore, to an infinitely greater degree than the offense received, the sovereignty whose sanctity has been wounded by the crime. No matter who the recipient is, the physical person of the sovereign is the one to be affected—who can only respond by sinking his or her own blows as deeply as possible into the body of the perpetrator. Hence the ceremony, both religious and military, that accompanies the condemned to the gallows: before the punishment of an offender comes the restoring a breached equilibrium, of asserting in all its glorious emphasis the absolute power of someone who, even in grammatical terms, is named by a superlative—not only *superior*, but *superaneus*, precisely because the sovereign is incomparably more powerful than any of his or her enemies and therefore obliged to destroy each of them, in body and soul. In order to pay for the crime that was committed, before it is dead, the offender's body must be humiliated, branded, flagellated, broken, and torn

98. In "Capital Punishment as a Problem for the Philosophy of Law," *New Centennial Review* 9, no. 2 (2009): 221–70, Adam Sitze rightly emphasizes the importance of Beccaria's rejection of clemency, which is obfuscated by Morellet's edition.

99. Beccaria, *Dei delitti e delle pene*, p. 94.

apart. Only in this way—through a penalty that is potentially infinite in duration and intensity—can retribution be made for a crime that, no matter whom it was directed against, is always ultimately one of wounded majesty. The violence infinitely inflicted on the body of the offender is the only adequate punishment for what, from the point of view of the sovereign, is analogous to a regicide. As Kant writes about this, "It is regarded as a crime that remains eternally and cannot be expiated (*crimen immortale, inexpiabile*), and it appears to resemble the kind of sin that the theologians call the sin that can be forgiven neither in this world nor in the afterworld."[100] Neither an entire life nor death alone is enough to atone for a crime of this sort—it must be a punishment that extends beyond death; or a death that dwells forever in life.

The most horrifying and glaring archetype of this infinite punishment was to be found less in the rituals of a worn-out ancien régime, now in rapid decline, than in the point of origination of Beccaria's own literary tradition. As the founding locus of Italian poetry, but also of Italian philosophical reflection, Dante's *Divine Comedy* is also the first, unsurpassed symbolic codification of the symmetrical relation between guilt and punishment inscribed in the heart of the Western legal system. If we return to that theater of horror which, in exact opposition to the perspective offered by Beccaria's proposed reform, was tagged by Foucault as "l'eclat des supplices" (the splendor and explosive glory of death by torture),[101] it is difficult to find a more vivid and comprehensive epitome than Dante's *Inferno*. As is generally known, the rule employed by Dante in assigning punishments to the damned is that of *contrappasso*: in other words, a strict relation of similarity or opposition between the sin and the punishment. It is based on the idea of a retributive justice that precisely correlates the weight of the penalty to the gravity of the crime committed. The descending cross sections that divide the circles of hell, like the graduated ascent through the circles of purgatory, also represent topographically the proper proportion between the intensity of the suffering and the severity of the crime. And yet, the further one advances into the poem, the more

---

100. Kant, *Metaphysics of Morals*, p. 97.

101. Foucault, *Surveiller et punir*, pt. 1, chap. 2, pp. 36–72. The translation of the phrase is from James Miller's "Carnivals of Atrocity: Foucault, Nietzsche, Cruelty," *Political Theory* 18, no. 3 (1990): 470–91.

one realizes that this proportion is continuously skewed by an excess of suffering. The assigned punishment by far overpowers the sin, which is punished in a fashion that the poet-spectator sometimes witnesses with compassion, sometimes accentuated with an attitude of mercilessness toward the damned, and even pleasure at their suffering. A shapeless mass of bodies—defiled, flogged, amputated, lacerated, boiled, frozen in ice, or thrown to the flames—stretches out before his eyes, and ours, in a crescendo of torment that no human code could have ever prescribed. It is true that some of these punishments were not unknown to Dante's time and were even practiced: such as quartering and continuing to torture the body of the criminal after death, exposing it to public ridicule, cutting it in pieces, and dragging it in the dust until it was almost completely consumed.[102] And yet, even compared to these extremes, in Dante's inferno there emerges something more, like a residue or, as we were saying, an excess. This is recognizable not only in a few famous episodes—like that of Count Ugolino, intent on gnawing the flayed skull of his enemy to the bone; or of Brutus, mangled in Lucifer's mouth—but, more generally, in the overflowing violence arranged to increase suffering beyond any conceivable limit. It is as if the representation of the punishment chased after a vanishing point that remains invisible, driven to a place that the poet's words can never reach, because its location lies beyond the barrier of human expression.

The answer he gives to the question about what kind of justice it is that excludes someone from salvation who died unbaptized because they came into the world before Christ seems to allude to this incommunicability: Dante himself says that this mystery is impenetrable to the human mind. We must be content to assume that the divine will is just—not in the weak sense that God always wants what is just, but in the stronger one, that what God wants is always just.[103] The theological-political segment destined to form the archeological nucleus of the modern paradigm of the sovereign already begins to take shape at this point—in the presupposed reconciliation of justice to the will of its author. But with the difference that while the modern paradigm will proceed by analogy, by

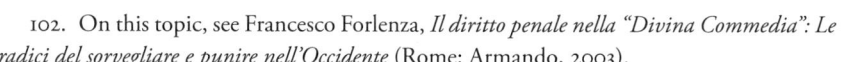

102. On this topic, see Francesco Forlenza, *Il diritto penale nella "Divina Commedia": Le radici del sorvegliare e punire nell'Occidente* (Rome: Armando, 2003).

103. See Patrick Boyde, "Justice," in *Human Vices and Human Worth in Dante's Comedy* (Cambridge: Cambridge University Press, 2000), pp. 198–224.

giving the sovereign the same constituent powers as the divine decision, Dante embodies in the divine will the attributes of *summa potestas* subsequently assigned to the sovereign. What governs the fate of human beings is not, in short, a monarch made in the image and likeness of God, as will indeed be the case shortly thereafter, but a God provided with the inalienable, and even despotic, powers of an absolute monarch. Having established the impossibility for those who were ignorant of the Christian faith to save themselves, it is through these powers that God may decide to contravene his own decision, as in the case of the Trojan Ripheus or the Roman Cato, who were pardoned in spite of being pagans. In these passages—cantos 19 and 20 of *Paradiso*—we have the foundation for the power of death, but also of grace, against which Beccaria protests in the twilight of the sovereign regime, precisely because of its theological-political roots. This power of restoring life to those who had lost it is in a certain sense an even more divine prerogative for the sovereign than the right to kill: because it expresses a ruler's power of decision to block his or her own decision, establishing a state of exception to the same system of rules he or she had imposed.

Without being able to dwell on the Platonic, Aristotelian, Augustinian, and Thomistic influences that alternate and meet up in the extraordinary melting pot of Dante's culture, we do need to place our attention on a critical juncture of his theological-juridical development. This is the theory, made explicit by Justinian's spirit—chosen as the point of synthesis of the entire Roman jurisprudence—of the perfect correspondence between the redemption of humanity and the apex of Roman power.[104] Echoing a theme introduced earlier in book 4 of the *Convivio* as well as in book 2 of the *Monarchia*, Dante interprets the history of Rome in a providential key—as if it had taken place directly according to God's will. This practice was already seen in the apologetic literature of the first centuries, by Eusebius, Prudentius, and Orosius. Dante not only seems to embrace it, he takes it even further, as also evidenced by his fierce condemnation of Brutus and Cassius as the murderers of Caesar. To say that Rome's progress was a product of divine, and not only human, intervention ("non pur per umane ma per divine operazioni, andò lo suo processo"; *Convivio*, 4.5.10),

104. On the theology of Dante's history, see Charles S. Singleton, *La poesia della Divina Commedia* (Bologna: Il Mulino, 1978), pp. 229 ff.; as well as Barbara Reynolds, *Dante: The Poet, the Political Thinker, the Man* (London: Shoemaker and Hoard, 2006).

or even that the hand of God was clearly at work from the beginning in the battle between the Albans and the Romans for control of the kingdom ("puose Iddio le mani proprie a la battaglia dove gli Albani con li Romani, dal principio, per lo campo del regno combattero"; *Convivio*, 4.5.18), means to make God the main character not only of civil history but also of Roman military history, granting Him the power of life and death normally given to a victorious condottiero. As we said, instead of depicting an emperor as delegated by God to exercise power, Dante has God himself directly guiding the history of the world, in first person, so to speak, through his chosen people. The excess that we found to characterize the system of punishments in *Inferno* stems precisely from this overlapping of divine law and Roman power, embodied by the imperial eagle. Its reconstruction is divided into the three conceptual steps structuring the speech of Justinian. The first is the one, in the name of the first emperor, that links the greatest Roman expansion to the advent of Christ. As Virgil had prophesied in his fourth *Eclogue*—the reason he was promoted to being the poet's guide in his otherworldly journey—only with Augustus did the world attain the *plenitudo temporis*, so as to be "optime dispositus" (*Monarchia*, 1.2.1) to welcome the coming of the Savior on earth. This is the theorization of the political monotheism—already in some way implicit in the Aristotelian equation between *unus deus* and *unus rex*—according to which only a single sovereign with unlimited power can exercise absolute justice, because there is nothing a sovereign can desire beyond what he or she already has.

Justinian adds a second step to this one that lends a further connotation to Dante's idea of divine justice, pushing it very close to that of vengeance. This is the task assigned by God to the third Caesar, Tiberius: namely, to preside from a legal point of view over the condemnation of Christ, which was necessary to exhaust the "vengeance for the ancient sin" (*Paradiso*, 6.93), or the original sin of Adam, in other words. Already in this vindictive characterization of justice, compared to its other functions of correction and prevention, we recognize that element of ulteriority of the punishment with respect to the crime that characterizes Dante's *Inferno*. The poet himself speaks of "just vengeance" on more than one occasion, as if to create an essential connection between the two terms through the theological-political nexus of Roman sovereignty. But Dante does not stop here: making the first vengeance against original sin a terrible offence against the person of Christ (although it is just with respect to the transgressor and all his descendants), he imagines that God entrusts Titus with the destruction of Jerusalem. In this way, not only is divine justice carried out initially through vengeance, it requires further vengeance to avenge it:

for the true Justice that inspires me
granted to it—in that next Caesar's hand
the glory of avenging His own wrath.
Now marvel here at what I show to you:
with Titus—afterward—it hurried toward
avenging vengeance for the ancient sin. (*Paradiso*, 6.88–93)[105]

When the poet asks Beatrice about the inherent contradictoriness of God avenging a vengeance previously declared to be just, once again by means of the Roman eagle, she can only answer, "You need no longer find it difficult / to understand when it is said that just / vengeance was then avenged by a just court" (*Paradiso*, 7.49–51). Even beyond the typically Scholastic explanation of the distinction between human nature—which, as such, is tangible—and the divine, intangible nature of Christ, the real reason for the apparent conflict lies in the interpenetration of divine justice and the imperial power of Rome. Like the power of Rome, although divine justice is oriented toward a criterion of proportionality between law and punishment, it, too, is free to express itself and contradict itself with no possibility of appeal because it rests on the prescriptive power of its invincible sword, much more than on a natural or rational basis.

This is what penetrates deep into the flesh of the damned. Of course, for this to be possible, their bodies need to be able to suffer, and, before that, to have some sort of substantiality. This opens up a question, an ontological one, so to speak, that doesn't appear to have attracted adequate attention in the endless exegesis of Dante's work. The souls of the damned belong, without exception, to dead people—otherwise they would not be where they are, a point they themselves stress repeatedly. And yet, death has always been considered a definitive liberation from pain rather than a condition of physical torment. This is exactly the opposite of what happens in *Inferno* and, in a more attenuated form, in *Purgatorio*, where even

105. Citations from the *Divine Comedy* are from the Allen Mandelbaum translation (New York: Random House, 1995).

those who have never suffered corporal punishments in life have to do so in an overabundant form, as we have just seen. Death, in this case, not only fails to put an end to suffering, it is what dramatically increases suffering. To make this possible, within the framework outlined by Dante, death must be something that can't be reduced to the simple cessation of life. It must involve something more—or less, depending on your point of view—than simple death, understood in its natural dimension as the opposite of life. There is no doubt that it takes place after life, but in an "after" that, rather than having a temporal status, seems to take on a liminal significance. This is an after that does not completely exclude the "before," and, indeed, in some ways brings it in and continually reintroduces it. The damned are dead for sure, but not entirely devoid of some sort of life—otherwise they would not be able to move, speak, and above all suffer, as they do eternally. It is almost as if their punishment were less like a death sentence and more like a "life" sentence—even if it is lived by the dead. What they are condemned to, more precisely, is not being able to die once and for all. In other words, they are condemned to dying continuously, an infinite number of times, and, in order to make this possible, to always coming back to life.

What they lack and long for in vain is not life, which they also seem to miss, but death—a real death—which they are not able to attain without being forced back into a kind of life that is inhabited, but never entirely extinguished, by death. Some of Dante's deliberately ambiguous expressions seem to allude to a zone of indistinguishability, or contiguity, between the two states, to a condition suspended between life and death— a life after death or a death in life.[106] For example, the words of Capaneus, spoken as a challenge: "That which I was in life, I am in death" (*Inferno*, 14.51); or the words spoken by the poet about himself, who, at the sight of Lucifer, exclaimed, "I did not die, and I was not alive" (*Inferno*, 34.25).

The starting point for addressing a question of this sort is clearly provided by how the nature of the soul is defined in relation to the body. As we know, Dante devotes a sort of dissertation to this topic, presented by the Latin poet Statius. According to his reconstruction, inspired by the Christian interpretation of Aristotle, the soul is separated from the body after death, only to rejoin it at the time of the Last Judgment. During this

---

106. See the part dedicated to Dante in the essay by Eugene Thacker, "Nine Disputations on Theology and Horror," *Collapse* 4 (2008): 119–56.

period of interregnum between the two events, the soul retains the capacity to experience infirmities and to manifest them externally. Without following the Averroistic thesis of the separation of the intelligent agent, perhaps under the influence of Siger of Brabant, Dante seems to go further than the position taken by Thomas Aquinas. While Thomas recognized some sort of sensitive capacity of the soul, now separated from the body, Dante attributes a particular formative force that allows it to imprint itself on the surrounding air space. By means of this capacity, the air that surrounds the soul takes on the shape of a body that is materially insubstantial but in all ways similar to the body prior to death. In this way, even in terms of appearance, a kind of unity of the spirit is reconstructed with its old corporeal shell. This allows the inhabitants of the afterlife to feel pleasure or pain—albeit in an attenuated way compared to what they will experience when, following the day of judgment, their souls will be physically reunited with their bodies. The problem of the "life of the dead" needs to be approached from this point of view. Like their body, it has a purely outward, or even symbolic, character, responding to the artistic need to make the souls in the poem act and speak, but also to allow the divine punishment to be carried out in the characteristic, overblown form that we have discussed. Only the presence of the sinners' bodies, no matter how virtual it may be, allows Dante's God to exercise His "just vengeance" in all its infinite expressive potential. In order to be punished with a violence at least equal to—in reality, infinitely greater than—the sin committed, the soul of the damned must be struck not only spiritually, but also physically, to the extent that we can make use of this term in Dante's lexicon. This explains why what is defined as "body" can never be completely destroyed by the tortures to which it is subjected in the depths of hell, to the point of having to be entirely reconstituted all over again when it is dismembered by devils, as in the case of the sowers of discord; or, in the case of thieves, reduced to ashes and eternally revived like the phoenix. Once death is removed from the realm of the instant and multiplied into the realm of duration, life also has to become in a certain sense eternal in order that it may be permanently negated.

Within these extreme limits, the body of the damned—what is understood to be such for whoever observes it—is subject to all sorts of mistreatment. Mortified—in the literal sense of being continually put to death—defiled, perforated, dissected, hooked, roasted, inflated, it is reduced to a rotting piece of meat in decay. Not only that, it is thrust into a dimension that retains very little of the human. Made to resemble all sorts of lower animals—snakes, dolphins, frogs—in the case of suicide, it is even transformed into a plant. Or into a thing—a wineskin, a lute, a lantern like his own head that the body of Bertrand de Born holds by the hair, making it swing. Even when the body retains an animal aspect, it is always on the verge of losing its individual contours in a kind of forced overcrowding that overlaps the limbs of one onto those of the other; or they are tied together in a monstrous knot that fights against itself, like the children of the Count of Mangona who are braided together by their hair, intent on butting their heads against each other like rams. For all of them, rather than a body, we should talk about an indistinct bodily material, reduced to its zero degree because it is deprived of any formal connotation. The paradoxical effect that emerges from this is that those who should be exclusively souls—and truly are, in principle—end up in the eyes of the reader as being nothing but body; and indeed, body reduced to a simple biological sludge, or even an inorganic object of ridicule and insult. If the Greek distinction between *bios* (a qualified form of life) and *zoe* (generic life with no formal quality) could be used in relation to Dante, we would have to liken the fate of the damned to the second—to a sort of general zoologization that deprives them of any identity.

Right here, however, the genius of Dante appears in all its inventive energy, reversing this objectivizing depersonalization into the creation of unforgettable individual characters, all the more pronounced the more inhuman the "biological" condition is to which they are reduced. From Francesca to Farinata, Pier delle Vigne, and Ugolino, it would seem that the poetic intensity of their identity is inversely proportional to the material degradation that their body undergoes—almost as if, in their case, *bios*, rather than opposing it, arises precisely from the *zoe* onto which it is crushed. Erich Auerbach has attributed this expressive miracle to the device of the "figure," in the technical sense that the term possesses in the medieval conception.[107] Contrary to the spiritualistic and Neoplatonic tendencies, the explosive novelty in Dante's approach is that he considers earthly life to be absolutely real in itself, but also, at the same time, a "shadow" or, as we said, a "figure" of what it will become when it dwells

107. I am referring to Erich Auerbach, *Dante: Poet of the Secular World* (New York: New York Review of Books, 2008), pp. 174 ff.

in the afterlife. Rather than dimming the features that are present in life, as they were in the classical tradition, for example in Virgil (with the partial exception of Dido's character), the afterlife accentuates them and fixes them eternally in their most characteristic moment. This explains why the great characters in Dante's work not only seem just as alive—this time in the sense of the "life form" that seemed buried in the indistinct magma of the bare biological matter—as those in flesh and blood, they also seem more vividly delineated, capable of pushing their emotions, and ours, to their peak.[108] The more the words seem to come out with difficulty from their deformed, oppressed bodies, as only the voices of human-beasts or human-plants can do, the more striking their astonishing expressive capacity; not the entire lived experience of whoever utters them, but precisely the decisive moment, the gesture, or the choice from which their eternal fate was hung. From this point of view, although they are separated from their corporeal shell, they show in an inimitable way the essential point of union between soul and body that permanently marked their lives. Nothing that has qualified it, in the unique and unrepeatable fashion of an individual habitus, is lost in the infinite instant of death. Of course, in the "second life," in addition to their terrestrial rank, they also lose the historicity that distinguished it, but not the indelible character that decided their fate, imprinting it with the mark of eternity. For this reason, in the sharing of a common suffering, thrust into the same vessel of pain, each of them speaks the utterly pure language—for Francesca, of love; for Farinata, of honor; for Ulysses, of knowing; for Ugolino, of hate—through which their existence was disclosed and consumed.

108. See Alison Morgan, *Dante and the Medieval Other World* (Cambridge: Cambridge University Press, 1990), pp. 170 ff.

philosophy
– is historically
determined.

Fourth Chapter

Thought in Action

① time
and thought
②

Whatever happens to
every individual is a
child of his time;
so philosophy too is

Philosophy and Resistance

1. The distinguishing feature of Italian thought in the first half of the twentieth century can be described as its complete historicization. What I mean by this is not only the acute awareness on the part of its chief exponents that their philosophy, like all others, is historically determined; but also the tendency—whether tacit or proclaimed—to make itself history. Or, to use a more resonant expression, to make itself "thought in action [pensiero in atto]"—understood in both senses of activity and actuality. Although one senses the influence of Hegel at the root of this attitude, it cannot be reduced to the German's formula of "its own time apprehended in thoughts"—which still expresses a cognitive type of relationship between separate elements. What we have here is something much more intrinsic, something that thrusts the philosophical work into the very heart of the real, even to the point of identifying with it. Of course, this process (or plan, at least) of mundanizing philosophy—the rejection of all dualism in favor of an immanence viewed as more and more absolute—implies a profound discontinuity with its traditionally speculative form, a rupture that was explicitly asserted by the philosophers of the period. To make itself world, to acquire worldly power, philosophical knowledge must somehow escape outside itself, it must incorporate its other—what is commonly considered to be "unphilosophical." In breaking with a traditionally intellectualist conception, twentieth-century Italian thought at the same time reconnected to the deeply formed features of its own ge-

nealogy. This was not only because it brought to fulfillment the practical or civil vocation that had characterized it from its beginnings. But also because it provided a radical answer to the question, posed dramatically during the previous period, regarding the unbridgeable gap between "science and life"—the excess manifested by life in the face of all attempts to understand it conceptually. The solution that was now put forward lay in flipping the lens through which the problem had been examined until then: instead of pointlessly attempting to force life into the formal parameters of philosophy, why not give philosophy the concrete characteristics of life? In order to be able to tap into a vital substratum that is refractory to the conceptual dimension, a thought that seeks to be worthy of its time must immerse itself in it, transforming itself into "living thought." But to make this possible—this is the last and most drastic step in this reasoning process—it must intersect with politics; or to be more precise, it must rediscover its inherent "politicalness." Only in this way, through practical action in the world, can philosophy truly revitalize itself, identifying itself in a historicity that is one with the inexhaustible movement of life.

As we know, the thinkers who took this assumption to its most extreme consequences, committing their entire lifetimes and even the circumstances of their deaths to its fulfillment, were Giovanni Gentile and Antonio Gramsci. Standing on opposing sides of a single barricade, they dramatically shared the project of making philosophical practice a potent historical force intended to change the world. Even without subscribing to the most extreme hypothesis (backed by arguments not devoid of plausibility) that their work is what fueled the creation, on the one hand, of fascism, and on the other, of the peculiar phenomenon that was Italian communism, the historical-political significance of their thought cannot be underestimated. To be sure, it is difficult to come up with two contemporaries in the philosophical landscape of the world who were as decisive in the conceptual development, and institution, of political regimes with such epochal significance. Still, while Gentile and Gramsci, in the forms we shall examine, represent the apex of this tendency, the third great thinker of this period, Benedetto Croce, was not extraneous to it. In spite of the claim he never tired of making regarding the gap between thought and action, he was rightly perceived as the extraparliamentary leader of the opposition to fascism. This fact is highly symptomatic of a drive toward politics that went beyond individual choices. Even his fierce resistance to what struck him as an unacceptable politicization of philosophy took on an inevitably political significance during this phase. Although expressed negatively—in the form of a withdrawal or a distinction—it was an integral part of the same process that simultaneously brought into play history and philosophy, power and life, decision and existence. That is why, despite their differences and even wide divergences, their thought must be analyzed together—in the tension that holds them in the same horizon of meaning.[1]

Beyond their irreducible personal and political conflicts, what connects them into a single trajectory, one that is totally unique on the European scene, as we have said, is the perception of a profound change in the role and purpose of philosophy. From this point of view, but without arriving at the same conclusions—indeed, taking a conspicuous distance from them—Croce was just as clear as Gentile and Gramsci in grasping the irreversibility of the transformation that was taking place. Contrary to those who continued to interpret philosophy as abstract knowledge separate from reality, he maintained that it had to be integrated into reality, to be put back into contact with the dilemmas and conflicts of life, and brought back to the clarity of ordinary language. This is why—contrary to what "pure philosophers" believe, not to mention those engulfed in academic disputes and quarrels—"new philosophical thought, or its germs, are often to be found in books not written by professional philosophers and not extrinsically systematic: for ethics, in books by ascetics and members of the clergy; for politics, in books by historians; for aesthetics, in those by art critics, and so on."[2] One glance at the Italian philosophical tradition whose genealogy we have reconstructed—from Machiavelli to de Sanctis, passing through Cuoco and Leopardi—makes it easy to understand whom Croce is referring to. What he means is that while philosophy stands in a recipro-

---

1. See especially Eugenio Garin, *Intellettuali italiani del XX secolo* (Rome: Riuniti, 1974); and his *Tra due secoli: Socialismo e filosofia in Italia dopo l'Unità* (Bari: De Donato, 1983), pp. 323–67. See also Biagio de Giovanni, "Sulle vie di Marx filosofo in Italia: Spunti provvisori," *Il Centauro* 9 (1983): 3–25. This issue also contains essays by Bruno Accarino, Michele Ciliberto, Marcello Montanari, and Roberto Racinaro, all relevant to the topic under discussion.

2. Benedetto Croce, "Aesthetica in nuce," in *Ultimi saggi* (1935; repr., Bari: Laterza, 1963), p. 33; text is translated directly from the Italian. This essay is available in English in *Philosophy, Poetry, History*, trans. Cecil Sprigge (London: Oxford University Press, 1966), pp. 215–47.

cal relationship with the other discourses of modern knowledge, it is also continually cut through and changed by them, in the sense that philosophy shares the same interests and objects, even though it places them in a different conceptual topology. The material of philosophy is not another philosophy, in a self-referential attitude that closes in on itself, but rather, precisely what is not philosophy because it coincides with life itself in its continuous and unpredictable development: since "philosophy has always originated out of the motion of life,"[3] it "can solve only those problems presented by life."[4] For this reason, once we have given up on any pretentions to solve the big metaphysical problems, we can only turn to "a historical and immanent philosophy, which draws its material from all the most varied impressions of life and from all intuitions and reflections upon life."[5] In these texts—but many more of them can be cited—the process of the historicization of thought we referred to at the start of this chapter reaches its apex. Philosophy is always historically determined in its questions and answers, which are obviously partial and provisional, but when it tends toward infinity it coincides with history. Not in the extremist sense, theorized by Gentile, which would have it constituted by history, but in the sense that philosophy arises out of history and returns to it as its sole horizon of relevance.

From this point of view, those who see in Croceanism something that is not quite a philosophy are right—on condition that they recognize its philosophical importance. Otherwise, following the same line of reasoning, we would have to reject the philosophical import of Heidegger's thesis on the "end of philosophy," or Wittgenstein's explicit adoption of ordinary language. What makes them closer to Croce, perhaps more than one might think—although without being able to compare his analytical framework and vocabulary to theirs, naturally—is the same search for a thought that is postmetaphysical and, thus, in some ways, also postphilosophical. But not antiphilosophical. In the case of the Italian thinker, this is attained

---

3. Benedetto Croce, "Suggestioni dell'estetica," in *Il carattere della filosofia moderna* (1940; repr., Bari: Laterza, 1945), p. 80.

4. Benedetto Croce, *Filosofia della pratica* (1909; repr., Bari: Laterza, 1963), p. 206; English edition: *Philosophy of the Practical*, trans. Douglas Ainslie (London: Macmillan, 1913), p. 304.

5. Benedetto Croce, *Teoria e storia della storiografia* (Bari: Laterza, 1917), pp. 145–46; English version: *History: Its Theory and Practice*, trans. Douglas Ainslie (New York: Harcourt, Brace, 1921), p. 162.

by sharply reducing the technical portion (the amount of jargon, in other words) of his theoretical expression, which leads it to adhere so closely to its historical object that it ends up almost inside it. It is as if the philosophical shell surrounding the concreteness of a real problem were to be thinned down to the point of making itself transparent—thus giving the impression of being absorbed by it. But never entirely, because what philosophy conveys of the historical event—whatever that may be—is not the direct image, but rather, a reflected awareness: the knowledge, that is, of its specific place in the circularity of the spirit that, for Croce, is the general form of the historical process. Thus, legitimizing, he can argue that "the particular task of philosophy" does not fade away—it simply no longer lies "above and detached from science and life, but inside them, as a tool of science and life."[6] The seemingly simplistic definition of philosophy as "an abstract moment of historiography" or even as its "methodology" can be traced back to this task. Without the light of philosophy, if history were removed from the work of thought, it would be nothing but a bare sequence of events without meaning; in the same way that if thought were devoid of historical material, it would lose itself in the desert of abstraction. Although located outside all schemas deriving from a philosophy of history (consistently rejected by Croce in order to safeguard the role of individuals compared to general causes), just as his philosophy is essentially historical, similarly, his historiography—every historical work that he effectively wrote—is inherently philosophical. How could it be any other way, starting from the principle that all history, both past and present, is contemporary? To argue that the historian's gaze, based on his or her real interest, enlivens any event by projecting it onto the moving screen of today is tantamount to regaining the horizon of actuality, from a different angle than the one taken by Gentile. Philosophy, history, and life are arranged on this horizon in an equilibrium that makes one the point of refraction of the other two. While philosophy can only draw from life through its own historicity, in the same way, but on another level, philosophy is what lends life an intensely historical character. Just as the categories of the spirit organize the historical sequence by distinguishing between its various moments, history transforms life from a messy jumble of conflicting impulses into a frame in which multiple threads are interwoven into a unified fabric.

6. Croce, "Aesthetica in nuce," p. 397.

2. And yet Croce was well aware that things are not quite so simple. He knew that the picture whose broad strokes he drew with unparalleled clarity was far from stable, and indeed was subject from the beginning to variations, pressures, and distortions destined to undermine its harmonious consistency. By studying the history of his notebooks, Gennaro Sasso has reconstructed the dramatic growth of this awareness in the philosopher's mind.[7] Something, from inside and outside the system, tends to loosen its joints and blur the distinctions—beginning with the one between thought and action that was crucial for keeping it intact. Specifically to prevent this potential dissolution—which would have inevitably led him down the path embarked upon by Gentile, both activistic and immobilizing at the same time—he had set up firm boundaries that strictly distinguished between the various faculties of the spirit, while joining them into a single, circular development: "For 'Westerners' or, more precisely, for healthy spirits," cautioned the philosopher, "the strength of civilization still resides in its continual distinction and opposition between thought and action, which is the only way they can nurture each other."[8] His warning against the "improper mixture of theory and practice"—which would lead the actualists to the "mutual corruption of philosophical meaning and political meaning—was never stated more forcefully than in a polemical text directed at Gentile entitled "Against Too Much Political Philosophy."[9] It was one thing to recognize the full historicity of philosophy—against all the intellectualistic revivals of those who had failed to grasp the antimetaphysical turn taken by contemporary thought; but it was quite another to carry out an unmediated politicization that would reduce knowledge to the direct expression of power—of forces and vested interests incapable of rising to a universal level. Not that forces and interests are not part of history. There was nobody who had championed their reality, and even their productivity, more than Croce, who never forgot the teachings of Machiavelli. But only if they were contained within a specific sphere, that of the useful or the economic, and were certainly not coextensive with the entire movement of the

7. See Gennaro Sasso, *Per invigilare me stesso: I taccuini di lavoro di Benedetto Croce* (Bologna: Il Mulino, 1989).

8. Benedetto Croce, "Teoretico e pratico," in *Conversazioni critiche*, vol. 5 (Bari: Laterza, 1939), p. 356.

9. Benedetto Croce, "Contro troppa filosofia politica," in *Cultura e vita morale* (1914; repr., Bari: Laterza, 1926), p. 245.

spirit. Precisely in defense of this necessary division—aimed at distinguishing the part from the whole, but also the sphere of facts from that of values—he had refused to attribute a philosophical character to Marxism. In this case, too, his opinion clashed with those of both Gentile and Antonio Labriola.[10] And yet it was precisely on this point—the autonomy of the category of utility, later expanded into the more controversial and problematic one of "vitality"[11]—that he began to encounter growing difficulties. This element was exactly what pushed against the walls of his system, both internal and external, threatening to pull them down. Not only did this category show itself to be barely containable within the terms assigned to it, sooner or later it risked overflowing into adjacent areas, destabilizing them, along with the entire system that supported them. Whether or not this discrepancy in the philosophy of the spirit stemmed from an internal contradiction or from an external factor has been discussed at length. The debate continues on whether its roots were theoretical or historical.[12] But clearly the two possibilities are not mutually exclusive; indeed, one implies the other. The very moment Croce superimposed philosophy onto history, almost absorbing the former into the latter, he flooded his theory with all the historical disorderliness that was marking the landscape of the time, in an increasingly threatening form. All the more so because of the absolute hermeneutic primacy of contemporary history: if, from the perspective of the person examining it, every event contracts into the immediacy of the present, how could his own philosophy not record the deep tremors that, between the two world wars, were making the global landscape tremble, to the point of devastation?

It comes as no surprise, then, that the relationship between history and philosophy, as it had been previously established, was precisely what at a certain point underwent a marked change. What failed to hold—dur-

10. On Labriola, see Roberto Dainotto, "Historical Materialism as New Humanism: Antonio Labriola's 'In Memoria del Manifesto dei Comunisti' (1895)," in *Annali d'Italianistica* 26 (2008): 265–82.

11. On the "vital" in Croce, see for example Giuseppe Cacciatore, *Filosofia pratica e filosofia civile nel pensiero di Benedetto Croce* (Catanzaro: Mannelli, 2005), pp. 59 ff.; as well as Corrado Ocone, *Benedetto Croce: Il liberalismo come concezione della vita* (Catanzaro: Mannelli, 2005), pp. 103 ff.

12. The clearest, most accurate reconstruction of the question in my opinion is by Giuseppe Galasso, in *Croce e lo spirito del tempo* (Milan: Il Saggiatore, 1990).

ing a period when European civilization as a whole appeared poised on the brink of the abyss—was the primacy of history over philosophy, a primacy which had stood as the self-reductive cipher, so to speak, of Croce's initial philosophy. In the 1920s he still believed that, compared to the normality of intellectual work—identified as the task of historiography—philosophy as such was an accident, like a disease that has to be overcome;[13] in the middle of the next decade this assessment appears to have been overturned. A comparison between the three *Histories*—of Italy, the Baroque era, and Europe—and *History as the Story of Liberty*, which came out only a year before the outbreak of the war, is illuminating in this regard. While the first three interpret the traumas and wounds of their time additionally in the light of subsequent restorations, the fourth fails to conceal, and even draws attention to, the signs of an increasingly ungovernable crisis. Or—this is the decisive point—a crisis that is only governable through an ethical-political intervention capable of dramatically altering the course of events. It would seem that only then—in the years when definitive choices about the fate of Europe and the world were being made—did the meaning of the principle that "all history is contemporary" get expressed to its full potential, revealing its intensely dramatic core. When modern history as a whole reached its fulfillment, and at the same time its deflagration, the actuality of the moment split into two opposing alternatives that could not be neutralized by the serene objectivity of a historical narrative, because they demanded a decision that put at stake the very possibility of what the author himself referred to as "the religion of freedom"—hardly a rhetorical term given the times. It was a lurch forward, but also the first crumbling of the rigid grid that structured the system of distinct concepts. The whole nexus of unity and distinction was now disintegrated and had to be reassembled in a form different from the original one. The relation of dominance between history and philosophy, now reversed in favor of the latter, gave Croce's discourse, if not a political tone, at least a metapolitical one. Of course we are still far from the extreme interpretation that, from opposing fronts during the same years, Gentile and Gramsci gave to the formula of "thought in action." But we are equally distant from the crystalline clarity of the dialectics of distinctions as it had been theorized in the first quarter of the century. The narrow cracks on the smooth wall of the system, once barely perceptible, had now

13. See Michele Ciliberto, "Malattia/sanità: Momenti della filosofia di Croce fra le due guerre," in *Il Centauro* 9 (1983): 71–103.

widened into deep fault lines that ran across, and corroded, the entire surface. What had earlier evoked rules and health—the shifting border of the historical present—now appeared as exception and disease. And the remedy that had been identified as historiographical research, also in terms of his personal history, was now sought in the ethical hold of a thought capable of governing historical processes and the very actions of human beings.

What marks these two phases—or rather layers, not always distinguishable in chronological order, and, indeed, often overlapping even in the same texts—is a continuous revisiting of the category of life that shows itself to be the pivot of all Italian philosophy, to which Croce is no exception. It should immediately be noted that this category never takes on a univocal semantics—it is not expressed exclusively in spiritualistic or biologistic terms. Rather, it oscillates between the two sets of connotations in different ways and in various proportions depending on the different times and contexts. Its relationship with thought is also far from univocal. On the one hand, as we have said, life, understood in the broadest sense of the expression, is the source of meaning for thought, the ground that the activity of thinking roots itself in—and outside of which it becomes arid and retreats uselessly into itself. However, when understood in its more specific modality as life force—in other words, as the conservative and expansive impulse, and also as the instinct to overcome whoever obstructs it—it is placed in its turn by philosophy into the categorial sphere of the useful or the economic. On the one hand, then, thought is contained in life as its originary horizon of unfolding; on the other hand, when assumed as a specific mode of existence, it is life that is included in thought. It is as if the two elements, always intertwined but never identical, chased after each other in an endless, restless race: "The infinite, inexhaustible by the thought of the individual," concludes the *Philosophy of the Practical,* "is Reality itself, which ever creates new forms; Life is the true mystery, not because impenetrable by thought, but because thought penetrates it to the infinite with power equal to its own; . . . no philosophical system is definite, because Life itself is never definite."[14]

The significance, and relevance, of Croce's philosophy lies specifically in his tense, dramatic perception of this irreducibility—of the necessity and, at the same time, the impossibility for thought to grasp life and

14. Croce, *Philosophy of the Practical,* pp. 590–91.

control it: its inability to contain the energetic charge within rationally mediated forms in order to prevent a potentially self-destructive explosion. All this—this ceaseless, although at times desperate, effort—largely calls into question the detached, clerical image with which he was depicted with surprising interpretative insensitivity during the years after the Second World War. It was precisely because he was aware—no less than Gentile and Gramsci, to limit ourselves to Italian authors—of the shock wave produced by life in all areas of contemporary experience that he tried to tackle it in the forms and tools that were proper to him. From this point of view, with all the idiosyncracies of his case, we can say that Croce provided one of the last (if not the last) fully modern philosophies to be deployed in defense of a civilization that had already exhausted its propulsive force, so to speak, in the 1930s, flowing back over itself in a tragic, dissolutive backwash. On these lines, his choice to resist to the bitter end should not be limited to his relationship with fascism, no matter how decisive this might have been: his resistance extended to the secularization processes that impacted Western society as a whole during those years, with unheard-of violence. His insistent appeal to the "religion of freedom" as well as his vindication of its Christian roots should not be explained away as simple metaphors, or even less, as cautious formulas intended to reassure the Catholic world. Rather, they express the rampartlike character—like a genuine *katechon*—that Croce consciously sought to give his thought. Croce's entire vocabulary, moreover, has unmistakably immunitary connotations: "bulwark [argine]," "curb [freno]," "health," and "protection," not without an explicit homeopathic inflection: "health is the balancing of imbalance, because it subdues and locks disease up inside itself . . . ; the spirit itself would perish were it not reined in and confined just like the other [special forms] that follow upon it and go by the same yardstick [tengono lo stesso metro]."[15] A historically responsible thought has the role of containing, restraining, and controlling the vital forces within confines able to channel its push, repress its fury, and cool its heat. It must prevent "contamination" of the moral forces,[16] by setting up a prophylactic belt against

15. Benedetto Croce, *La storia come pensiero e come azione* (1938; repr. Bari: Laterza, 1973), pp. 43–44; text is translated directly from the Italian. Another English version can be found in: *History as the Story of Liberty*, trans. Sylvia Saunders Sprigge (New York: Norton, 1941), p. 56.

16. Croce, "Forze morali e forze vitali," in *Il carattere della filosofia moderna*, p. 241.

the pandemic spreading throughout modern civilization and threatening to drag it back into its primitive past.

3. But the characterization of Croce's thought as "immunitary" is not based solely on a protective attitude toward the set of impulses, pulls, and excesses attributed to the category of vitality. This would place him in a classically conservative position that, as such, would not be able to account for all the different tones of his complex intellectual performance. Not that an attitude of this sort—defensive and even reactive in the face of the momentous transformations he was witnessing—was foreign to him; objections put to him from opposing points of view by both Gentile and Gramsci. The dialectic of distinctions also arose out of the urgency to oppose the attack launched by Marx against the framework of the "Christian-bourgeois" society. To enclose the economic, and also "the political," within a specific sphere—endowed with a certain autonomy, to be sure, but destined to be integrated and surpassed in qualitatively superior times—also responded to the need to safeguard the existing social equilibrium in the face of possible radical change. On a more purely cultural plane, while partly sharing in the semantics of the philosophies of life offered by Georges Sorel, Henri Bergson, Georg Simmel, and the young Georg Lukács, his system was able to provide a more reassuring answer to the questions they posed during those same years: rather than being opposed to forms, life constitutes the raw material that will itself become form in an infinite circular rhythm, but directed upward. However, this argumentative strategy of Croce's did not definitively settle the accounts with his interlocutors: we have already seen how it proved fragile even in the eyes of its author. Not that he thought it wrong enough to abandon —something he never did, always rehashing it, albeit formulated in different tones and with varying emphases. But it certainly must have seemed inadequate to him when, at the height of the 1930s, first Italy and then Europe as well, began to fall prey to forces that were imbued with unprecedented destructive violence. His categorial distinctions were not a sufficient response: although valid in themselves, they were more suited to a normal stage of development in the European spirit than to an era that had already slid into a permanent state of exception. What needed to be deployed was a potency just as intense and all-encompassing as that of the enemy. The only adequate response to a concentrated attack from

the forces of evil was a call to gather together positive energies endowed with the same vigor.

In Croce's theoretical dispositif, this change in pace was accompanied by the gradual centrality that the ethical-political discourse assumed with respect to the others—which did not disappear but were subordinated to its primacy. Against the increasingly pronounced and pervasive rise in irrational and selfish, if not brutal and demonic, instincts, for Croce, the "call to arms" of the moral forces was the only way to preserve and revitalize universal reasons for action. Of course, the concept of the ethical-political, like the dialectic of distinctions over which it was superimposed, causing its seams to burst, arose out of a need for immunization against the outbreak of enemy forces, but with a difference that was anything but negligible in terms of the effects it had on Croce's lexical apparatus. What he eventually arrived at was a more sophisticated and complex use of the immune paradigm. Like an antiviral medical procedure, instead of combatting it head-on, Croce prescribed the use of the same force he sought to neutralize—consisting, as we know, in the tumultuous potency of life. Already in the *History*, cited earlier, he was careful to point out that all forms must be restrained and controlled by means of others that "go by the same yardstick": meaning, made of the same vital element that from the beginning had put the system in crisis, but would now serve to strengthen it. Not only negatively—as a point of dialectical contrast in defining the other degrees of the spirit. But positively as well—as propulsion fuel for their development. A whole series of texts, crucial for understanding the internal movement of Croce's thought, referred to the impossibility of eliminating the vital impulses, including the animal ones, which were described not only as traversing human beings but also, to a large extent, as constituting them. On this line of thought, many years earlier he had recalled—"For friends who seek the 'transcendental'"—that "Humankind, the human spirit, will never escape outside . . . the circle that is life. To accept the reality of the very things that we must confront and condemn and tear down, and in doing so, feel them and judge them to be evil, falsehood, and ugliness in order to create goodness, truth, and beauty, is to accept the force of animal life (useful, hedonistic, economic), without which the highly spiritual and moral life would lack its material as much as it would its instrument."[17] Only to conclude, at the end of his career, that

17. Benedetto Croce, *Etica e politica* (1931; repr., Bari: Laterza, 1956), p. 453.

"in conflict and in dialectics, which is the law of history, the moral action of human beings does not stand alone, abstracted in an abstract world, but always in connection with what is together its material and its instrument, its opponent and its ally; namely, the life force."[18] Not only are the moral forces not abstractly separable from the vital forces, they must incorporate them and make use of them in order to strengthen themselves. Hence, even that dreadful, amoral force—of vitality—which periodically drags civilization down into barbarism, should not be eliminated; rather, it should be put to use to re-create the conditions of its rebirth. To this end, when one historical cycle is winding down and another is starting up, the moral principles faced until a short time before by the telluric powers must be endowed with the same "virtues of the barbarians, by arming ideas with strong arms, gripping hands, and hooked claws."[19] In these passages it is impossible to miss the echoes of Machiavelli and Vico, who are read in the light of the twentieth-century catastrophes, but also in the light of the positive upheavals consequent to the fall of fascism and the end of the war. Like his distant predecessors, Croce too recognized the simultaneously destructive and constructive force of vitality as the source of politics and history. For a new history—or a new politics—to begin, it must draw its foundational energies from the regenerative depths of life. The fact that life contains within itself primordial instincts that are savage, or even bestial, does not put their necessity into question at a time when other, hostile forces must be combatted and defeated. Only later, when its roots are well established and its enemies are vanquished, can history be diverted into a channel that is ethically controlled and logically recognizable in the circular course of the spirit.

However, this distinction between the historical process and its origin is exactly what comes into conflict with the general perspective in which it is inscribed—and which, as we mentioned, Croce would never have given up on. How are we to reconcile the gathering of all history into the circularity of the spirit with the dissimilar and even distorted form of its extralegal beginnings?[20] The moment vitality is no longer solely containable within the economic sphere, it first becomes the material and then the energetic

---

18. Benedetto Croce, "Soliloquio di un vecchio filosofo," in *Discorsi di varia filosofia* (Bari: Laterza, 1945), vol. 1, p. 295.

19. Croce, *Forze morali e forze vitali*, p. 239.

20. Regarding this basic contradiction in the Crocian "system" see Gennaro Sasso, *Benedetto Croce: La ricerca della dialettica* (Naples: Morano, 1975).

engine of the entire circle of the categories, ultimately situating itself on a plane that is not entirely coextensive with it. Croce does not conceal this irreducible dissonance between origin and history—the impossibility of a full historicization of the origin. In his "Remarks on Prehistory" he notes:

Even if we succeeded in converting from prehistory into history a few centuries or a few peoples that now stand outside it, we would push back a threshold, but we would not conquer prehistory, because . . . the exaggerated interest we feel in the primitive ages stems from the illusion . . . of being able to arrive at our origins through them . . . and of ripping the veil away from the mystery of humanity. A hope of this type fails to acknowledge that facts are never "originary" but have always "originated" from the unique source, the living Spirit; and that, therefore, the attempt to discover our origins by way of facts is an impiety of sorts.[21]

What the philosopher is covering up here with the veil of mystery is the ontological difference between history and life that the system is incapable of absorbing—and, indeed, that it continuously reproduces as the very precondition of its functioning. To claim, as he always did, that history is rooted in life—or that life is at the bottom of history—means introducing a thin differential margin between the two that prevents their reciprocal identification. To be sure, only from the magmatic layer of life can history draw the potency it requires for its development. But that potency is always also a form of "prepotency," or "prevalency," which the historical movement fails to dominate completely because it somehow precedes and predetermines the historical movement as a prior fact that can never be reduced to a simple fact: "Anyone who is moderately honest . . . surrenders to and indulges in the vital force they have inside them and which would not be potency if it were not also able to be prepotency."[22]

Certainly, what resounds most strongly in these remarks is the realism of someone who knows that it is impossible to definitively separate reason from force; or even, more than ever, force from violence. But what we also sense is a contradiction involving the very foundation of Croce's thought—situated as it is at a liminal point in the history of Italian thought, still vacillating between two different, and opposing, modes of understanding the philosophical task. He was aware that purely specula-

21. Benedetto Croce, "Considerazioni sulla preistoria," in *Indagini su Hegel e schiarimenti filosofici* (1952; repr., Bari: Laterza, 1967), pp. 195–96.
22. Croce, "Il peccato originale," in *Indagini su Hegel*, p. 148.

tive philosophy was coming to an end, but not willing to see it directly transposed into politics; he was convinced of its fully historical dimension, but not enough to see history as its product; and he was a theoretician of the contemporary interest of all past events, but careful not to reduce the historical fact to an act of thought. From this point of view, too, the significance of his perspective is inseparable from his resistance to the general movement in which it was objectively inscribed. Hence the feeling of a battle being waged within his own philosophy, the dramatic tension that, especially from the mid-1930s on, would continue to mark its development: "The human mind tries to settle this fight or at least regulate it, but the attempt is futile and the fight continues with the same violence and the same torment."[23] At the end of the war, with new totalitarian risks looming—when he realized that fascism was not, in reality, a periodic disease of the spirit but rather the destructive side of the origin, the emergence of a malevolent potency underlying history that was always poised to come to the surface the instant the conditions were right—he grasped the empty spot on which European history rested,[24] and realized that "life and history deserve to be called tragic."[25] Yet, despite this acute, painful awareness, Croce never resolved to take the final step: to see in this vortex not only the crisis of modern history but also its exhaustion. He did not feel, or would not admit, that the forces threatening the orders at that time had arisen from its own belly, and thus were not governable with tools and categories derived from it. The current then set in motion—which we can label as nihilism—was no longer containable from outside. It could only be confronted from within, in a project destined to overwhelm any distinction through a total superimposition of thought and action, philosophy and life.

In interiore homine

1. This is the path Giovanni Gentile traveled to its end, with a radicalism that brought modern thought simultaneously to its completion and to its dissolution. Along these lines, those who have compared his perspec-

23. Benedetto Croce, "La vita, la morte, il dovere," in *Indagini su Hegel*, p. 49.

24. See also Paolo Bonetti, *Introduzione a Croce* (Rome-Bari: Laterza, 1984), pp. 120 ff.

25. Benedetto Croce, "L'utopia della forma sociale perfetta," in *Terze pagine sparse* (Bari: Laterza, 1955), vol. 1, p. 96.

tive to Nietzsche's are right, based on the destructive energy with which it put an end to an entire philosophical tradition—without opening up another, however, and, indeed, making the old one impracticable from within its own categories. There is something extreme in this peremptory character of Gentile's philosophy—a trait that pushes it even beyond those of Husserl, Heidegger, and Wittgenstein,[26] to which it has also been compared—locking it into a solitary, separate orbit. While all these philosophies had continuations in the second half of the twentieth century—whether phenomenological, ontological or analytical in nature—Gentile's thought seems to have died along with him during the tragic weeks leading up to the civil war and then to the end of fascism. And yet, by a singular fate, this brusque interruption which prevented its development lends it remarkable relevance today [*attualità*] compared to other lines of research whose potentials have been thoroughly explored and exhausted by their own unfolding. It is as if its irreducibility, and irrelevance even, to the horizon of the twentieth century preserved a nucleus of meaning inside it that has remained unconsumed, and which has only now come to the surface, albeit with characteristics that are difficult to decipher. This hermeneutic difficulty is not only due to the sometimes rhetorical or convoluted lexicon in which it is expressed, but also to a more inherent antinomy, that, like a perspectival rotation pin, renders all Gentile's statements convertible into their specular opposite. Because of this, whatever is affirmed—for this very reason—is simultaneously negated or, at least, identified with its contrary. Even the question of his adhesion to fascism, still controversial and prone to conflicting interpretations, can be attributed, as far as its beginnings and significance are concerned, to this self-destructive instinct that may also be described as nihilistic (in a particular sense of the term to which we will return). To claim that this improvident choice was linked to his philosophy does not mean, therefore, that it ensued from the contents of his philosophy,[27] or, even worse, that his philosophy was determined by it; rather, it had to do with the inherently contradictory form

26. See E. Severino, "Giovanni Gentile distruttore degli assoluti," in various authors, *Giovanni Gentile: La filosofia, la politica, l'organizzazione della cultura* (Venice: Marsilio, 1995), pp. 57–59; as well as the important book by Salvatore Natoli, *Giovanni Gentile filosofo europeo* (Turin: Boringhieri, 1989).

27. On this topic, see the observations made by Gennaro Sasso in *Le due Italie di Giovanni Gentile* (Bologna: Il Mulino, 1998).

a herently contradictory)

of his philosophy. Gentile's choice in favor of fascism, in short, is not the result of his activistic philosophy, as Croce claimed from the outset; nor of his immanentism, as later argued by Del Noce.[28] Rather, it stems from an activism converted in its turn into an abstract theorizing, and of an immanentism internalized in hypersubjective terms.

This self-dissolutive dialectic is recognizable in all the decisive passages of his thought, starting with the notion of "praxis" which, from many points of view, is its genetic locus and driving force. It represents the tip of that "thought in action" that characterizes twentieth-century Italian philosophy, and also a kind of mobilization that, as such, is not to be found in other traditions. The fact that a debate of international scope on the philosophical importance of Marxism was initiated in Italy, in a form and with a quality that cannot be reduced to the dispute between revisionist and orthodox schools,[29] is certainly not unrelated to the fruitful tension between history, politics, and life that constitutes the base and penchant of its thought. In the same way, the wholly Italian genealogy—from Bruno to Spaventa via Vico—that Gentile traces for the concept of praxis is also symptomatic of this tension. True, the concept of praxis had to wait for Marx's critique of Feuerbach to establish itself as the locus where subject and object, doing and knowing, coincide in a single principle constitutive of the world. However, the fact remains that—already potentially latent in Vico's criterion of the *verum factum* principle—it was only in Spaventa's Hegelian formulation that the concept was definitively recognized as that "knowing which is not simply knowing, but, inasmuch as it is knowing, also acting, doing [operare]."[30] It is thanks to this vocation of the Italian tradition, oriented toward practice from the outset, that the performative capacity of Marx's philosophy only received an adequate reading in Italy.

Croce was much more sheltered and cautious compared to the compelling force of the theoretical and historical connections that Gentile made in the brief two-year period between 1898 and 1899. Always careful to avoid a perverse short circuit between spheres and languages that he believed

---

28. See Augusto Del Noce, *Giovanni Gentile: Per una interpretazione filosofica della storia contemporanea* (Bologna: Il Mulino, 1990), especially pp. 283 ff.

29. For a complete reconstruction of this question, see Giacomo Marramao, *Marxismo e revisionismo in Italia* (Bari: De Donato, 1971).

30. Giovanni Gentile, "Introduzione a B. Spaventa," in *Opere* (Florence: Sansoni, 1972), vol. I, p. 112.

should remain separate, Croce staked out his resistance along a line of defense that Gentile had already quickly overpassed. The attack that Gentile launched moved precisely in these two converging and, indeed, overlapping directions: the relation between philosophy and history on the one hand, and the relation between philosophy and politics on the other, which Croce refused to follow to the end, remaining midway between identity and difference. As to the first—the relation between history and philosophy—it is in itself compatible with Croce's system, but in a restricted form, limited to the historically determined character of thought, which was far from satisfactory in Gentile's eyes. In proposing a way for it to be completed, Croce effectively overturned its meaning in a sensational way: "I would say, in conclusion, not that philosophy finds its truth in history, but that abstract philosophy finds its truth and resolves itself in history. This must be kept clearly distinct from concrete philosophy, which is not beyond history but is history itself, inasmuch as true history is the history of philosophy, and this is the true philosophy. Whence, the circle does not really close in history, qua history, but in philosophy."[31] If all past events acquire meaning only in the present interest of whoever interprets it at any given time—according to Croce's principle that all history is contemporary history—this means that by interpreting an event, the interpreter produces it at the same time. And thus, that history is in itself, and not only indirectly, philosophy; indeed, strictly speaking, it is not even possible to establish a relationship between the two, since, in the eternity of the creative act, they are the same thing right from the beginning.

As to the second relationship—between philosophy and politics—the node is even more binding and constitutive for both terms. What is at stake in this case is precisely the integration between thought and life that Croce failed to fully achieve by presupposing, or overlapping, one term over the other. This is the main focus of the essay entitled "Politics and Philosophy," which Gentile specifically devoted to the topic. "A philosophy that is immanent to politics," he begins, "and which politics can therefore not do without, is not an abstract philosophy, which, placed over and above life in order to understand it, is alienated from it and closes itself off in the purely ideal world of speculation; but that concrete philosophy, which, as we can and must understand today, is inseparably associated with

31. Giovanni Gentile, *Il circolo della filosofia e della storia della filosofia* (1907), now in *Opere filosofiche*, ed. Eugenio Garin (Milan: Garzanti, 1991), p. 309.

life, and is life itself, one might say, in the full vigor of its own awareness."[32] As we know, Croce had also distanced himself from a speculative, abstract conception of the philosophical task. But he had stopped at an intermediate, and therefore self-contradictory point (which Gentile left far behind him) by setting up an alternative with no middle terms between a classic conception of philosophy—intellectualistic and naturalistic—that placed reality before thought; and a modern one, which identified them in the eternally productive actuality of the living spirit. While for Croce, the activity of philosophizing can begin only after the necessities of biological life have been taken care of, according to the old Aristotelian paradigm that separated *oikos* from *polis;* for Gentile, knowledge coincides from the outset with a life that is indistinguishable from political activity. Once history has been resolved into the fullness of the present—according to what can well be defined as an "ontology of actuality"[33]—the productive flow of life becomes the shifting terrain of identification between philosophy and politics. If this is the case, Gentile concludes, "a philosophy that is not blended with life, namely the life of its time and its country, which for everyone is the life by which they live the universal life, is senseless."[34] This degree of indifferentiation between thought and life was unprecedented, and not just in Italian philosophical culture. At least, never had the category of life so thoroughly filled those of politics and history, to the point of being identical with them, in a theoretical device that made one the spiritual substance of the other.

But, as always happens in Gentile, this drawing of philosophy back to life is only the upside-down topos of an equally complete reduction of life to philosophy—and thus an abstraction from its living body. He himself confirms this in response to Croce, who had objected to an excess of vitalism in his work: "When you say that 'my pure act' could also be called Life, Feeling, Will, or in any other way, you are perfectly right . . . but with the caveat that thought is life, because life, the one physiologists call life, is not properly life, but thought."[35] Philosophy entirely permeates life,

---

32. Giovanni Gentile, "Politica e filosofia," in *Dopo la vittoria* (1920; repr., Florence: Le Lettere, 1989), pp. 138–39.

33. See G. Marramao, "Un filosofo al potere?" in *Giovanni Gentile*, pp. 45.

34. Gentile, *Politica e filosofia*, p. 153.

35. Gentile, *Intorno all'idealismo attuale: Ricordi e confessioni* (1913), in *Opere filosofiche*, p. 393.

but only if life is nothing other than philosophy. This is the inversion, or semantic conversion between opposite meanings of the same concept—thus exposing it to the incumbent pressure of its negative—that we mentioned earlier. The identification between politics and philosophy can be looked at from the political angle, but also from the standpoint of philosophy. In Gentile's language, to say that philosophy is inherently political is a proposition that is perfectly reversible by exchanging its terms. Hence "if modern thought does not accept a politics that is not itself thought, then, on the one hand, any philosophical thought that keeps politics out of philosophy will be unacceptable; but on the other hand, any politics that disregards philosophy will also be inconceivable."[36] But what is a perfectly philosophical politics, if not a politics governed by an idea that excludes any event not referable to it? It is the relationship that exists between the most absolute of freedoms—consequent to the absence of any foundation outside its act of making itself [*farsi*]—and the necessity for it to be precisely this: nothing but *this* freedom, inevitably presupposed by the exclusion of any other possibility. Not being conditioned in the slightest—coinciding entirely with its own ideal development—history itself, as a whole and in its individual expressions, cannot be different from what it is from one occasion to the next. This means that the current identity with its own idea preventively protects it from an event external to it, but also from a judgment that is not included—and therefore neutralized—in the praxis that comes into being from one occasion to the next. From this standpoint, Gentile's relationship with fascism—his full collaboration even—is, if not inevitable, at least recognizable in the interior fault line that his thought continuously digs within itself.

2. The same reversibility between philosophy and politics that makes one both the form and the matter of the other also affects the relation between subject and world. At stake here, too, is the question of immanence: the dynamic epicenter toward which all the rays of Gentile's thought seem to converge.[37] It must immediately be said in this regard that it is hard to find an equally radical and potent formulation on the twentieth-century philosophical landscape—with the exception of a line of thought that, be-

36. Gentile, *Politica e filosofia*, p. 154.
37. On this topic, see Antimo Negri, *Giovanni Gentile* (Florence: La Nuova Italia, 1975), vol. 1; and Giorgio Brianese, *Invito al pensiero di Gentile* (Milan: Mursia, 1996), pp. 109 ff.

cause of its idealistic inspiration and lexical register, is otherwise entirely remote: that of Gilles Deleuze. It is striking that in order to better define his position, exactly like Deleuze, Gentile also traces out a kind of genealogy of immanence based on his predecessors that is marked by the failure, or at least the internal contradictoriness, of all attempts to theorize it. While Bruno—to whom we also owe the first transposition of the divine into the productive expression of infinite life—cannot avoid a relapse into transcendence, Spinoza, too, who picks up on this heritage, ends up reproducing an ontological gap between reality and knowledge of reality. Even Hegel, who can be credited with the most developed foretaste of the "method of immanence,"[38] gets caught in a realistic residue—recognizable, on the one hand, in the distinction between the plane of logic and that of phenomenology; and on the other, in the tripartite division of his system into logic, natural philosophy, and philosophy of the spirit.[39] By making the process of constituting reality attached to a result that is already posited prior to its development, he precludes that dialectical solution that made it possible in the first place, one that only the philosophy of action, also through the mediation of Spaventa, could arrive at fully. In order for immanence to be absolute, and for its method to be implemented, the entirety of reality must be brought back to thought, without anything being excluded, anticipated, or delayed. This means that everything is history—and thus philosophy—including that vital protrusion that Croce never succeeded in subduing, and that he retained in the seminatural dimension of prehistory. From this point of view—that of "putting into action" even life's origins—we can say that, certainly in his language, Gentile brought to completion the full transposition of nature into history that was prefigured by Marx in the communist society. While not overlooking the obvious differences, in both cases the unqualified life that the Greeks called *zoe* is entirely recuperated into the circle of *bios*—into an entirely historical form of life.

And yet, once the method of immanence has been defined, there still remains a basic question about the subject in Gentile's formulation—and even before that, about whether or not immanence has a subject other than

38. Giovanni Gentile, "Il metodo dell'immanenza (1912)," in *Opere filosofiche*, pp. 350–81.

39. A different reading of the relationship between Gentile and Hegel—whose overall aim is to diminish the theoretical scope of Gentile's philosophy—has been recently put forward by Vincenzo Vitiello in *Grammatiche del pensiero: Dalla kenosi dell'io alla logica della seconda persona* (Pisa: ETS, 2009), pp. 33–52.

itself. If it did, if there existed any subject of which immanence was the predicate, immanence would no longer be such, since a gap would be opened up inside it, between it and itself. In response to this risk, as always in these cases, Gentile sets up a double-faced theoretical dispositif, which is open to two interpretations: these coincide formally but differ in their effects of meaning. On the one hand, we can say that the process whose immanence we assert has no other subject than its own unfolding. In this case, that which is immanent would be nothing but immanence itself, with no subjective mediation distinguishing between levels. Gentile does not exclude this hermeneutic possibility in principle. We have already seen how the concept of praxis incorporates the subject of action, transforming it along with the object. In its creative expression, praxis does not refer to a subject outside its own movement. If anything, it causes the subject to be outside itself: in order to generate reality, like a moving vector, it must push itself outside its own confines. Action, in its perennial actuation, initiates a similar process of externalization: "The truth is in us, we ourselves are it," Gentile says, "but we are not the individual egoistically closed in on himself, who is only for himself, but the individual who goes outside himself; the moral subject who lives and who loves; not the individual who is, but the individual who *makes* himself."[40] We, therefore, are a subject—but a subject defined by its no longer being such, because it coincides with a "making itself" that continuously projects it beyond itself, into something that Gentile defines as "world" or "life" or, even better, as "life of the world." What we call subjectivity "is never more than the resolution of this duality between us and the world, so that our life is the same life of the world and the world is one, in its development, with our existence."[41] From the point of view of immanence, properly speaking, existence does not have a subject—which, if this were the case, would be posited prior to it, turning immanence into a simple predicate. To exist, in the infinite becoming of action, the subject cannot remain as such—subject—but must pass through the form of its own desubjectification.[42] Only in this way can it realize itself—diminishing its role,

40. The passage from Gentile is reported by Eugenio Garin in his introduction to *Opere filosofiche*, p. 52.

41. Giovanni Gentile, *Introduzione alla filosofia* (1933; repr., Florence: Sansoni, 1958), p. 159.

42. For this interpretation of Gentile's immanentism, see Natoli, *Giovanni Gentile filosofo europeo*.

until it dissolves entirely into the happening of the world. For this reason, referring to what he calls "pure experience," Gentile cannot conceive this in transcendental terms, as the experience of a given subject. Just as there is no object of experience, there can be no subject, whether divine or human. In fact, not only is his thinking irreducible to a simple form of subjectivism, it is far from any classically humanist inclination. Human beings do not take the place of God in the role of subject of history; rather, both are resolved in a process that dissolves any substance, including the human substance. In this distancing from anthropocentrism, there is something that recalls Bruno's centerless universe. Gentile's thought also lacks a center intended to unify the infinite variety of the world under its control. Not surprisingly, his greatest student—taking this line of thought to its limit—does not hesitate to speak of a world or a history that can easily do without humankind, according to the most extreme signification of the Copernican revolution.[43] Without arriving at similar conclusions, we can say that, for Gentile, as for Bruno earlier, the human being is but one of the myriad forms in which the unity of life is expressed.

However, as for everything else, this is just one of the possible interpretations of the relation between subject and world, to which another one leading in the opposite direction can be juxtaposed, or at least superimposed. As always happens in Gentile, this does not involve a conflict internal to his thought, or even a real hermeneutic divergence, but rather, a rotation of the view which, without canceling out the first perspective, assumes it through its reverse, thereby englobing it. From this angle, what appears to be—and in some ways, effectively is—a philosophy of the world, goes back to expressing itself as a philosophy of the self. Not because it denies the process of mundanization that pushes the subject out of itself, but because it attributes this act of exteriorization to the same subject that disappears inside it. The subject itself is the agent of its own dissolution, in an ecstatic form that makes it difficult to identify the various steps, because the negative coincides from the start with the positive. When Gentile writes, for example, that "thought neither presupposes nor posits the subject as its antecedent; rather, it *is* the subject. . . . There is no such thing as me and my thought: rather, I am my thought,"[44] he is saying

43. I am referring to Ugo Spirito. See particularly his *Inizio di una nuova epoca* (Florence: Sansoni, 1961), p. 303 ff.
44. Gentile, *Intorno all'idealismo attuale*, p. 397.

simultaneously that the thinking thought has no subject; and that it is the only subject, outside of which there is nothing. The thinking thought is the subject of something that has no subject—the locus, although always subjective, of a process of desubjectification. The logical transition from one plane to the other—in reality, a single plane with two faces—consists in the transition from the particular to the general. What dissolves on each occasion is the particular subject—not the universal or total one—which arises precisely from its nullification: "The person who thinks," explains the author, "is not an object, but a subject of thought; not a particular subject, but the subject in its totality or infinity, that is, the All as a thinking subject."[45] The problem is thus shifted, but without being resolved. On the contrary, the individual subject risks being nullified along with the exteriority that it implies. What appeared in the rigorous terms of the method of immanence as an escape of the self into the world is turned into a kind of incorporation of the world into the self—since nothing is external to the self-creative movement of the "I." In this way we pass seamlessly from a philosophy as world to a philosophy as Self.

This is not a mere linguistic deficiency: it is a conceptual contradiction which is all the more important in a logical system that resolves the conflict between thesis and antithesis in the actuality of a priori synthesis. This means that actualism can be seen alternately, or even simultaneously, as the thought that is least tied to the figure of the subject—understood in the sense of modern individualism—and the most subjectivistic, if compared to the plane of Self-awareness. The sacrifice of finite subjectivity, in short, is the expressive vehicle for a transcendental subjectivism. The question of how this sort of transcendental—any transcendental—can be in agreement with a radically immanentistic perspective, such as what Gentile would like his to be, remains to be answered. In this case, immanence is not the coextensiveness of life with itself—or the coextensiveness with itself through life—but rather, the refolding of an unfolding: the reclosure, in subjective terms, of the opening of the subject to its outside. Therefore, rather than expressing immanence as a philosophy, Gentile develops it himself as a religion; also in the technical sense of the Incarnation of the divine and the eternity of the living spirit—*manet Deus in nobis* (God dwelleth in us). Since the body is the externalization of the soul, the soul is

45. Gentile, "Il carattere religioso dell'idealismo italiano," in *Discorsi di religione* (Florence: Vallecchi, 1920), p. 152.

the essence of the body—that immaterial trait that brings the outside back into the inside, and makes the inside the truth of the outside. From this point of view, if Italian philosophy is a thought of immanence, or aspires to be one, it must be said that Gentile takes a step backward in relation to Bruno. To be sure, like Bruno, Gentile denies the immortality of the individual soul; and like Bruno, he rediscovers it only in the infinite life of the Mind. But while Bruno launched the first triumphant attack against the concept of personhood, both human and divine, Gentile remained caught up in its semantics and failed to develop the perspective of immanence in a thought on the impersonal: "Action," he writes in *The Philosophy of Art*, ". . . can only correctly entail the first person."[46] Not by chance, then, his entire philosophy is declined in the first person—as the work of an infinite "I" that can be the compendium of all the individual "I's," thereby nullifying them as such. Against the risk of the third person— which would allow an uncontrolled current to course from the *ego cogitans* to the *homo cogitat*, all the way to the bare *res*—Gentile keeps a firm hold on the language of the "I." And, in fact, Del Noce rightly concludes that he both fulfills Spinozism and at the same time negates it. He makes it "pass from the third person to the first."[47]

3. We need to examine the question of the "religion of immanence" more closely, however, if we want to capture the full resonance of an expression formed by the union of two apparently contradictory terms. As to the first of these—religion—it needs to said immediately that it should not be reduced to the mere metaphor of a philosophical faith. As is well known, in spite of some of the public stances he took, particularly on matters pertaining to the concordat and the rejection of a transcendent God, Gentile always insisted on declaring himself a Catholic. And, indeed, he not only continued to write extensively about religion, he also interpreted his thought ultimately in religious terms. No differently, for that matter, even if under much less favorable circumstances, from how "his" Bruno acted, when the Nolan defended the autonomy of philosophy from dogmatic interference *usque ad mortem* (even unto death), without denying

46. Gentile, *La filosofia dell'arte* (1931; repr., Florence: Sansoni, 1943), p. 50; text translated directly from the Italian. An English version is available: *The Philosophy of Art*, trans. Giovanni Gullace (Ithaca, NY: Cornell University Press, 1972).

47. Del Noce, *Giovanni Gentile*, p. 268.

the opportunity, and even the necessity, of the popular faith as a source of moral values and social bonds. This first requirement, in the broad political sense—which explains his decision to keep the teaching of religion in the lower classes as part of his school reform—was accompanied in Gentile's aims by a second, no less cogent reason: namely, to not weaken, and even to strengthen, one of the most profound traits of the Italian character, which consists in the Catholic tradition. His youthful rediscovery of Rosmini and especially of Gioberti, as the most faithful interpreters of the spiritual substance of the nation, can in some way be associated with this intention. It allowed him to channel his rejection of liberalism, and of modern culture in general, into a nonrevolutionary direction, oriented instead toward a restoration of the national virtues, which, at some point, he imagined as being accomplished (or at least accomplishable) by fascism. On this spiritualistic horizon we can also include his progressive and increasingly profound appreciation for Mazzini, whom he interpreted less as a political author than as an apostle of the faith required to gain, and then defend, the unity of Italy from the disintegrative impulses threatening its permanence. In this case, too, a sort of religion—of duties placed prior to the individualistic claim of rights but also opposed to them—opened up an alternative route, one leading backward, so to speak, with respect to the avenue that was being traveled at a faster and faster speed by modern secularization.

This first meaning of the expression "religion of immanence" should not obscure another one that is more expressive of the second term, though. The idea that religion is immanent for Gentile primarily means that it is not separable from the rest of his thought: on the contrary, it is an inner necessity that arises out of his thought. Far from placing philosophy and theology on two distinct, separate levels, united only by a need for mutual legitimacy, Gentile identifies them in a single spiritual dynamic coinciding, in turn, with the actuality of thought. Philosophy does not relate simply to faith—it itself is the true faith, because it expresses the most prominent function of the Christian God, that of creating the world. Clearly, this does not take away from the relation of religion to politics, and in fact it makes it even more intrinsic: since, as we know, philosophy is in itself political, then philosophical theology—or theological philosophy—cannot also be, in its most exacting form, political theology. On a closer look, this is precisely the outcome of the peculiar immanentism that we identified as the constant element, and rotational pivot, of Gentile's thought as a whole. Located on a plane of absolute immanence, theology must make itself, or reveal itself, as essentially political. No wonder the locus of its historical externalization is the state. Which is not limited to being the secular extension, or even the counterpoint on earth, of God's power as it is in classical or modern political theology. Instead, the state is identical to the divine power: "The state secularizes itself by becoming an end in itself. . . . And it cannot become an end itself by negating all ends, but rather by asserting itself as an end; itself, I repeat, as something absolute, endowed with divine value: deifying itself in some way."[48] We need to be careful not to tone down this claim: the state is not *like* God; rather, at least in its most universal expression and always in a state of becoming, it is itself God. From this standpoint, it is easier to understand the reproach mentioned earlier that he directed at Hegel for not taking the method of immanence to its completion. By subordinating the state to a subsequent figure of the Spirit and distinguishing it, internally, from civil society, and externally, from other states, Hegel failed to recognize its fully divine character. It is true, says Gentile, that the German philosopher considered the state far superior to the individuals it represents, but he did not consider it to be inside them—constitutive of their most intimate interiority, as was the case with Augustine's God.

This is the great theme of the state as *in interiore homine*, rather than *inter homines*, first appearing in his *Foundations of Law* and arriving all the way to his last, most inspired work. *Genesis and Structure of Society* is really, in every sense, the book of his life and death. It is the locus where his thought reaches its apex and at the same time its point of maximum internal contradiction. Lodged at its core is the dialectic between community and immunity that runs through all Italian philosophy, like a great semantic commutator. On the one hand, the state Gentile examines is indistinguishable from *communitas*, understood in the most powerful sense of the term. It has nothing to do with creating identity, in the naturalistic or biological sense. As he wrote with a trenchancy that he never retracted: "Theories of *race, environment, heredity, economic factors*, etc., are now generally looked upon with disdain and historians make every effort to avoid them."[49] Since the state is posited prior to, not after, the nation, it is not rooted in the land and the blood; it does not arise from a past that somehow constrains its eternal becoming. The state is not what it was, or, properly speaking, what

48. Gentile, *Educazione e scuola laica* (Florence, 1908), p. 107.
49. Gentile, "La storia," in *Introduzione alla filosofia*, p. 109.

it is; the state is only what it will be in the consciousness of the individuals in which it inheres. Not only that, but what counts even more toward community, this consciousness in each of the individuals is never self-consciousness. Rather, it is consciousness of the other, of one's own originary alteration into the estranged figure of the *socius* (associate), more internal to us than ourselves. Gentile pushes this line of discourse—one that has a deconstructive effect on all forms of personal identity—to the point of including in the "I" not only the associate but also the enemy, who is to be kept alive always so that the self can recognize itself: not like the Hegelian "slave," which is still external to the "master," but as an integral part of the self. The other is internal to the subject, to the point that, inside itself, it experiences the death of the subject, dying partly with it in the form of a "community of death" that perhaps only Georges Bataille, during the same years, conceived in an equally extreme fashion. Nothing is so "common" as death, because one never dies for oneself—as Heidegger claimed—but only for an other and in an other: death "is the other who is *our* other, reduced to other with no relation to us; no longer ours."[50]

But the death theme—which Gentile felt intensely in the months leading up to his own end—is in fact the least theoretically convincing aspect of his thought. In the name of death, *communitas* is reversed into the most total, and totalitarian, form of *immunitas*—it immunizes itself in advance from its own most radical significance. The "I" attains its immortality by dying with the other and in the other, by making itself "we": "And this We cannot be bypassed without losing the same experience— the only one possible—of death. And thus the 'I' is immortal."[51] What survives to infinity is the We that is inside us only to the extent to which we ourselves belong to it in a mutual incorporation through which the individual is swallowed up by the totality. With the usual movement that makes community and immunity perfectly reversible, the state is situated in individuals only if these are also, in their turn, located inside the state, to the point of being dissolved in it. From this point of view, always superimposed over and not opposing the first, the criticism of person implicit in the transcendental dialectic of *societas*, instead of initiating a thought of the impersonal, slips into a new and more inclusive personalization, con-

50. Gentile, *Genesi e struttura della società: Saggio di filosofia pratica* (1946; repr., Florence: Le Lettere, 1987), p. 170.

51. Ibid., p. 170.

stituted, as we have said, by the immortal Person of the State.[52] The relationship between *ego* and *alter* does not call into question the third person; instead, the relationship is reflected in a specular fashion onto the first—from the subject to the subject through the subject. What we have here is the extreme, paroxysmal fulfillment of a political theology that ends up placing the entire thought of Gentile in a stranglehold. This does not reside so much in the sovereign identification of politics and state, or solely in the absorption into the state of the entire social sphere of existence, both public and private; but rather, in the immediate transposition of religious monotheism into ethical-political monism. In this horizon, closed in on itself in an absolute identification between self and other, every particular is an evil, an error, a past that must be suppressed and surpassed in the name of the actuality of the Whole, which is in perpetual becoming. Within the all, it has the same role as death does in relation to immortal life. The single individual dies because, even before being born, singularity is on the side of death. More than an affirmative possibility—as it still is in revealed Christianity—eternal life, in Gentile, is intended as a double negative: the death of death, the annihilation of nothing. Gentile's nihilism is this and nothing else: not abandonment to death, not the assumption of finiteness, and not the revealing of evil. Rather, his nihilism is the functional negation of the life of the whole. The filling up of the difference that brings human beings into a communality in the undifferentiated unity of their identity. What is nihilistic is not absolute immanence—the abolition of every presupposition—but its inner reversal into a new, undifferentiated subjectivity: the breaking point between a plane of immanence and a thought of multiplicity, which converts the outside into the inside, the other into the same, and the common into the immune.

Thought-World

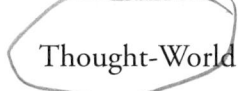

1. In relation to the comparison—and confrontation—between Croce and Gentile, where should Gramsci's thought be situated, and how does it define itself? After the first phase—during the postwar period of Gentile's eclipse—in which the only possible term of comparison was Croce's histori-

52. See Remo Bodei, *Il noi diviso: Ethos e idee dell'Italia repubblicana* (Turin: Einaudi, 1998), pp. 7 ff.

cism, an examination of the conceptual background that Gramsci shared with Gentile began in a form that separated both of them from Croce. Unlike Croce, rallying in defense of the great liberal tradition against the dual threat posed by fascism and communism, and with drastically different strategic objectives, Gentile and Gramsci converged in their acute perception that the political and philosophical categories of modernity were exhausted, and in seeking to surpass these through a political "activation" of philosophy.[53] This interpretive schema, whose basic outlines are generally valid, should not be pushed beyond a certain limit, however. Otherwise we risk losing sight not only of the area shared by Croce and Gentile, we also lose sight of what is clearly specific to Gramsci's position with respect to the each of the others. Staying with the triangle formed by these three authors, we might say instead that Gramsci uses the other two against each other, separately or simultaneously, only to leave them behind by taking off in a direction that goes far beyond them, and in some way even beyond his own time.

There is no doubt, in fact, that Gramsci's criticism of Croce—of his philosophical and political resistance to change—although not directed at him with the same intention as Gentile, is expressed in the same language: Croce fails to achieve a philosophy of immanence, he remains entangled in remnants of transcendence, because he recognizes neither the philosophical character of history nor the political character of philosophy. It is this double blind spot that, in spite of Croce's grasp on the historicity of thought, concealed from him the most powerful significance of his time—precluding him from that ontology of actuality which Gentile, instead, grasped and distorted: "Croce's proposition regarding the identity of history and philosophy is richer than any other in critical consequences: 1) it remains incomplete if it does not also arrive at the identity of history and politics . . . and 2) thus also at the identity of politics and philosophy."[54] To

---

53. This is the thesis first put forward by Augusto Del Noce in *Il suicidio della rivoluzione* (Milan: Rusconi, 1978).

54. *Quaderni*, 10, 1241; Boothman, p. 382. The Italian references to the quotes from the *Quaderni del carcere* by Antonio Gramsci refer to the critical edition by Valentino Gerratana (Turin: Einaudi, 1975). The first number refers to the notebook, and the second, to the page. The English versions are indicated by the name of the translator, the volume (if relevant), and the page number. Notebooks 1–8 are available in *Prison Notebooks*, ed. Joseph A. Buttigieg (New York: Columbia University Press, vol. 1, 1992; vol. 2, 1996; vol. 3, 2007). Quotes from the other notebooks come from *Selections from the Prison Notebooks of Antonio*

get there—instead of pulling back toward a still speculative conception of philosophy—Croce should have historicized his own thought by recognizing its resistant character, not only to fascism but also to the social dynamics fascism responded to in terms of "passive revolution." Gramsci's ability to grasp the paradox of a philosophy that expresses its politicization precisely by asserting its distance in principle from politics is remarkable. This is what he is getting at when he argues that "establishing with precision the political and historical significance of Crocean historicism means precisely cutting it down to its real import as immediate political ideology"[55]—which, as we have said, is that of containing the crisis that was taking place at that time by neutralizing the long-term conflicts that rippled through European civilization, tearing it apart. When Gramsci asks himself the questions, "Can one write a history of nineteenth-century Europe without an organic treatment of the French Revolution and the Napoleonic wars? And can one write a modern history of Italy without the struggles of the Risorgimento?"[56] he is explicitly alluding to the immunitary function that Croce's thought assumed in the face of traumas in the modern conceptual horizon that had by then become unmanageable. Ultimately, this immunitary function is what lies behind both the idea of the separation between intellectuals and the people—which takes social knowledge away from those who should be the first to make use of it—and the whole dialectic of distinctions, intended to enclose the explosive power of the economic inside a sphere that is independent and subordinate to the others. This is why although Croce's thought expresses a "greater adherence to real life . . . than any other speculative philosophy,"[57] it fails to translate it fully into history. Whence that prehistoric or metahistorical protrusion of something "vital" that oscillates continuously between a content without form and a form without content: if we ask ourselves about its connotation—remarks Gramsci—"there would always remain the assertion that what is 'vital' and inviolable is the liberal form of the state, i.e. the form that guarantees every political force the right to move and campaign freely. But how

Gramsci, ed. and trans. Quintin Hoare and Geoffrey Nowell Smith (London: Lawrence and Wishart, 1971); and from *Further Selections from the Prison Notebooks*, ed. and trans. Derek Boothman (London: Lawrence and Wishart, 1995).

55. *Q.*, 10, 1327; Boothman, pp. 375–76.
56. *Q.*, 10, 1209; Boothman, p. 330.
57. *Q.*, 10, 1216; Boothman, p. 337, slightly modified.

can this empirical fact be confused with the concept of liberty, that is to say of history?"[58] This is only possible in a sort of "preconceptualised history . . . that tends to enervate the antithesis, to break it up into a long series of moments, i.e. to reduce the dialectic to a process of reformist 'revolution-restoration' evolution, in which only the second term has any validity."[59]

One might very well say that all the criticisms of Croce that Gramsci makes—on the failed politicization of philosophy, on the residual separation between history and life, on the absence of a mass education for the working classes—are echoed more than once in the positions Gentile took during the same time. Provided that this echo is understood to be reversed. This is the point that seems to escape even the most acute critics, like Del Noce: Gramsci doesn't criticize Croce starting from Gentile—but from his opposite. While Croce failed to push far enough forward along the path of immanence, Gentile went all the way, but in the opposite direction to the one taken by Gramsci. When Gramsci observes that "the term 'immanence' has here acquired a special meaning which is not that of the 'pantheists' nor any other metaphysical meaning but one which is new and needs to be specified,"[60] adding that "the philosophy of praxis is absolute 'historicism,' the absolute secularisation [mondanizzazione] and earthliness of thought,"[61] he is opening up a breach in the thought of Gentile that pushes it outside itself, tipping it over to its outside: "The philosophy of praxis is bound up not only with immanentism but also with the subjective conception of reality in so far as it turns this latter upside down, explaining it as a historical fact, as the 'historical subjectivity of a social group.'"[62] This explains the profound significance of the opposition—anything but a rhetorical figure—between "the real 'impure' act, in the most profane and worldly sense of the world,"[63] and Gentile's pure act. "Impurity" or "profanity"—from within "thought in action," within the actualization of thought—in this case signifies the refutation of the absoluteness of the subject, the breakdown of its inner rhythm, its exposure to the density of the world. From this point of view, all the contents of Gentile's

58. *Q.*, 10, 1327–76; Boothman, p. 376.
59. *Q.*, 10, 1328; Boothman, p. 377.
60. *Q.*, 11, 1437; Hoare, p. 465.
61. *Q.*, 11, 1437; Hoare, p. 465.
62. *Q.*, 10, 1226; Boothman, p. 347.
63. *Q.*, 11, 1492; Hoare, p. 372.

thought are reversed into their opposite: starting with the definitions of "concrete" and "abstract."[64] What for Gentile is abstract, the material grain of existence, for Gramsci is concrete; and what is concrete for Gentile, the immaterial development of the spirit, for Gramsci becomes abstract. The same applies to the synonymic relationship between philosophy and politics—looked at by Gentile from the perspective of philosophy, and by Gramsci from that of politics, to the point of being able to say that "everything is political, even philosophy or philosophies . . . and the only 'philosophy' is history in action, which is life itself."[65] It is quite true that Gentile could also have used the same words, but with a significance that had the opposite effects of meaning. While for him politics in its essentially philosophical status is internal to the self-creative movement of the subject, for Gramsci it is philosophy, which is intrinsically political, that becomes an integral part of the world until it thoroughly coincides with it in a sort of *thought-world* contrary to Gentile's *world-subject*.

I don't know how much this difference, or even divergence—made even more acute by being inscribed in the same epochal horizon—is due to a different interpretation of Hegel, or to the influence in Gentile of Fichte, mediated by Mazzini.[66] Certainly the element that Gramsci specifically focuses on in the Hegelian dialectic is the antithesis, which, rather than neutralizing or mediating it as Croce would, Gentile tends to cancel out tout court in the apriority of the synthesis. Out of the elision of all antagonism in political action, the monistic—and therefore theological-political—tendency is generated that is destined to engulf the individual in the state the moment it makes the state the soul of the individual. To counter this, in some respects, Gramsci even seems to use Croce's distinction, or at least as far as it pertains to the internal structuration of the state form: while "Gentile's actualism corresponds to the positive phase of the state," Croce criticizes it as "antihistory." While "Croce wants to maintain a distinction between civil society and political society, between hegemony and dictatorship . . . Gentile posits the (economic-)corporative phase as an ethical

64. See André Tosel, "La philosophie de la praxis comme conception du monde intégrale et/ou comme langage unifié," in *Modernité de Gramsci?* ed. André Tosel (Besançon: Annales Littéraires de l'Université de Besançon, 1992), pp. 435–56.

65. *Q.*, 7, 886; text translated directly from the Italian.

66. This is the thesis of Domenico Losurdo, "Gramsci, Gentile, Marx e le filosofie della prassi," in *Gramsci e il marxismo italiano* (Rome, 1990), pp. 91–114.

phase within the historical act: hegemony and dictatorship are indistinguishable, force is no different from consent; it is impossible to distinguish political society from civil society; only the state exists and, of course, the state-as-government."[67] Indeed, what in Croce is a distinction—aimed at guaranteeing the autonomy of the individual from the absorbing intrusiveness of the state—in Gramsci becomes a more complex maneuver, directed once again against Gentile, that deconstructs the assumed identification between politics and state. Political action exists before, after, and even at the same time as the institution of the state, which does not coincide with it; its role is first to establish the state institution and then to renew the established power according to the relations of force that arise at different times. While not believing in the myth of the state's extinction, Gramsci works at loosening its sovereign bond by introducing into it something that traverses and, at the same time, surpasses it. This is the ambivalent role of the "civil society" lodged at the heart of his political perspective. It is made up of various powers and forms of knowledge, needs and interests, classes and social groups which, while not opposed to the state, make its internal dynamics more fluid, dividing it into a plurality of segments that are irreducible to a single form of control.

— Does this mean that Gramsci abandons Leninist ideology? That he moves toward a democratic perspective? That he breaks decisively with all forms of political theology? This is not quite the way things stand. The fact that he retrieves Gentile's term *totalitarianism* for his own conceptual lexicon—to indicate the need to overcome any dichotomy between public and private, theory and action, politics and economics—attests not only to a linguistic proximity but also to a deeper bond with his opponent, one that he never succeeded in severing. As we said, Gramsci reverses the content of actualism, but within the same subjective form, replacing the transcendental subject of Gentile with a collective subjectivity. Admittedly, this secularization—in the literal sense of belonging to the *secolo* or the earthly world—already undermines the monistic framework of Gentile's immanentism, but without reinstating the relationship, which he denied, between immanence and multiplicity. It is true that, for Gramsci, political life—the only one possible for him—is cut through by an unresolvable conflict between opposing powers in the struggle for he-

67. *Q.*, 6, 691; Buttigieg, vol. 3, pp. 9–10.

gemony. But it is equally true that, instead of preceding the conflict, the powers are always constituted differently from one period of time to the next, and in a different way from the initial modality. The general class and philosophy that first theorized their antagonism are also subject to this continuous transformation, but in a direction whose outcome is an exhaustion of the conflict, since "in the reign of 'freedom' thought and ideas can no longer be born on the terrain of contradictions and the necessity of struggle."[68] His most famous—and infamous—texts, on the "modern Prince" who "takes the place of the divinity or the categorical imperative,"[69] and on the necessary incorporation of individuals into "the collective man,"[70] refer to this dimension, one that is inevitably organismic[71]—and thus "total" in the strongest sense of the term. To interpret them merely as homages to the Leninist tradition in view of a national path to socialism is both inadequate and untrue to a thought that lived its time deeply, and in all its shadows. But to lock up inside these texts a philosophy that for the first time had the ambition, and strength, to make itself one with the world hinders us from grasping the features of it which, piercing through that time, have come down to us today.[72]

2. There are essentially two vectors in Gramsci's discourse that extend from his historical horizon to interpellate us from a closer distance, both of which are connected to the question of Americanism:[73] one in a geopolitical key and the other in a mode that to all intents and purposes can be defined as biopolitical. Of course what is meant here are planes of analysis that are tightly connected into a single semantic block. Breaking

68. *Q.*, 11, 1488; Hoare, p. 405.

69. *Q.*, 13, 1561; Boothman, p. 133.

70. *Q.*, 13, 1566; Boothman, p. 242.

71. As Franco Sbarberi rightly argues in *Gramsci: Un socialismo armonico* (Milan: Angeli, 1986).

72. On this topic, see the passionate work by Giorgio Baratta, *Le rose e i quaderni: Il pensiero dialogico di Antonio Gramsci* (Rome: Carocci, 2003).

73. For a thorough examination of Americanism in Gramsci, please see Massimo Montanari's introduction to Gramsci, *Pensare la democrazia* (Turin: Einaudi, 1997); also by Montanari, *Studi su Gramsci* (Lecce: Multimedia, 2002); the essays by Giuseppe Vacca, Mario Telò, and Michele Ciliberto appearing in the book edited by Giuseppe Vacca, *Gramsci e il Novecento* (Rome: Carocci, 1999); and finally the work by Francesca Izzo, *Democrazia e cosmopolitismo* (Rome: Carocci, 2009), pp. 147 ff.

it down for expository purposes is legitimate only if we keep in mind its meaning as a whole. The first concerns the relationship between territorialization and deterritorialization, which is typical and in some ways even constitutive of Italian political culture. In place of these terms, we could use the more familiar ones of *national* and *international*—but in doing so we would lose out on an important aspect involving the complex dialectic Gramsci establishes between territory, state, and nation. These three concepts are so tightly implicated in his vocabulary that they are mutually complementary, without, however, being completely superimposed on each other. As always happens with Gramsci, this is not just a terminological or abstractly philosophical question, but a political-historical problem concerning the history of Italy; one which has never been resolved, except in inadequate and distorted ways. Gramsci starts from the dual premise that "there can be no talk of the national without the territorial,"[74] but also that a modern form of state cannot arise out of the territorial as such, in the absence of the national—in other words, without an ethical, passionate content capable of uniting the inhabitants in a symbolic bond. For politics to perform its proper function, it must be rooted in a land defined by precise boundaries. But this land should be seen in its turn as the common place in which a people recognizes the genesis and significance of its history. Without this—outside this deep connection with nationality—the territory remains a mere geographical expression. This is precisely what happened to Italy, unlike other European countries where the virtuous symbiosis between land and nation enabled the formation of strong state bodies. The root of this discrepancy—the lack of a national ethos in the Italian territory—is identified by Gramsci as residing in an age that is very remote from today, namely, in the epochal passage that led from the Roman republic to the Roman empire. This is when first Caesar and then Augustus, by transferring the center of the imperial hegemony from the Italian peninsula into a supranational space, shifted the pillars of world history, leaving Italy in a secluded position. This choice, although leading to an unprecedented expansion of the Roman empire, in effect prevented a complete nationalization of the Italian territory, says Gramsci. This failed to materialize during the decentralized, municipal phase of the city-states; during the cosmopolitan period of the Renaissance; and, lastly,

74. Q., 17, 1935–36.

during the time of the Risorgimento, which remained uncompleted because of the narrowness of its social bases, only to then be occluded by the fascist reaction.

Into this negative picture, no different in its essential outlines from the one sketched out by de Sanctis in his *History*—in terms of the corporative closure of the intellectual class and the antinational role of the Church of Rome—Gramsci introduces something regarding the general crisis of the state form that is new and potentially explosive. It is an extraordinarily important theoretical step that places the author well beyond the national/ popular limits within which an entire tradition of interpretation sought to confine him, and launches him into the midst of a European debate that allowed him to overtake both Croce and Gentile. While both of them, albeit with opposite intentions, continued to reason from the perspective of the state, Gramsci took for granted the state's precariousness in the face of unprecedented but unstoppable dynamics that seemed to unify the world in a different, epoch-making horizon. There is no doubt that he moves to a level of analysis that, with the exception of Santi Romano, and with markedly different goals and conduct, in those years was achieved only when Carl Schmitt declared the end of the *jus publicum europaeum*— which hinged on the category of the sovereign state—and the beginning of a new era. This does not mean, of course, that for Gramsci state bodies have outlived their purpose—he is always skeptical about the communist prognosis of extinction—but rather, they are no longer able to neutralize conflicts generated by powers [*potenze*] which now extend largely beyond their national boundaries. Starting with the power of the economy, which in the contemporary world seems to have taken the place of politics as the ground of definition and transformation of power relations between individuals and peoples. This is a turning point—from political control to economic production—equal in intensity and starkness to the one that inaugurated the modern era, when politics took over the role previously exercised by theology. If secularization bears the signs of politics, globalization, which had begun to arise in all its ambivalence starting as early as the 1930s, was thrust into being by the economy. From that moment on, geography seemed to become not only the object but also the subject of history; in the sense that whatever happens anywhere in the world is immediately refracted in all the others with a double effect of historicization of space and spatialization of time. But the innovative force of Gramsci's reading lies in its ability to grasp not only the importance of the geopolitical factor—the interweaving of national and international, involving all places on earth—but also the entropic consequences brought on by this coimplication. The loss of hegemony experienced by politics is itself a political factor with which the analysis must contend. This—not the primacy of the economy as such, but the desire of politics to take it back—is precisely what gave rise first to the war and then to fascism. The warmongering nationalism and drive toward imperialism were the most brutally reactive ways in which European politics responded to its own marginalization. But none of the political responses that came from Europe appeared equal to the times or to the complexity of the problems that they brought with them. Certainly not the authoritarian fascist corporatism that was destined to plunge the world into the catastrophe of war; but not French republicanism or German Social Democracy either, which continued to view the state as the main engine of innovation. Even the revolutionary movement, which Gramsci felt himself to be a part of, threatened to shut itself up inside the asphyxiating boundaries of state sovereignty, with the Stalinist project of building socialism in a single country.

At the bottom of this apparent unresolvability there is a structural contradiction in the fact that "whereas economic life has internationalism, or better still cosmopolitanism, as a necessary premiss, state life has developed ever more in the direction of 'nationalism,' of 'self-sufficiency' and so on."[75] But Gramsci adds something that is even more insightful. He says that the global crisis is caused by the perverse intersection of two concomitant factors: first, the attempt by politics to govern in a nationalistic form a power [*potenza*] like the economy that is global and deterritorialized by nature; secondly, and simultaneously, the breakdown of the immunitary mechanism that counterbalanced—thereby containing—the paradoxical effects generated by the first impulse. The crisis is generated by the

intensification of certain phenomena, while others that were there before and operated simultaneously with the first, immunizing them [immunizzandoli], have now become inoperative or have completely disappeared. In brief, the development of capitalism has been a "continual crisis," if one can say that, i.e. an extremely rapid movement of elements that mutually balanced and immunized [immunizzavano] one another. At a certain point in this movement, some ele-

75. Q., 15, 1756; Bootham, p. 220 [trans. note: slightly adapted based on original].

ments have gained predominance and others have disappeared or have become irrelevant within the general framework.[76]

What does not work anymore, because it leads to recessionary and aggressive effects, is the return to the land that Italy experienced in other periods of its history and that was at that time recurring in different but consistently regressive ways in Nazi Germany and Soviet Russia. Compared to this backward, violent scenario, the only national reality that seemed to Gramsci to move in step with the incipient globalization and its direction was the American one. Instead of aiming for an impossible reterritorialization of the world, Americanism fostered economic deterritorialization, adhering to its spontaneous flow. By privileging the category of production over that of decision, it broke the old European circle that ran between sovereignty, administration, and territory. Rather than repoliticizing the economy, as Europe sought vainly to accomplish, America made of the political a channel for the universal deployment of the economy. This is how it had established its global hegemony—which was all the more strong and widespread the less it identified with political power and the more it was directed toward financial and sociocultural expansion. Naturally, Gramsci did not look on Americanism as a final outcome of his own perspective.[77] In his eyes, it still expressed a form of passive revolution that had to be surpassed by taking a much more radical direction. Similarly, he did not see the fate of contemporary civilization as lying in economic or technological depoliticization. On the contrary, he worked on developing a new political form that would be capable of dealing with the points of no return created by the current turn of events, by integrating them. But for this to be possible, the new politics had to exceed the limits of state sovereignty, from both inside and outside it. This did not mean losing sight of the question of the nation—which remained at the center of Gramsci's focus. But only if the nation were to be introduced into an international context that would dramatically restructure it: "The national personality (like the individual personality) is a mere abstraction when considered outside the international (or social) nexus."[78] What

76. *Q.,* 15, 1756–57; Bootham, p. 220.

77. See Jacques Texier, "Gramsci face à l'américanisme: Examen du Cahier 22 des *Quaderni del carcere,*" in *Modernité de Gramsci?* ed. Tosel, pp. 347–78.

78. *Q.,* 19, 1962.

Gramsci attempts to conceive as the future of the contemporary world is an insoluble mixture of local and global, regional and continental, national and international. A nation is such—a living body, that is—when, instead of shutting itself up in its own territorial identity, it is able to deterritorialize itself, to look at itself from the outside, and to take from the outside world whatever aids in renewing and developing its own roots, rather than obstructing them. This applied equally to the newly started process of European unification—upon whose completion, says Gramsci, "the word 'nationalism' will have the same archaeological value as 'municipalism' has today"[79]—as it did to Americanism, which, even before being ridiculed by what Vico had dubbed the "conceit of nations," was dismissed offhand by the "conceitedness of the learned [boria dei dotti]" in ways that Gramsci did not hesitate to call both "stupid" and "comical."[80] In any case, despite its immune syndrome, "old Europe" will still be transformed by a land like the United States, which was deterritorialized from its beginings, but not denationalized, by the melting pot of ethnicities, religions, and cultures that formed it. This will mean a quantum leap in civilization, says Gramsci, only if the relationship is two-way—that is, only if once Europe has been transformed by America, it is able to have an impact on the United States, in turn, by giving a political soul back to the technological and financial globalization. Italy can and must also do its part in this global dialectics. Indeed, according to Gramsci's analysis, in spite of the fascist regression that was currently underway, Italy was in an advantageous position compared to other European countries, precisely because of its historic lack of state sovereignty. With a stroke of genius, Gramsci reversed the negative judgment on Italian cosmopolitanism that was expressed by his own tradition, provided that it was able to detach itself from its elitist origins and place at its center the material production of life within the globalized world: "Traditional Italian cosmopolitanism has to become a modern type of cosmopolitanism such, that is, as to ensure the best conditions for the development of Italian humanity-as-labour in whatever part of the world it is to be found. . . . The Italian people is that people which is 'nationally' more interested in a modern form of cosmopolitanism."[81]

79. *Q.*, 6, 748; Buttigieg, 3, p. 61.
80. *Q.*, 5, 635; Buttigieg, 3, p. 356.
81. *Q.*, 19, 1988; Bootham, p. 253.

3. This leads to the second vanishing point of Gramsci's perspective—passing extremely close to us—that we can connect back to the biopolitical sphere. It may come as a surprise that this has never received adequate attention in the now considerable literature on Gramsci, or from scholars of the genealogy of biopower who have been at work on the topic for some time.[82] Although it bears saying that Gramsci never presented it as a paradigm that he developed himself, but rather as a historically determined product of that broad economic deterritorialization process we just spoke about. Moreover, even when a remarkably insightful conceptual innovation is recognized, it must still be located in the author's lexicon; especially, in this case, with regard to the predominant, continuously active category of "civil society." While these observations may suggest hermeneutic caution, they do not lessen the innovative scope of this, the most radical, part of his discourse. Indeed, they make it even more meaningful to the extent that they end up locating it in a horizon that is external to—or later than—the modern one of state sovereignty. The impression conveyed by Gramsci's text is that the exhaustion, or at least the weakening, of the role of the state is precisely what opens up a space (a problematic one, to be sure) for the direct connection between the sphere of politics and the sphere of life that took the name of biopolitics. We know that, from the beginning, Gramsci conceived the theory of praxis as an interpenetration of philosophy, politics, and economics, such that each of them could be converted or transposed into the other. But, as we have just seen, early globalization, which was recognized and at the same time generated by the American model, shattered this equilibrium, making the economic category of production the epicenter of all socially influential dynamics. Along these lines, we can say that it penetrates life not only in terms of form—tracing out new and unprecedented forms of life—but also in terms of its immediate biological content.

We have already stated that in Americanism Gramsci did not see the characteristics of a society free from oppression. Nor did he see a full-on break with European civilization, of which America remained a direct inheritor. He viewed it rather as nothing more than a passing phase in capitalist development whose function was to overcome one of its struc-

---

82. It did catch the attention of Francesco Fistetti, in *La crisi del marxismo in Italia* (Genoa: Il Melangolo, 2006), pp. 33 ff. Étienne Balibar also brings together Gramsci and Foucault in "Gramsci, Marx et le rapport social," in *Modernité de Gramsci*, p. 269.

tural crises. But he was far from underestimating its novelty or the force of its impact on the rest of the world. By avoiding parasitic sedimentations and bureaucratic constraints that block or slow down the productive pace of European capitalism, American capitalism managed to enlarge the sphere of consumption while increasing the level of wages. To achieve this dual aim, which reverses the downward trend of profit, it was forced to change not only the economic cycle of American society but its entire shape. Having made the factory its dynamic center, it also reorganized the space external to the production process according to the rhythms and objectives of the factory, thus creating an overlap between work and life that made one the foundational and developmental sphere of the other. Starting from this historical and sociological premise, Gramsci began the analysis—a biopolitical one, in the full sense of the term—that led him to anticipate with extraordinary clarity of vision the reflection initiated by Foucault in the mid-1970s. He was more than aware that the process he was examining was barely in its genesis, one that was anything but complete and destined to undergo a series of internal metamorphoses whose final outcome was difficult to predict: "In America rationalisation has determined the need to elaborate a new type of man suited to the new type of work and productive process. This elaboration is still only in its initial phase and therefore (apparently) still idyllic. It is still at the state of psycho-physical adaptation to the new industrial structure."[83]

What is clear, on the one hand, is the anthropological profundity of the change; and on the other, its repercussions on people's bodies and minds, in such a way as to subordinate one to the mastery of the other. The strength of the Fordist and Taylorist model lay precisely in the ability to delegate the control of the worker's body to his or her mind. To ensure that each worker produced as much as possible in the shortest possible time, his or her body movements had to be uniform with those of all the other workers, in order to create a single production body similar in every way to a machine: "American industrialists are concerned to maintain the continuity of the physical and muscular-nervous efficiency of the worker. It is in their interests to have a stable, skilled labour force, a permanently well-adjusted complex, because the human complex (the collective worker) of an enterprise is also a machine which cannot, without considerable loss,

83. Q., 22, 2146; Hoare, p. 286.

be taken to pieces too often and renewed with single new parts."[84] But if the body of the workers was strictly modeled according to production needs, the attention given to their mind was equal and opposite—in the sense that the mind was freed for the performance of higher skills precisely through the complete automation of the body's muscles: "Once the process of adaptation has been completed, what really happens is that the brain of the worker, far from being mummified, reaches a state of complete freedom. The only thing that is completely mechanicised is the physical gesture; the memory of the trade, reduced to simple gestures repeated at an intense rhythm, 'nestles' in the muscular and nervous centres and leaves the brain free and unencumbered for other occupations."[85] But the freedom acquired in this way by the brain, rather than also bringing about the freedom of the body, was directed at suppressing it through a series of self-impositions that the brain carried out on itself, not due to external constraints, but consensually, by voluntarily complying with the objectives of the entire productive mechanism. What Gramsci describes, in pages of rare analytical intensity, is a true system of discipline consisting of introjected rules that regulate and control every aspect of the worker's life—from reproductive activities to hygiene and health, which is also oriented to optimizing work performance. Birth, nutrition, health, housing, and immigration are all vital spheres subjected to the same "psycho-physical adaptation to specific conditions of work. . . . This is not something 'natural' or innate, but has to be acquired,"[86] with a self-repressive effort that reached its apex in the "sexual question," examined not in isolation, but precisely for its bioeconomic and biopolitical relevance:

It is worth drawing attention to the way in which industrialists (Ford in particular) have been concerned with the sexual affairs of their employees and with their family arrangements in general. Once should not be misled, any more than in the case of prohibition, by the "puritanical" appearance assumed by this concern. The truth is that the new type of man demanded by the rationalisation of production and work cannot be developed until the sexual instinct has been suitably regulated and until it too has been rationalised.[87]

84. *Q.*, 22, 2166; Hoare, p. 303.
85. *Q.*, 22, 2170–71; Hoare, p. 309.
86. *Q.*, 22, 2149; Hoare, p. 296.
87. *Q.*, 22, 2150; Hoare, pp. 296–97.

Without transferring Gramsci into a theoretical orbit that does not concern him, it is difficult not to view this extension of his discourse as the base for the discussion that Italian philosophy would relaunch onto the international scene only a few decades later. Prefigured in his most inspired pages, still wrapped up in the language of the "war of position," is the shift of the entire perspectival axis of political analysis from the sphere of institutions and subjects to that of dispositifs and "docile bodies." While it is true that Italian reflection of today is premised on the work undertaken twenty years earlier by Foucault, it is also true that, although not directly informed by them, the French thinker had the extraordinary insights of Gramsci behind him.

PASSAGE IV: THE UNBEARABLE

The identification between history and life, recognized or otherwise postulated by Gentile and Gramsci, was not destined to last long. Only a decade after the war, Pier Paolo Pasolini's *The Ashes of Gramsci* marked the first, obvious, rift.[88] The marked dissonance of this text with the neorealist literature of its time was understood from the outset, particularly by Marxist critics, in terms of the conflict expressed by the poet himself between "passion" and "ideology": in other words, between the conditions—both emotional and social—of an intellectual with a middle-class background, and a commitment alongside the working class and its political organization. But when Pasolini, standing in front of the *cinera Gramscii* at the English Cemetery in Rome, described "the scandal of contradicting myself, of being / with you and against you; with you in my heart / in the light, against you in the dark viscera,"[89] it seemed as if the existential gap between poetry and politics had deepened into a wider fracture between the sphere of history and the horizon of life. This is the angle from which the work of Pasolini not only enters in its own right into the picture we have outlined so far, it represents an unusually insightful point of it. True, in his first poetic experiments he endeavored to keep these two polarities linked together, by depicting his own vitality in the guise of an ideological choice in favor of people from rural areas [*il popolo contadino*] and the urban underclass. But what attracted him about the rural people was neither their political struggle nor their historical consciousness. Instead, he was drawn to their natural, even biological dimension—expressed in pre-political and even prehistoric terms—that could not be transposed into Gramsci's national-popular project, to which he nevertheless declared his intellectual allegiance. Pasolini remained

attracted to a proletarian life
prior to you, religion for me is

its joyfulness, not its millenary
struggle: its nature, not its
consciousness.[90]

88. Pier Paolo Pasolini, *Le ceneri di Gramsci* (Milan: Garzanti, 1957).

89. Pasolini, *Le ceneri di Gramsci*, in *Le poesie* (Milan, 1975), p. 73. [Translator's note: All citations of Pasolini prose and poetry are my own.]

90. Ibid., p. 73.

What "drags him back" to the "joyfully earthly," "idle time" of the "humble people [umile gente]"[91]—despite the need to "understand" and "act"—is a visceral adherence to a vital, pulsing matter that both precedes and exceeds the ideological framework of a historically determined task. Although itself the expression of a centuries-old historical development, this "eager," "animal," "bodily" life with which the poet identifies in his very flesh, is by now situated on the outer edge of history, in an anthropogenic stratum that is indistinct and chaotic, without any formal characterization—not a "form of life," but, in the literal sense of the term, a stripped-down life, coinciding in every way with its bare presence:

that life is nothing but a shiver;
bodily, collective presence;
you feel the absence of all true
religion; not life, but survival
—maybe happier than life—like
a population of animals, in whose arcane
orgasm there is no passion other than
for their daily functioning:
humble fervor which gives a sense of festivity
to humble corruption.[92]

This reference to the body, in opposition to, or at least outside of history— "Something has widened / the chasm between body and history"[93]—has generally been interpreted by Pasolini critics in terms of a regressive attitude toward the postwar development of Italian society, or even resentment in reaction to it. Something of the sort is undeniable—the poet himself makes it explicit in an insistent and often poignant evocation of the originary, primordial qualities of his own biographical experience. But, as we have also seen at other times in the Italian tradition, the call to the prehistoric or prerational origin is never exhausted in a mere reference to the "force of the past," which Pasolini also claims to embody; rather, it pushes forward, projecting itself beyond the line of the present:

I am a force of the Past

. . .

91. Ibid., p. 51.
92. Ibid., p. 78.
93. Pasolini, *Poesie incivili*, in *Le poesie*, p. 313.

I look at the twilights, the mornings
over Rome, over the Ciociaria, over the world,
like the first acts of Posthistory,
that I witness, thanks to my date of birth,
from the far edge of some buried
age. Monstrous are those born from
the viscera of a dead woman.
And I, adult fetus, wander about
more modern than any modern person
in search of siblings who are no more.[94]

Contrary to those—such as in the neo-avant-garde literature of the 1960s, for example—who identified their modernity in an emphatic break with the origin, it was precisely in the paradoxical relationship with the origin that Pasolini recognized a passageway leading us, for better or worse, beyond the modern age. In this sense, that absolute or dissolute life (because it lacks any formal mediations) that causes friction with history and diverges away from it, while certainly being what precedes history, is also what follows it: the "post-" toward which modernity rushes along in a seemingly unstoppable current. This explains why the poet's gaze is torn between two worlds that, although continuing to coexist for some time, are already in conflict. The first is intent on molding the vital impulses to its historic objective, with an increasing lack of success; while the second represents a life that is no longer containable inside the closed circle of history, destined in its biological density to leave it far behind. As the last message of "Gramsci's Ashes" expresses it:

The rain and the sun are mixed together
in a joy that perhaps is preserved
—like a splinter of the other history,
no longer ours—deep in the heart
of these poor travelers:
alive, only alive, in the warmth
that makes life greater than history.[95]

For the generation oppressed by fascism, that trust in the progressive forces of history in which Gramsci still sought the meaning of life had resulted in

94. Pasolini, *Poesia in forma di rosa*, in *Le poesie*, p. 344.
95. Pasolini, *Le ceneri di Gramsci*, p. 134.

its withering away as soon as the goal had been reached, and life seemed to withdraw into itself as a function of mere survival:

the disappointment of history!
Which makes us arrive at death
without having lived,
and, because of this, remain in life
to contemplate it, like a wreck
a wonderful possession that doesn't belong to us.[96]

    This allusion to death identifies something more than just a point of contrast with the vitalistic tension of the poet. Starting from the homage to Gramsci's remains (concluding a cycle of Italian poetry inaugurated by Foscolo's *Sepulchers*), death constitutes the emotional and lexical horizon with a slant destined to traverse and in some way influence Pasolini's entire experience, all the way to his tragic end. Without resorting to the radical hypothesis of a consciously planned sacrifice,[97] there is no doubt that death, taken as a "frame around the furious gift of life,"[98] represents an essential interpretive key for his entire oeuvre. The author himself, moreover, on several occasions identifies death as the only place from which the meaning of an individual life can be understood, in a remarkable correlation with what Auerbach said about Dante's conception of the "figure." We must die in order for the message of our life, otherwise confused, to be deciphered in all its significance. But what demands our attention is the role that death plays during life—not "after," but from inside it, as Pasolini stresses: "my idea of death, then, was a behavioralist and moral idea: it wasn't concerned with what comes after death, but with what comes before it—not with the hereafter, but with life. Thus, with life understood as fulfilment, as a desperate, uncertain tendency toward its own expressive perfection that is continually in search of support, opportunities, and relationships."[99] Our task, of course, is to understand the sense of this in-

    96. Pasolini, *Poesia in forma di rosa*, p. 378.

    97. I am referring to the perspective of Giuseppe Zigaina, in *Pasolini e la morte* (Venice, 1967).

    98. Pasolini, *Poesia in forma di rosa*, p. 379.

    99. Pier Paolo Pasolini, "I segni viventi e i poeti morti," in *Empirismo eretico* (Milan: Garzanti, 1972), p. 256; English version: "Living Signs and Dead Poets," in *Heretical Empiricism*, trans. Ben Lawton and Kate I. Barnett (Bloomington: Indiana University Press, 1988), p. 249.

fluence of death, which would change over the course of time during the different phases of Pasolini's artistic commitment. But what characterizes the first stage, up to the early 1960s, is precisely the indissoluble interpenetration between life and death, their mutual immanence. Death is not, at least for now, what comes from outside to destroy life, but rather an inner force—the magnet to which life gravitates in order to be able to explicate itself in its uncontainable natural potency. The pivot around which "life whirls,"[100] consuming itself without limits, burning its energetic force in an intoxicating and at the same time destructive mixture that is one with the freedom to surrender oneself completely, allowing oneself to be possessed by one's own other: "Freedom. After giving a lot of thought to it, I understood that this mysterious word doesn't mean anything else, in the end, in the long run, except . . . the freedom to choose death."[101] Hence its indissoluble link with the realm of sex, in the transgressive meaning that Pasolini gives to it—death as the "twin" of love and desire.[102] Desire, never able to fully realize itself, destined to remain short of full enjoyment, is always, ultimately, a "death wish,"[103] an oscillating edge along which the instinct of life is identical to its opposite—"Perhaps no one has lived at such a height / of desire—funereal anxiety / whose breeze fills me like the sea."[104] This is also how the unconsciously sacrificial impulse of almost all Pasolini's characters should be interpreted—from Vittorio in *Accattone*, to Ettore in *Mamma Roma*, to the protagonist of *A Violent Life*: what is violent, in reality, is not any life in particular but rather life as such; when left to itself, when removed from the flow channel of history, like the life of the "ragazzi di vita," the hustlers who are all without distinction exposed or promised to death, as that which conducts life to its animal regression or sacred excess.

But this ambivalent relationship with life is not the only vector in Pasolini that is tangential to the deeply formed characteristics of Italian

---

100. Pasolini, *Poesie incivili*, p. 295.

101. Pasolini, "Il cinema impopolare," in *Empirismo eretico*, p. 273; text translated directly from the Italian. English version available in "The Unpopular Cinema," in *Heretical Empiricism*, pp. 267–75.

102. Pasolini, "Il cinema impopolare," in *Empirismo eretico*, p. 273; text translated directly from the Italian.

103. Ibid., p. 315.

104. Pasolini, *Poesia in forma di rosa*, p. 356.

thought. One could even go so far as to say that the relation of obliquity, or externality, between his intellectual experience and the traditional institutions of literature is the same as the relation Italian philosophical reflection entertains with the canonical texts of modern philosophy. This dissimilarity is already perceptible in the deliberately anti-aesthetic character of his poems, forged as they are for the purposes of practical intentionality—of accusation, protest, prophecy—that in itself deprives them of the style the poet had initially looked to as the established sphere of poetic practice. To this must be added, on the one hand, the programmatically unfinished, or at least uncomposed, character of his writings,[105] long before death dramatically interrupted his last work; and on the other hand, their hybrid structure, achieved through overlapping stratifications, including heterogeneous materials taken from news reports on politics, the judiciary, and morals. But, as has been rightly pointed out,[106] this stylistic break on the artistic plane is only a first level of infraction, one that, with varying degrees of success, historical avant-garde artists had already experimented with. To this must be added a second, much more incisive one, because it relates to the mutually conflictual relationship between the poet and the literary institution as a whole. Moving in the opposite direction from the diminishing role of the author (displaced by the automatic function of writing as theorized by late twentieth-century structuralist criticism), rather than disappearing behind the autonomy of his work, Pasolini made his art a sort of living appendix of himself. Not only did he refuse to shield his texts from the emotions, sensations, and excitements that he felt, he literally filled them up with his feelings, sucking his writings into his overflowing, subjective experience. The impression given to the reader is that they couldn't have been written by anyone else—at least not in the form, or to be more precise, in the nonform or antiform that they have. It is as if he had purposely intended, through his own exhibited "impurity," to contaminate literature by dragging it into the same maelstrom into which he himself was slipping deeper and deeper. The ultimate effect (at times intensely poetic) of his writings is inseparable from his rejection of poetry as an immunitary body—both protected from and protective of the violent life by which he, instead, was relentlessly inter-

---

105. See Antonio Tricomi, *Sull'opera mancata di Pasolini* (Rome: Carocci, 2005).

106. In the excellent portrayal traced out by Carla Benedetti in *Pasolini contro Calvino: Per una letteratura impura* (Turin: Boringhieri, 1998).

pellated, seduced, and violated. Just as we have repeatedly observed about Italian thought, the most explosive content—the significance and the truth—of Pasolini's poetry lies in this exteriority, which is identical with the subjective experience of its author.

But what is even more characteristic, as far as our discussion is concerned, is that this subjectivity should not be understood in the interiorized sense of the author's "person," but rather in the sense of his body, experienced in all its paroxysmal, biological intensity. It was his body that occupied the Italian literary scene, disrupting it, for at least two decades—until it was found, lifeless, at the Ostia water airport—like some tragic experiment in body art, in which the artist is both subject and object of his or her performance.[107] In a poem entitled "Poet of Ashes," when Pasolini announces that he intends to express himself "with examples. / Throw my body into the fray,"[108] adding that "the actions of life . . . will be themselves, poetry, / because, I repeat, there's no other poetry than real action,"[109] he sets up a short-circuit between action, life, and body that has no equal in contemporary poetry: poetry means nothing unless it expresses a force for changing reality, by taking a stance in the conflicts that run through it. But this struggle, rather than being about abstract ideals, hinges on the fate of the living body. Starting from these assumptions, it comes as no surprise that his entire interpretation of contemporary society, beginning with the protest movement of 1968 and lasting until the time of his death, had a clear biopolitical valence.[110] His ideas on the "anthropological mutation" of the Italians—their false tolerance and social uniformity, and the pernicious influence of television—are too well known to have to be recalled in detail. But what makes his arguments so intensely relevant today, even beyond their specific content, is the interpretative filter—the point of view that knits them together—which consists in the vicissitudes of the (individual and collective) body of the Italians. Long before the restructuration of power passes through ideologies, it works through the modification of

107. See ibid., pp. 139 ff.

108. Pier Paolo Pasolini, *Bestemmia: Tutte le poesie*, ed. Graziella Chiarcossi and Walter Siti (Milan: Garzanti, 1993), vol. 2, p. 2082.

109. Ibid., p. 2083.

110. Along these lines, see Lorenzo Chiesa, "Pasolini and the Ugliness of Bodies," in *In Corpore: Bodies in Post-Unification Italy*, ed. Loredana Polezzi and Charles Ross (Madison, NJ: Fairleigh Dickinson University Press, 2007).

bodies, which are both its cause and effect: "I *live*, existentially, this cata-clysm, which, at least for now, is pure degradation: I live it in my days, in the forms of my existence, *in my body*. . . . All my ideological discourses issue in conclusion out of this existential, immediate, concrete, dramatic, *corporeal* experience."[111]

All the traumatic transitions that in Pasolini's view had marked Ital-ian society were ultimately attributable to a kind of dematerialization of the bodily dimension which, until a few years previously, had been kept vital or even intact by the lower classes who were not yet affected by con-sumerism. If, until a few decades ago, he writes "the last bastion of reality seemed to be the 'innocent' bodies with the archaic, dusky, vital violence of their sexual organs," now that innocence "has been violated, manipu-lated, tampered with by the power of consumerism: indeed, this violence against bodies has become the most macroscopic datum of the new human era."[112] This was so much the case that the bodies had modified them-selves, adapting themselves to the psychological degeneration and literally mutating their appearance. Young people, onto whom the poet had once projected his hopes and desires, were the living testimony of this transfor-mation. Just as their faces had become expressionless and their language had regressed to a kind of inarticulate slang, even their long hair, or their beards, which up to a certain point had represented a sort of "antibody" or a counterbody against the soft body of bourgeois society, had now become its mere ideological reverse. Because of this, the same body that when com-posed of "lower-class dough [pasta popolare]" spoke of "health, innocence, barbarism, delinquency: anything but guilt, banality, and vulgarity,"[113] was now the locus of an anonymous, disturbing devastation: "Their physical appearance is almost terrifying, and when not terrifying is annoyingly un-happy. Hideous furs, grotesque heads of hair, pale complexions, dull eyes. They're masks for some barbaric—squalidly barbaric—initiation. Or else they're masks of some diligent, unconscious integration, which doesn't in-

111. Pier Paolo Pasolini, "Sacer," in *Scritti corsari*, now available in *Saggi sulla politica e sulla società*, ed. Walter Siti and Silvia De Lande (Milan: Mondadori, 1999), p. 382.

112. Pier Paolo Pasolini, "Abiura dalla 'Trilogia della vita,'" in *Lettere luterane*, now in *Saggi*, p. 600; translated directly from the Italian. An English version, entitled "Repudia-tion of the Trilogy of Life," can be found in the expanded edition of *Heretical Empiricism*, trans. Ben Lawton (Bloomington: Indiana University Press, 2005).

113. Pier Paolo Pasolini, *Petrolio* (Turin: Einaudi, 1992), p. 187.

spire compassion."[114] Not only that, this integration was also capable of projecting its own grim, threatening shadow onto the past, through a retroactive mechanism that by the light of the present deconstructs what once seemed flourishing and exuberant. This is the reason why in the 1970s the poet, now also a director, could no longer make films with a luminous quality like those in the so-called *Trilogy of Life*—*The Decameron*, *The Canterbury Tales*, and the *Arabian Nights*—because that life is now also looked at through the reversed cone of its opposite: "Today, the degeneration of bodies and genitals has taken on a retroactive value. If those who were like this or that *then*, have now become like this or that *now*, it means they were already potentially that way: thus, even their way of being *then* is devalued from the present. If the young people and kids from the Roman subproletariat—who are the ones I projected onto the tough, old Naples and then onto the poor countries of the Third World—are *now* human garbage, it means they were also that potentially *then*."[115]

This annotation brings to light a further point of intersection between Pasolini's perspective and the nucleus of Italian thought. It relates to a notion of temporality that is layered and anything but linearly progressive: if the entropy of the present implicates, or induces, the entropy of the past, it is because instead of simply following on one another they are also in some way contemporaries. The theme we pointed out earlier, of the advent of a new prehistoric time after the exhaustion of modern history—in addition to recalling the European debate on the *posthistoire*, developed variously by Kojève, Jünger, and Gehlen—refers to a founding topos of the Italian tradition: when the underlying stratum of history is opened up, the language of myth resurfaces in all its vital and mortal ambivalence. His cinematic works like *Oedipus Rex*, *Medea* and *Pigsty*—but also *Theorem*—must be interpreted in this light. But what is even more important, in terms of what we discussed in the previous chapters, is that myth is not used by Pasolini in an antihistorical fashion; rather it is used metahistorically or, rather, infrahistorically, in the particular sense that it is embedded, like an archaic shard, inside history. Or else it envelopes history like its extratemporal shell. Both in *Oedipus* and *Pigsty*, history and unhistory, the archaic and the actual, take turns alternately embedding themselves in one another—like a dual, chained perspective which, when

114. Pasolini, "I giovani infelici," in *Lettere luterane*, p. 543.
115. Pasolini, "Abiura," p. 601.

set into motion, allows a more penetrating look into both. While not theorizing it in any systematic way, what Pasolini clearly allowed to be understood is that just as the origin is never graspable as such, because it is always moved backward and projected ahead, similarly, the contemporary world cannot speak to us if it is flattened onto itself, if it is not illuminated through contrast with what precedes it. There is no historical consciousness outside the tension with the unhistorical core that dwells inside history and unsettles it. Pasolini asserts this in what is essentially a philosophical interview, entitled "The Dream of the Centaur." When asked if "by giving preference to the return of myths rather than engaging in current political affairs, aren't you turning your back on all forms of realism?" he replies that his "precise opinion on this point is that only people who believe in myth are realists, and vice versa. The 'mythical' is nothing but the other face of realism."[116] This coexistence of opposites alludes to the doubling of the centaur, in *Medea*, which is both separated and constituted by the superimposition of origin and actuality. The fact that the two centaurs coexist rather than follow one another in time is meant to signify that as much as history entails "a continuous superseding of data . . . , these data are never deleted; they're permanent."[117] Similarly, in opposition to a linear idea of secularization, the profanation caused by both power and antipower does not put an end to the sacred—indeed, it constitutes the everyday place of its resurgence: "This encounter, this coexistence, in other words, of the two centaurs, means that the sacred thing, once desecrated, doesn't disappear as a result. The sacred being remains juxtaposed with the desecrated being."[118] From this angle, too, those who identify the oxymoron as the originary figure of Pasolini's poetry and life are not far off the mark.

At some point, however, the rope stretched between the opposites snaps. The antinomy inside which Pasolini had inscribed his extraordinary creations over the course of twenty years violently slams shut on itself, crushing everything contained inside it. The author shows himself to be perfectly aware of this in his "Repudiation of the *Trilogy of Life*," when, in reviewing the twists and turns of his career, he declares his historical

116. Pasolini, "Il sogno del centauro," in *Saggi*, pp. 1461–62.
117. Ibid., p. 1474.
118. Ibid., p. 1473.

and biographical defeat. All the spaces of authenticity he had endeavored to keep or view as open—from the village in Friuli to the working-class suburb of Rome, from the medieval world to the unspoiled areas of India and Africa—reveal their illusory nature under the irresistible force of standardization. What vanishes—even before specific places on the earth or in the spirit—is the very possibility of difference in a world that has been totally homogenized. What Pasolini grasps with a lucidity that is rarely to be found elsewhere is the strategic change of neocapitalistic power, which has passed from the logic of exclusion to that of inclusion—or, more precisely, to their perfect superimposition in a dispositif of exclusionary inclusion. When he observes that "at present, neocapitalism seems to follow the path that coincides with the aspirations of the 'masses,'"[119] he brings into focus a question that we are still grappling with today, more than thirty years later. Far from opposing the desire of the "masses" for enjoyment—of any kind—the new biopolitical regime coopts it, stimulating this desire, or even prescribing it as a sort of new categorical imperative. It is precisely this perverse identification between power and subjects— one whose entire phenomenology is only now becoming recognizable to us—that blocks any possible escape route. Whence the repudiation; which does not mean disavowing what we have done, but acknowledging the impracticability of alternatives when dealing with a present that is totally flattened onto itself. Not only would it be absurd to celebrate the youth of the emarginated class—since it, too, has been included—it is no longer even viable to deconstruct reality through myth, since the same reality has "mythicized" itself by proclaiming itself to be eternal. This is what Pasolini calls "hell,"[120] which doesn't mean just a place of suffering, but even worse, the absence of any other option. It is the consequence of breaking with the origin, on the part of a society that, in addition to losing all hope in the future, has lost all memory of the past. But, as always happens in these cases, when the vital, energetic side of the origin has been barred, it returns in a ghostly, spectral form, unleashing its violence on those who thought they could do without it.

The most complete representation of this dynamic is the film *Salò; or, The 120 Days of Sodom*, which was immediately banned and only came back into distribution after many long years of censorship. In *Salò* we

119. Ibid., p. 1448.
120. Ibid., p. 1448.

again recognize the figure of the Unbearable, by which I mean some-thing—like Dante's inferno, or Da Vinci's battle, or Vico's forest—that is literally unimaginable, something we have to avert our gaze from to protect ourselves from its blinding vision. This is the effect that Paso-lini himself sought to create, which becomes clear from his answer to the question of whether he was concerned about being misunderstood: "No, because mine is a mystery; it's what's called a *misteri*, the medi-eval mystery: a sacred play, and so it's very enigmatic. It's not supposed to be understood."[121] Before asking ourselves what it is that's not meant to be understood, it must be said that the director does everything he can to not attract his audience—and indeed to make them leave the theater. He does this through a plain set design, lacking anything spectacular and frozen into a haunting fixity; and, even more, through the story, or rather, the narrated nonstory, immobilized in the chilling repetitiousness of the actions that mark off the days. Not only does Pasolini do noth-ing to curry favor with his audience,[122] he somehow manages to involve them in the abjection represented on the screen, making them partici-pate in it despite themselves, or even causing them to be ambiguously attracted to the obscene ceremony. He involves the spectators by repel-ling them, and repels them by involving them. In August 1975, just three months before his death, when he says that he's shooting an "infernal" film,[123] we need to take this term in its literal meaning. If all the artistic activity of his last years—from *Divine Mimesis* to *Petrolio* (Oil)—can be entirely inscribed within the framework of Dante's *Inferno*, this especially holds true for this film, which, based on an inspiration probably origi-nating with the Marquis de Sade himself, is divided into pits and circles of increasing atrocity. The allusion to the Dantesque archetype is wholly appropriate to the carnage the bodies of the prisoners are subjected to in accordance with Sade's law, transposed into the putrescent regime of the Republic of Salò. Under its dictates, the life that was celebrated in Pa-solini's early poems, and even recast in mythical form in the *Trilogy*, is entirely invaded and swallowed up by death. The bruised and bloodied

121. Pier Paolo Pasolini, "De Sade e l'universo dei consumi," in *Per il cinema*, ed. Walter Siti and Franco Zabagli (Milan: Mondadori, 2001), vol. 2, p. 3020.

122. See Serafino Murri, *Pier Paolo Pasolini: Salò; o, Le 120 giornate di Sodoma* (Turin: Lindau, 2007), pp. 10 ff.

123. See Giuseppe Zigaina, *Pasolini e l'abiura* (Milan, 1993), p. 15.

bodies of the victims are in ▮
kept alive only for the pleasure ▮
from the episode of the young m▮
put to death again and again. When▮
ecutioner's act, the act of sodomy can ▮
times, the Bishop replies that the same ca▮
interrupt it just before going through with ▮
his victim, "how could you have thought that▮
you know we intend to kill you a thousand times▮
if eternity could have an end."[124]

We have yet to arrive at the heart of the Unbearab▮
lies not in the distance between victims and executione▮
closeness. From the standpoint of the executioners, this pr▮
pressed by the absolute lack of distinction between law and crim▮
words, by the structurally anarchic character of power. The four ▮
who lead the dance of death do not present themselves as transgressor▮
as representatives of the law that they themselves proclaimed. This is w▮
they adhere so strictly to a ritual that has the cold cogency of law, punish-
ing anyone who commits the slightest infraction of the code with death—
to which the victims are in any case destined. On the basis of this logic,
the initial warning that Blangis addresses to the prisoners sounds perfectly
consistent and not at all contradictory: "You are beyond the reach of any
legality. No one on earth knows you are here. As far as the world goes, you
are already dead. . . . And here are the laws which will govern your lives
in here."[125] The new law, the only one they are bound to obey without exception, is the exact opposite of traditional legality. But this doesn't give it
any less force of law; on the contrary, it presents itself as so superior that
its validity even extends to its opposite: the law of illegality. Probably without being fully aware of it, this allows Pasolini to delve into the originary
core of sovereign power, understood as the ability to not only impose or
lay down the law, but also to impose its deposition. This is what he himself
calls the anarchy of supreme power: "We fascists," argues Blangis, "are the
only true anarchists. Naturally . . . once we've become masters of the state.

124. Pier Paolo Pasolini, Script for *Salò*, in *Per il cinema*, vol. 2, p. 2055. An English version is available online at Drew's Script-o-Rama, www.script-o-rama.com/movie_scripts/s/
salo-script-transcript-pasolini-sodom.html (accessed June 11, 2012).

125. Ibid., p. 2036.

he fact that un-
...nation—there is
...s, that is based on
...he same time. From
...hat, in its empty for-
...by the limitlessness of
...power, in addition to
...ualizes and what it codi-
...archy, in other words."[127]

In fact, the only ...uld not be interpreted in a
derlying *arche-*...t in specifically genealogical
somethin...ment implicit in every power
noth...wer, in its very founding prin-
...r—in any power, whether leg-
...its practice, it does nothing but
...al and blind violence of the strong

...to the most repulsive underbelly of
...ul—the role played by the weak in the
...This is what gives a point of reference
...extremism and even ulteriority of Pasolini's thought
...red to the contemporary critique of power as practiced, for example,
by the Frankfurt school. On several occasions the author had shown how
the logic of exchange makes the functions of the executioner and the victim
reversible: "Me as the victim," exclaims the Woman in *Orgy*, "you as the executioner. The victim who wants to kill, you; the executioner who wants to
die, me,"[129] since "every martyr martyrs himself through the conservative
executioner."[130] But in *Salò* there is something that becomes increasingly
disturbing that doesn't involve just the symmetry of the roles, but also their
contamination—namely, the passing of the victims onto the side of the tor-
turers. This—the destruction of the idea of innocence—is the Unbearable
that causes spectators to close their eyes. "There are no innocent children,"

126. Pasolini, script for *Salò*, in *Per il cinema*, vol. 2, pp. 2041–42.
127. Pasolini, "Il potere e la morte," in *Per il cinema*, vol. 2, p. 3014.
128. Pasolini, "Appendice a *Salò*," in *Per il cinema*, p. 2066.
129. Pasolini, *Orgia*, in *Porcile, Orgia, Bestia da stile* (Milan: Garzanti, 1979), p. 143.
130. Ibid.

survival strategy

Pasolini had written earlier about children's conflict with their fathers.[131] The same thing applies to the victims in *Salò*. Along with their complete objectivization, the film also records their gradual corruption. Their enjoyment of the collective torment that devastates them grows and grows— with the exception of Enzo, who is riddled with bullets with his arm still raised and fist still clenched—to the point that they end up denouncing each other and taking part in each others' torture. Until they sing the same song with the republican soldiers, abandoning themselves to the vile acts of their executioners. It is the same vortex of corruption that ends up enveloping the audience-voyeurs, who are fascinated by what they reject in horror. Deep down, isn't this the same ambiguous, accommodating relationship that the writer entertained with the literary institutions he nevertheless criticized? Or that the director maintained with the cultural industry that he nevertheless claimed to keep at a distance? Unless we turn to another, more subtle interpretation,[132] not necessarily an alternative to this one, whereby the victim's participatory sharing of the executioner's desire would be the only way to deny the executioner's desire while at the same time denying himself or herself. We know that the masochistic fervor of the victim takes away the object of the sadist's pleasure, exposing the originary impotence that underlies the delirium of omnipotence[133]—the void of meaning upon which the sovereign power rests. By stepping out of the role of the suffering victim, by enjoying his or her own destruction, the masochist demonstrates to the sadist that the pleasure the latter would like to feel, without ever fully succeeding, does not belong to him or her, but to an Other. The limitless enjoyment to which the sadist aspires is impeded by his or her own will to power, because the place of the object of desire remains perpetually empty. If so, if this is the message of the film, then the lashes in the air of the Bishop's whip or the frenzied dance of the executioners around the corpses of the victims would become the tragic emblem of the insubstan-

131. Pasolini, "I giovani infelici," p. 546.

132. See the Lacanian reading of *Salò* by Fabio Vighi, "Il dolore della liberazione: Violenza, masochismo e anticapitalismo secondo Pasolini," in various authors, *La nuova gioventù? L'eredità intellettuale di Pier Paolo Pasolini* (Novi Ligure: Joker, 2009); as well as Erminia Passannanti, *Il corpo e il potere: "Salò o le 120 giornate di Sodoma" di Pier Paolo Pasolini* (Novi Ligure: Joker, 2008).

133. On the destructive passion of hate, see Massimo Recalcati, *Sull'odio* (Milan: Mondadori, 2004), especially pp. 33 ff.

tiality of power—the disastrous collapse of the sovereign throne. Similarly, the fact that the tortures are not carried out by the Masters themselves but only observed at a distance, and in the end through binoculars, would signify the impossibility of their orgasm, and therefore the self-destruction of power. This too, this extreme possibility, along with its horrifying opposite, is safeguarded in the unbearable mystery of *Salò*-Sade.

E is doing the same to Pasolini.

The Return of Italian Philosophy

Immanence and Antagonism

1. The violent deaths of Gentile and Gramsci, along with the gradual drying up of Croce's thought, mark a threshold beyond which the direction of twentieth-century Italian philosophy sharply reversed itself. Apart from individual thought-contents that were picked up and sometimes profitably developed by students and inheritors, it was the general framework of their philosophies that showed itself to be exhausted. Although sometimes extending to the furthest reaches of the modern tradition (at least in Gramsci's case, but in some ways, in Gentile's too), in the end it reproduced one of modernity's distinguishing features: what we have defined in its most general terms as "theological-political." Without being able to dwell on the semantic polyvalence of the term, the meaning we can give to it is the presupposed reconciliation of the different points of view into a single perspective that is apparently endowed with universal validity. Whether this is epitomized in Croce's notion of the ethical-political, in Gentile's state that resides *in interiore homine*, or in Gramsci's party-cum-church, the multiplicity of languages and plurality of interests become preventively unified, and thus neutralized, into an a priori synthesis that leaves no room for difference and conflict. It is as if, in order to take form, the political representation has to exclude from the picture all conflicts irreducible to it, because they cannot be made to fit inside its normative model.

In opposition to (or at least outside) this representational synthesis, Italian thought appears to have entirely renewed itself after a period of complete retreat, rediscovering some of the qualities of its original inspiration. *Operai e capitale* (Workers and capital), a book published in 1966 by Mario Tronti, offers an early, significant example of this renewal. It needs to be historically situated in the open political confrontation that, starting in the 1960s, took place within the communist left, which was soon divided between those who identified with the Italian Communist Party (PCI) and those who, remaining outside it, subsequently gave life to reviews like *Quaderni rossi* (The red notebooks), *Classe operaia* (Working class), and *Contropiano* (Counterplan).[1] But, without neglecting the historical and political significance of these events—later grouped under the broad label of *operaismo* ("workerism")—the specifically philosophical importance of the dialectic between capital and the working class advanced by Tronti lies in the problematic and, indeed, inherently antinomic relationship between the language of conflict and the logic of immanence. The question he posed—in a form that implicitly evokes the Machiavellian paradigm of a conflictual order—is that of the violent separation of something (in this case, the working class) from the historical horizon that alone is capable of making it what it is. How are we to conceive of the autonomy of a class that is necessarily inherent in capitalist society? And, even before that, what might an immanent antagonism be, inside of what it seeks to separate itself from? Or an antagonistic immanence, split into two opposing camps? The author begins by breaking open the synthetic—and as we have said, theological-political—model inside of which the Gramscian tradition had enclosed the dialectic between capital and labor. Against the idea that the working class should share the responsibility of social development with the bourgeoisie, by virtue of a common national interest, Tronti declares from the outset the necessity for a decision, understood in the etymological sense of "partition"—of opposition between the part and the whole to which it belongs: "The possibility, the capacity of synthesis, has remained entirely in the hands of the working class. The reason for this is easy to understand: because synthesis today can only be *unilateral*, it can

1. On this topic, see Steve Wright, *Storming Heaven: Class Composition and Struggle in Italian Autonomist Marxism* (London: Pluto, 2002); Guido Borio, Francesca Pozzi, and Gigi Roggero, eds., *Futuro anteriore: Dai "Quaderni rossi" ai movimenti globali: Ricchezze e limiti dell'operaismo italiano* (Rome: DeriveApprodi, 2002); and *Gli operaisti: autobiografie dei cattivi maestri*, ed. Guido Borio, interviews with Romano Alquati (Rome: DeriveApprodi, 2005).

only be consciously knowledge [scienza] of class, of a class. On the basis of capital, the whole can be understood only by the part. Knowledge is tied to struggle."[2]

While capital has every incentive to represent class as an integral part of its mechanism for creating value, the working class cannot acquire political substance except by separating itself from its antagonist. On this line of argument, the ontological primacy that Carl Schmitt gives to the enemy over the friend is strengthened by the Machiavellian principle of the perspectival difference between the noble and the popular points of view: from above and below, respectively, the two intersect, in contrasting fashion, on the same object. The object is constituted by the focal contrast of two opposing gazes: the one aimed at integrating, and thus canceling out, the other. There is no such thing as neutral knowledge, a general methodology from which to derive models of behavior deductively—as Hobbes and the modern conception in general would have it, contrary to Machiavelli. It is, on the contrary, the partial or partisan political choice, made under conditions of alternating "fortune," that is, of continuous contingency, that also determines in reverse the coordinates of the theory which recognizes it. If subjectivity is not given in advance, but is instead created by the alterity that is opposed to it, the only way for the working class to define itself as such is by overthrowing the synthetic point of view of those who deny their autonomy. Hence the "Copernican revolution," already theorized by Tronti in the first issue of *Classe operaia*, which consists in rejecting the adversary's perspective, thereby reestablishing the logical and historical primacy of the working class over capital. Living labor precedes capitalist accumulation and determines it, but so does the struggle of those who provide the labor. As Foucault would later say, if power produces resistance, resistance, in turn, anticipates and reproduces power. This is precisely what Tronti is attempting to theorize: the resistance *before* and within power. In reality, capital also presupposes inevitable worker antagonism as a given, but by seeking to enclose it within the sphere of economics, capital makes the antagonism dialectically functional to its own technological innovation. In opposition, the working class must break this dialectic, po-

2. Mario Tronti, *Operai e capitale* (Turin: Einaudi, 1966), p. 14, text translated directly from the Italian. English versions of some of the essays collected in this book can be found online at the Reocities Web site, www.reocities.com/cordobakaf/tronti_social_capital.html (accessed June 11, 2012).

litically duplicating the objective antagonism; transfer it, that is, from the economic to the political sphere. While capital has to unify the two into one, the class must break the one into two—separating what is presented as united. If capital offers conditions of peace from time to time, even bearing the social cost itself, the antagonistic class, in order to identify itself as such, should reject these and remove itself from the negotiations carried on by its party or trade union. The political category of the working class is war, not peace. Therefore it must also reject the representation of the "sovereign people," the bearer of the general will, since will, like interest, is always particular, partisan [*di parte*], and never belongs to all. The greatest risk is not the exploitation or the alienation imposed by the factory—which, indeed, is the prerequisite of the revolutionary response—but the neutralization of a conflict with the counterpart that must always be kept alive.

But the language of conflict—this is the wall Tronti's idea hits up against—is made problematic, if not aporetic, by the logic of immanence that is posited prior to it. Although he insists on the opposition between working class and capital, rather than interpret them as independent poles external to each other, he views them as two halves of the same whole. While "the mistake of the old maximalism lay in conceiving this opposition, so to speak, from the *outside* . . . , the working class must materially discover itself as part of capital, if it then intends to oppose *all* capital to itself."[3] The problem, as it is posed by Tronti, lies in the duel relationship between whole and part, and between representation and reality. On the one hand, the working class must escape from the representation that seeks to reduce it to a simple part of a whole that encompasses it. But on the other hand, it must recognize that it effectively is this—that it is internal, not external, to that which it nevertheless seeks to oppose. Since the identity of the class is generated by antagonism, it could not exist outside the relations of production that include it, since "a class—by itself—does not exist. There is no such thing as a class without struggle against the other class."[4] This applies, of course, to capital as well, which is unimaginable without the labor force that produces it; but with the difference that, while capital must keep alive its "enemy within" and improve its performance, the working class, on the contrary, can and must try to destroy its class antagonist. This is the last conflict—as Schmitt would say at his most ex-

3. Tronti, *Operai e capitale*, p. 55.
4. Ibid., p. 158.

pressionist—"between two classes that mutually give life to each other, but only one of which holds the death of the other in its grasp."[5]

But how is this possible? How can the working class eradicate what keeps it alive without also causing its own death? How can its antagonism be unleashed to its full extent without snapping the cord that binds it to the inexorable fate of its opponent? Tronti is well aware of the problem, and in some ways also of its irresolvability: as Machiavelli well knew, beyond a certain threshold, conflict eventually breaks up the inherence between the terms that it opposes; while this inherence, in its turn, tends to push conflict out of the picture. Immanence threatens to absorb conflict and conflict tends to bring down immanence, despite Tronti's efforts to theorize them together. In fact, on the one hand he argues that the working class should not hinder, but rather should encourage the social, technological, and even political innovation promoted by capital to productively overcome its cyclical crises, since the weakening of capital would mark a setback for the class. On the other hand, and at the same time, it should use its economic power as a weapon to put pressure on the political framework inside of which it remains compressed. In short, the class must be "inside" and "against"—to use an expression that Tronti continues to employ even today. But how can "inside" and "against" be kept together? How can an "inside" also make itself "against"? And how can an "against" frontally oppose what constitutes it? This is where the antinomic outcome of the entire dynamic looms up—namely, the transfer of the separation from the relationship between capital and class to the relationship between the economic dimension and the political dimension of the class. It is as if, unable to fully exercise its oppositional action against the system inside of which it is situated and from which it draws its lifeblood, the working class were forced to internalize the line of division, splitting even from itself. This is indeed the conclusion Tronti comes to, although he presents it with a curious dialectical reversal as a contradiction of capital: "To struggle against capital, the working class must struggle against itself as capital. This is the greatest point of contradiction, not for the workers but for the capitalists. . . . The working class, today, has only to look at itself in order to destroy capital. It must recognize itself as a political power [potenza]. It must negate itself as a production force."[6]

5. Ibid., p. 248.
6. Ibid., pp. 260–61.

At this point the contradiction affects Tronti's entire discourse, to the point of reversing it with respect to its own premises. Starting out from the Marxist need to reconnect political action to its economic roots in class—negated by the "old distinction between economic struggle and political struggle . . . which has always guided reformism"[7]—Tronti ends up theorizing their divergence himself, gradually shifting the axis of political subjectivity from the class to the party: if the working class must be autonomous from capital, the party must be independent from the class. But in this case, on the plane of immanence there begins to loom a point of transcendence destined to extend itself to the point of undermining it. Although we can't follow the author along the controversial path that led him in later years to reverse the relation of dominance between class and party—now attributing to the latter the autonomy that he once assigned to the former—the structural aporia that his theoretical dispositif slides into is clear. It is as if its two logically opposed poles of conflict and immanence were to react to each other, eventually canceling each other out. While the criterion of conflict destabilizes the logic of immanence, this, in its turn, discharges it all onto the antagonistic subject, which undergoes a series of divisions, either following upon one another or interlinking: the first is between economics and politics; and then, within the latter, between class and party, now openly invited to emancipate itself, as far as operating practices are concerned, from the demands of the class.[8] It is almost as if, at some point, Tronti had resigned himself to putting up with an apparently insurmountable given: in a logic that is rigorously immanent, separation can only occur inside itself, doubling itself to infinity until it implodes. The fact that in this way immanence runs the risk of yielding to a new transcendence—the risk, in other words, that once political theology has been refuted from the perspective of conflict, that it will come back into existence through its subject—was confirmed by the author of *Workers and Capital* himself some forty years later: "Political theology arose upon the node of the irresolvability of the political problem, in the dimension of immanence alone."[9]

7. Ibid., p. III.

8. The turn that Tronti took in this direction is evident in his discourse in *Sull'autonomia del politico* (Milan: Feltrinelli, 1977).

9. Mario Tronti, introduction to Giuseppe Trotta and Fabio Milano, eds., *L'operaismo degli anni Sessanta: Da "Quaderni rossi" a "classe operaia"* (Rome: DeriveApprodi, 2008), p. 47.

2. The second influential paradigm of the new Italian thought on politics is represented by reflection on the "impolitical." The philosophical problem that it translates—of a negative which, although attempting to come into being, does not take shape as another positive pole—is inscribed in a horizon that is intrinsic to the issue we have just examined regarding the aporetic relationship between separation and immanence. Again, as in theory on the political, the starting point is the rejection of the theological-political synthesis, understood both in the Catholic sense (as the representation of the Good on the part of power), and in the secular sense (as the unitary representation of different interests). In both cases, although in different fashions, it is the same translatability between different discourses—theological, political, economic—that is presupposed and which achieved its fulfillment in the philosophy of Hegel. Despite the presence of an intractable remainder, consisting of the "plebe,"[10] the Hegelian state appears to be the outcome of a logical-historical process in which the opposites mutually recognize each other in a higher unity. Contrary to a premise of this sort, "negative thought"—as theorized by Massimo Cacciari starting in the early 1970s—is precisely what drastically denies this possibility.[11] Far from being a dialectical vehicle for a future reconciliation, in this case, the "negative" should be understood as whatever declares this to be absolutely impossible. As Schopenhauer and Kierkegaard first attested—still in a partial and contradictory form—and then, Nietzsche, in an exhaustive fashion, this symmetry turns out to be completely powerless to represent the actual dynamics that have long governed the world. Since the advent of modernity, the ancient theological symbol lies shattered in a thousand fragments that can no longer be reunified, except in increasingly ineffectual utopias. The task, or the destiny, of the political in the modern era under these conditions is not the regressive one still played out by the socialist tradition of delaying this inevitable drift, but rather of cutting across it, so as to turn the dissolutive consequences into positive outcomes. Contrary to popular belief, in reality the crisis does not mark a contingent setback in development or the definitive collapse of the system, but rather the opportunity for its productive conversion suitable for a new order. In this analytical framework, "the autonomy of the political," still proposed by

10. See Massimo Cacciari, *Dialettica e critica del politico* (Milan: Cacciari, 1978).

11. See Massimo Cacciari, *Krisis* (Milan: Feltrinelli, 1976); and also by Cacciari, *Pensiero negativo e razionalizzazione* (Venice: Marsilio, 1977).

Tronti in a provisional way, becomes an objective given to be assumed in its irreversibility rather than a subjective choice. On the one hand, it indicates the limits that circumscribe the specialist sphere of politics, distinguishing it from those of the other discourses; and on the other hand, it points to the possibility, which this heterogeneity allows, to strategically negotiate the rules of their mutual relationship. Without going into the merits of choosing one camp over another, it is a matter of defining a valid method for anyone seeking to achieve their objectives. The underlying logic remains the same whether interpreted by the forces organic to capitalist rule or by the forces who contest it. What determines the success of political action is not the perspective that motivates it but the operational tools it employs. What thus emerges is a scenario that is thoroughly riddled and, indeed, constituted by the power [*potenza*] of nothingness.[12] It surrounds the various discourses, shaping each of them according to their peculiar difference. It penetrates to their cores, corroding anything of substance in the interest of pure efficacy. Now emptied of any ideal essence, the entities are ready to be manipulated on the basis of subjective interests that are irreducible to a common telos. Devoid of an ontological foundation and any transcendental finalities, political action is flattened into a technical ability to simply manage what is in existence.

The impolitical is both the critical counterpoint of this entropic movement and its silent witness. Contrary to what Thomas Mann theorized with the same name (*unpolitische*), the "impolitical [impolitico]" Cacciari examines in a 1978 essay dedicated to Nietzsche does not oppose some value to the political that the latter is supposed to have betrayed; on the contrary, he criticizes and deconstructs the claim for some residual value.[13] Consequently, the impolitical does not occupy a space outside the political of an antipolitical or apolitical type, as it still did in Schopenhauer and Kierkegaard when they identified a subjective dimension in asceticism or faith that was removed from the process of politicization. For Nietzsche, on the contrary, *nothing* escapes the dynamics of power relations and the

---

12. For more on this segment of Italian thought see Matteo Mandarini, "Beyond Nihilism: Notes Towards a Critique of Left-Heideggerianism in Italian Philosophy of the 1970s," in *The Italian Difference Between Nihilism and Biopolitics*, ed. Lorenzo Chiesa and Alberto Toscano (Melbourne: re-press, 2009), pp. 55–79.

13. Massimo Cacciari, "L'impolitico nietzschiano," in Friedrich Nietzsche, *Il libro del filosofo*, ed. Marina Beer and Maurizio Ciampa (Rome: Savelli, 1978), pp. 105–20.

conflicts that it reproduces. For him, the fact that life is, in itself, the will to power means that there is no reality other than the one that is constituted, and continually transformed, by the struggle that pits people against each other in a conflict with no motivation and no final outcome. Now this very "nothing [nulla]"—or "no"—is the positively inexistent focus of the impolitical. The thought that posits it is negative in this self-reflective sense, so to speak: not because it negates the effective reality in favor of an alterity, no matter how it is defined; but because it denies this alterity, asserting that the effective reality is the only one that is possible and, therefore, the only one that is real. Already from these first indications we catch a glimpse of the contradiction that the impolitical fails to resolve and, indeed, expresses. By not allowing itself to take on a positive form—which would make it an alternative or opposing entity to the reality of politics—on the basis of its own negative status, it ends up affirming what it should be differentiating itself from. From this point of view, as was argued in the discussion devoted to the topic in the 1980s,[14] when the impolitical tends to infinity, it coincides with the same political realism that was taken to its most radical form by Machiavelli. This traces out another avenue, different from the one taken by Tronti, for the return of Italian thought on politics to the source of its tradition. Contrary to all political philosophies of a normative type, the impolitical adopts the Machiavellian point of view of those who recognize no reality other than the effectual one of the conflict between powers and interests. As Thucydides had argued, even before Augustine, true peace, like true justice, is not feasible in the earthly city, which is torn by instincts and desires oriented in opposite directions. The impolitical, far from refuting this analysis, strengthens it, removing it even more intransigently from any form of political theology, whether idolatrous or mythological.[15]

But this isn't all. If this is how it were, if the impolitical coincided entirely with realism, if it were limited to repeating its prohibitions, it would

14. For more on the Italian debate of the 1980s, in addition to Francesco Fistetti, *La crisi del marxismo in Italia* (Genoa: Il Melangolo, 2006), see Dario Gentili's introduction to *La crisi del politico: Antologia de "Il Centauro"* and the interview with Biagio de Giovanni, published as an appendix to it (Naples: Guida, 2007). Starting from the 1980s, de Giovanni has developed a critique of modernity from within its own confines. See, among others, his essays "Presente e tradizione," *Il Centauro* 13–14 (1985): 67–82; and "Apologia del moderno contro il pensiero debole," *Il Centauro* 17–18 (1986): 48–70.

15. See Roberto Esposito, *Categorie dell'impolitico* (Bologna: Il Mulino, 1988, 1999).

we can see what the political cannot be.

not be distinguishable, as such, from its political opposite. Its "negative" would be nothing but the self-celebration of a positive made absolute by the lack of possible alternatives. Certainly, the very premise of the impolitical is that there is no such thing as a space that is not securely occupied by power. But this absence does not eliminate the difference, or the divergence, of perspectives from which this power is looked at. While the theory of the political sees it from inside—as fully adhering to the object of its gaze—the theory of the impolitical regards it from outside, or, rather, from its reverse: from the point of view of what the political *cannot* be. From the nothingness that surrounds it like its negated possibility, its silent language, its canceled trace. Already in Machiavelli, when his work is read outside the usual interpretative schemes, this "not said" reverberates: this tacit reference to what could be if people were *not* exactly what they are and what they cannot *not* be. The authors of the impolitical[16]—namely, of that hidden tradition that cuts diagonally across institutional political philosophy, deconstructing it—dig even deeper into this underground fault line, questioning that "wall of booming silence" that "the human voice cannot pass through,"[17] without coming into direct contact with what is not of this world. This is what Simone Weil meant when, still in the midst of war, she wrote that "there is no other force on this earth except force. That could serve as an axiom. As for the force which is not of this earth, contact with it cannot be bought at any lesser price than the passing through a kind of death."[18] The point of constitution of the impolitical lies precisely in the gap, imperceptible yet profound, between the negation contained in the first part of the sentence—the nonexistence of a force other than the one that always governs relations between human beings—and the statement expressed, in a politically unspeakable form, in the second. The problem—unresolved and unresolvable—is the impossible overlap between the two: the insuperable contradiction of an affirmative negation, or of a negative affirmation, in a language that is political and, even prior

16. See *Oltre la politica: Antologia del pensiero impolitico*, ed. Roberto Esposito (Milan: Mondadori, 1996).

17. Hermann Broch, *Die Schlafwandler* (Frankfurt am Main: Suhrkamp, 1974); translated from the Italian version: *Gli incolpevoli* (Turin: Einaudi, 1960), p. 673.

18. Simone Weil, *L'enracinement: Prélude à une déclaration des devoirs envers l'être humain* (Paris: Gallimard, 1949); English version: *The Need for Roots: Prelude to a Declaration of Duties Towards Mankind*, trans. A. F. Wills (London: Routledge, 1996), p. 211.

to that, metaphysical, based precisely on the principle of noncontradiction. In order for the negation of the impolitical to make itself positive, it should first negate—or deny—itself, establishing itself as another reality alongside, or against, what it declares to be unique. It would thus adopt the Gnostic perspective, with a dualistic framework that pits the realm of good against that of evil. But in so doing, it would contradict the principle of immanence outside of which the entire argument loses its force of impact. The impolitical—if it wants to avoid being reduced to an apolitical or antipolitical attitude—can only be conceived as inherent to the political. It can't locate itself on the outside—if it did, it would reestablish a new dimension of transcendence. But, on the other hand, if the immanence completely canceled out the difference, the category would implode into its opposite. It would end swallowed up inside the political reality from which it must still, even if only imperceptibly, remain different. This is why thinkers of the impolitical always tend—although unsuccessfully—to cross over that threshold, one that is more logical than historical, that keeps them within the worldly horizon. The furthest point they can reach is the awareness of the antinomy in which they are caught without being able to free themselves: "But then where are we really?" asks Elias Canetti. "We are in the tough clarity with which we see and record all of this."[19]

This means, to put it another way, that it is not possible to politicize the impolitical except by inverting it into its opposite—into a category of the political. For this to happen without compromising the coherence of the category, a subject needs to be identified who does not coincide with the subject who is the holder of power from one time to the next. But specifically this—a subject of antipower—is considered impossible by all the authors we have mentioned, since, in the logic of political representation, the subject is made such precisely by the possession of power, or at least by the aspiration to hold it. Conversely, in the same way, power is always understood as a sovereign attribute of one or more subjects. A "power" is always a subject and the subject, no matter what it is, can do nothing but exercise, or at least desire, power. This is the conclusion reached not only by Canetti and Weil, but also by the great writers of crisis, from Franz Kafka to Hermann Broch to Robert Musil. In reality they do not entirely exclude an operating, and even

19. Elias Canetti, *Die Provinz des Menschen: Aufzeichnungen, 1942–1972* (Munich: Hanser, 1973); translated from the Italian version: *La provincia dell'uomo* (Milan: Adelphi, 1978), p. 329.

subjective, mode of the impolitical. But, as is typical of the category in question, it must be such as to incorporate in itself the contradiction that characterizes its entire movement. What we are talking about here is action that includes within itself its own opposite: nonaction. Not in the simple form of inactivity. But in the mode—addressed again by recent Italian thinking—of an activity that is capable, at the same time as it acts, of deactivating itself, and hence, of separating itself from the fruit of its own action: "Man: mixture of power and passivity. Being a creature, a partial being, can only find purity in pure passivity."[20] The impolitical subject—if you can use this expression without contradicting both its terms—has to act, but passively, by virtue of that "passive power" that is the only thing able to break the indivisible bond between subjectivity and property, making the subject something "improper" to the extent that it is prompted to undo what it does: to bring its inevitable doing back to the nondoing from which doing itself originates; to expose activity to the return, or advent, of inactivity.

Whether a political significance can be attributed to this antinomic transition remains largely problematic. Even the author who has risked this transition more than anyone else—Georges Bataille—experienced no dearth of difficulties. Between the 1930s and 1940s, when he attempted a politicization of the impolitical that was incompatible with all the contemporary positions on the right and on the left, he demonstrated his grasp of the problem, but without being able to arrive at a solution. The path that he opened up in a solitary fashion passes through a clear gap between subjectivity and politics. Only outside the metaphysically compromised figure of a subject that produces its own essence can the impolitical give rise to a political outcome—or, conversely, can political action translate itself into a language of the impolitical. This does not mean completely escaping outside the category of subject—which would be impossible—but rather, twisting it to such a degree that it is emptied of its individual and general character, so as to push it toward the equally problematic conjunction of the singular and the common.

3. The third philosophical and political question posed by contemporary Italian philosophy is that of the constituent power in its elusive and enigmatic relationship with the constituted power on the one hand,

20. Simone Weil, *Cahiers II* (Paris: Librairie Plon, 1972); English version: *The Notebooks of Simone Weil*, vol. 1, trans. Arthur Wills (London: Routledge, 2004), p. 246.

and with the sovereign regime on the other. Again, as for the two previous dispositifs, what we are talking about is the difficult intersection between immanence and transcendence—this time made even more difficult by the attempt to escape political theology through a notion that itself has theological roots: that of *creatio ex nihilo.* Who, or what can become subject of "creation from nothing" once it has been inverted into radically worldly terms? And how can a power that lacks foundation ensure the perpetuity of what it founds? Finally, how can this origin be prevented from being incorporated, and thus, neutralized, by the institution from which it is generated? This problem, which neither jurists nor philosophers have managed to get to the bottom of (as Donoso Cortés observes),[21] is the need to hold together two elements—moment and duration, origin and originated, constituent and constituted—that are led by their internal logic to overpower each other in turns. They are both inseparable and divergent: they imply each other in the form of mutual exclusion. Just as the constituted power logically presupposes the principle that brought it into being, similarly this principle is only made recognizable by the institutional reality that has issued from it. But this implication, far from reducing the contrast between mutually conflicting elements, has the effect of accentuating it: while the constituted power always feels threatened in its stability by the possible return of the constituent power, the latter in turn runs the risk of being incorporated, and hence shut down, by the normative system to which it originally gave rise. It is the same dialectic, both conjunctive and disconjunctive, that exists between politics and law: between the political act, or in other words, the coup de force that necessarily lies outside the law and initially creates the legal order, and the system of rules that follows from it. Without an event, often a violent one, to establish it in the absence of law, positive law would not exist. But, considered apart from the legal order that it founds, that originary event would be lost, mixed up in the general violence of the extra-legal state. This is the recursive circle, necessarily declined in the future perfect mode, that Machiavelli had made central to his own narration when he recognized in the murder of the founder Romulus something that only later, once the founding had taken place, would have received its justification, according to the maxim that "reprehensible actions may

21. Juan Donoso Cortés, "Lecciones de Derecho politico," in his *Obras completas* (Madrid: Biblioteca de Auctores Cristianos, 1970), vol. 1, pp. 39 ff.

be justified by their effects" (*Discourses on Livy*, 1.9). The irreducibly anti-nomic character of the question lies in the singular fact that the law ends up legitimizing what it prepares itself to declare illegal and what, from that moment on, it is therefore committed to suppress. It thus includes in fact what it excludes in law, assuming internally what on a more temporal plane remains transcendent to it.[22]

One could interpret modern history in entirety, including its contemporary outcomes, as a never-ending struggle between the inextricable and opposing principles of the constituent and constituted powers—complicated by the advent of the sovereign regime, first in its absolutist form and then in its democratic version. While in Hobbes it is precisely the paradigm of sovereignty that secures the primacy of the constituted power over the constituent power—only active at the time of the contract and then forever extinguished—Rousseau recognizes the right of the latter to challenge, or change, the former, but only if the constituted power has been preventively unified in the (also instituted) form of the sovereign people. In the confrontation between founding principle and founded reality, in short, the victor, in any case, is whoever embodies the sovereign power from one time to the next. It is this assumption of sovereignty, even with respect to its own institution, that is the unique theological-political hallmark of "the political" in the modern era: not so much the primacy of the founded [*istituito*] over the founding [*istituente*], as their shared submission to the logic of sovereignty. This is why, although marking the end of the old regime through a spectacular reactivation of the constituent power, not even the two revolutionary transitions—by the American people and the French nation—profoundly altered the categorial framework out of which they burst forth, as Hannah Arendt also had to admit.[23] In spite of everything, what they failed to change is the need, implicit in the assumed logic of the sovereign paradigm, to inscribe even the most striking novelties inside an order legitimized by tradition. Because of this, although destabilizing the former regime, the constituent power presents itself already in the preconstituted sovereign form of the people or the nation. That is why the first effect of the new constitution, created by the revolution, was to definitively bring the revolution itself to an end. Since then, we can say that the overriding purpose of con-

22. On this line of thought, see Thomas Berns, *Violence de la loi à la Renaissance* (Paris: Kimé, 2000).
23. See Hannah Arendt, *On Revolution* (London: Penguin, 1963).

stitutional law has become to deny the very reality of an originary power existing prior to the constitution of all the others. This preventive need to cancel out the origin, generated by fear of the French Revolution, became so pressing that it prompted Kant to declare that "a people should not *inquire* with any practical aim in view into the origin of the supreme authority to which it is subject, that is, a subject *ought not to reason subtly* about the origin of this authority," since not only are these "subtle reasonings" into the historical origins of this mechanism "altogether pointless. . . . But it is punishable to undertake this inquiry with a view to possibly changing by force the constitution that now exists."[24] In fact, if the tacit agreement upon which liberal constitutions are founded is never to raise the issue of their beginnings, in contemporary democracies the constitutional rule of parliamentary sovereignty ends up erasing even the memory of a political principle which precedes it and is constitutive of it. This is the essential reason why our democracies are blocked today.

Antonio Negri's book on constituent power had the merit of reengaging this issue—one that had apparently been shut down by the increasingly obvious shift of the problem of the constitution from the political lexicon into the juridical. Against this process of depoliticization, he identified the constituent principle as the only force able to revitalize a dialectic—by radically renewing it—that had turned inward on itself and was seemingly blocked by the assumed predominance of the constituted power. The only power capable of restoring to democracy the absoluteness contained in its revolutionary genesis is one that is never exhausted (as Hobbes would have it) by the initial institution of the state order. Rather, it must be a power that reemerges whenever the constitution is reduced to merely stabilizing the existing order. Of course, Negri immediately realized that, to this end, it is not enough to rescue the constituent power from the inhibitory grasp of the constituted power. It must also be distinguished from the sovereign principle, which is stronger than both the powers because it is assumed prior to their relation, to which it ultimately also serves as arbiter: "the concept of sovereignty and that of constitutive power stand in absolute opposition. We can thus conclude that if an independent way of developing the concept of constituent power exists, it has excluded any reference

24. Immanuel Kant, *The Metaphysics of Morals*, ed. and trans. Mary McGregor (Cambridge: Cambridge University Press, 1996), pp. 95 and 112.

to the concept of sovereignty."[25] But the difficulty of this task, apparently with no way forward, lies precisely in this distinction.[26] How can the creation *ex nihilo* of the constituent power be distinguished from the equally unconditional creation of the sovereign decision? Do they not both derive from the notions of divine creation and of miracle (teleological ones to all intents and purposes), so that, when the memory of divine creation dies out in people, a miracle can always come to revive it? Negri responds to this objection using a two-pronged argumentative strategy, from the perspectives of genealogy and conceptual history. To begin with, like all the authors we have examined so far, he goes back to Machiavelli. Wasn't it the Florentine who, against the Hobbesian contractarian model, theorized the inexhaustible energy of the origin and the need to return to it whenever the political body showed signs of withering? And hadn't he given this—literally, reconstituting—"cure" the characteristics of a politics of life, down to its lexical attributes? Here, traced out in this argument, perhaps for the first time in contemporary Italian thought, is an early opposition of the biopolitical paradigm to the sovereign regime. Negri does not stop at recognizing its genesis in Machiavelli's "political biology." He initiates a wide-ranging genealogy that, instead of linking Machiavelli first to Hobbes and then to Schmitt, as Tronti does, places him at the source of a different current which, passing through Spinoza, arrives at Marx, and then extends to Foucault. What results is a fundamental partition cutting diagonally across the whole of modernity, between a thought on power [*potere*]—both constituted and sovereign—and a thought on potency [*potenza*] that hinges on the triad formed by Machiavelli, Spinoza, and Marx.

Without entering into the merits of the accuracy of this reconstruction—not always clear in terms of historiography—the most conspicuous effect stemming from it with regard to the question of the constitution is a

25. Antonio Negri, *Il potere costituente: Saggio sulle alternative del governo* (Milan: Sugarco, 1992), p. 32; English version: *Insurgencies: Constituent Power and the Modern State* (Minneapolis: University of Minnesota Press, 1999), p. 20.1.

26. On this issue, see the remarks by Gaetano Rametta, "Le 'difficoltà' del potere costituente," *Filosofia Politica* 3 (2006): 391–402. Giuseppe Duso has worked on the categories of power and its constitutive antinomies from a conceptual history perspective. See, for example, the volume he edited entitled *Il potere: Per la storia della filosofia politica moderna* (Rome: Carocci, 1999), and *Oltre la democrazia: Un itinerario attraverso i classici* (Rome: Carocci, 2004).

timely expansion of its semantics from the political-juridical realm to that of the ontological-metaphysical, implicit for that matter in the Latin term *constitutio*.[27] By connecting to an Italian tradition that as early as the 1940s, with Constantine Mortati, had asserted the material character of the constitution, Negri takes it far beyond its borders, filling the constitutive process with social and vital contents derived from the Marxist category of "living labor." But the insistent use of this category, which ontologically roots the constitutional discourse in the socioeconomic terrain, had an entropic effect with respect to its original political meaning. Just as the economic, or the social, risks swallowing up the political, in the same way immanence risks absorbing conflict. This is exactly where the divergence opens up with those in the "workerist" culture who asserted the centrality, if not autonomy, of political conflict. When faced with the impossibility of reconciling immanence and conflict, Tronti chose conflict; Negri, by contrast, chose immanence, sacrificing the political form of conflict in favor of the social being. What separates them, despite their shared rejection of legal formalism, is the very definition of ontology—intended by Negri in a fully immanent sense, but pushed increasingly in a transcendental direction by Tronti.[28] This explains the drastic distance Negri maintains from an author like Carl Schmitt, who was always shown to defend the inexhaustibility of the constituent power (rendered in the English translation as "the constitution-making power"). Why doesn't Negri ever refer in a positive way to the only jurist who believed that "the constitution-making power is not thereby expended and eliminated, because it was exercised once."[29] The answer can be found in a later passage in *Constitutional Theory*, in which Schmitt, after comparing the constitutional theory of Sieyès to the metaphysics of Spinoza, splits them apart by taking a stand for the first:

In some of Sieyès's writings, the *pouvoir constituant* appears in its relationship to every *pouvoirs constitués* as a metaphysical analogy to the *natura naturans* and

27. On the relation between ontology and politics, see Antonio Negri's conversation with Cesare Casarino, *In Praise of the Common* (Minneapolis: University of Minnesota Press, 2008).

28. For more on the relationship and disagreement between Tronti and Negri, see Alberto Toscano, "Chronicles of insurrection: Tronti, Negri, and the Subject of Antagonism," in *Italian Difference*, pp. 109–28.

29. Carl Schmitt, *Verfassungslehre* (Berlin, 1928); English version: *Constitutional Theory*, trans. and ed. Jeffrey Seitzer (Durham, NC: Duke University Press, 2008), p. 125.

its relationship to the *natura naturata* of Spinoza's theory: it is an inexhaustible source of all forms without taking a form itself, forever producing new forms out of itself, building all forms, yet doing so without form itself. But it is necessary to distinguish the positive theory of the constitution-making power, which inheres in every constitutional theory. . . . They are in no way identical with one another. The metaphysic of the *potestas constituens* as well as that of the analogy to the *natura naturans* is part of the theory of political theology.[30]

Apart from the accusation of political theology—easily reversible from one position to the other depending on the meaning given to it—what separates Negri from Schmitt, placing him on the side of Spinoza, is a different assessment of the relationship between potency and act. While Schmitt, in rejecting the overlapping between politics and ontology, cannot conceive of a potency that is not translated into action, in this very possibility Negri sees the rescue of constitutive power from the grasp of constituted power. What is at stake is the role of subjectivity. Choosing Spinoza against Schmitt, Negri seeks to keep the subject on this side of the line of sovereignty. But, in doing so, by opting for a potency not translated into action, he ends up losing, along with sovereignty, a politically determined subject as well—severing the relationship between politics and subjectivity. To avoid slipping into constituted power, in order to remain what it is, constituent power cannot assume a subjective connotation that defines it in sovereign terms. Unlike what happens in Schmitt, Spinoza's *natura naturans* does not have a subject other than life itself in its complete immanence. It is only through this work of desubjectification that the biopolitical semantics can escape the clutches of sovereignty. But—this is the contradiction that takes hold of his discourse, pushing it toward an undecidable outcome—without a subject who embodies it, the constituent power is incapable of producing politics. In fact, not surprisingly, the category of "production" used by Negri alongside that of "living labor" never goes beyond the economic sphere: it involves the social dynamic, but not the political one, unless we imagine, on the ontological plane of immanence, an immediate identification of politics with the economy and society. However, this would mean that the political would be entirely absorbed by ontology, as indeed the author invites the reader to do, recalling that ontology is "more fundamental than politics. . . . In postmodern

30. Ibid., p. 128.

philosophy, this ontological primacy is absolute because ontology has absorbed the political."[31] But, once sucked inside ontology, what sort of determinacy remains to politics? And inside ontology, what distinguishes one way of being political from another? At this point the absoluteness of constituent power claimed by Negri, rather than existing in perpetual tension with constituted power, becomes its pure negation. In this way, removed from the task of establishing a durable political form, what the constituent power loses is precisely its constitutive strength, thus risking regression into a deprivative power.[32] The paradigm of constituent power, which was rightly revived to rescue politics from its gradual slide into the juridical, like those of the autonomy of the political and the impolitical before it, bounces back against itself without reaching an affirmative horizon.

Origin and History

1. Like thought on the political, Italian reflection on history also passes through the question of the origin. What is the relation between origin and history? And, even before answering this, is the relation logically conceivable? Or are these mutually contradictory terms, destined to negate each other in turn? The answer to this question, one that is decisive for the pursuit of our inquiry, depends on where the origin is situated with respect to the line of historical development. But wherever this may be, the coexistence between the two terms appears to be more than problematic. If the origin is located outside of history—before its temporal beginning, in other words—then the value of history will necessarily be diminished, measured in negative terms from how distant it is from the origin. If, on the contrary, the origin is placed inside history, hence also historicized, it will inevitably become dissolved in the flux of its own becoming. The originality of Italian thought in the last few decades—but what also makes it problematic, one might say—lies precisely in its ability to sidestep this binary choice, or at least in its attempt to complicate it through an oblique gaze that brings

31. Antonio Negri, *Kairós, Alma Venus, Multitudo: Nove lezioni impartite a me stesso* (Rome: Manifestolibri, 2000), p. 136; English version: "Kairós, Alma Venus, Multitudo," in *Time for Revolution*, trans. Matteo Mandarini (London: Continuum, 2003), p. 234.

32. This is the criticism Miguel Vatter directs toward Negri in "Resistance and Legacy: Arendt and Negri on the Constituent Power," *Kairos* 20 (2004): 191–203.

into view a third option: on the basis of which the origin is both historical and unhistorical, because it, too, is traversed, but not resolved, by history. The long shadow cast by Vico's thought is easily recognizable in this
detour, or diversion, in the face of an overly stark set of alternatives. To him
we owe the first different genealogical model in all of modern philosophy:
a two-pronged model, so to speak, by which secular history, although issuing from the same origin as sacred history, does not coincide with it, and
indeed, tends to continually diverge from it, with results that are always
uncertain and sometimes catastrophic. By means of this initial splitting,
which eventually branches into the various profane histories, the origin remains somehow external to the time it nevertheless generates.

Recent Italian thought has submitted the influential theoretical paradigm known as "secularization" to an inevitably antinomic complication of
this sort. In the early 1980s, well ahead of other, later studies, when Giacomo
Marramao brought the topic back onto the center stage of Italian thought,
reconstructing its nineteenth-century genealogy with hermeneutic finesse,[33]
it had already been challenged by an author who has still not received due
consideration; partly, perhaps, due to the impossibility of assimilating him
to other established traditions. What distinguishes the philosophical work
of Augusto Del Noce is indeed a particular version of the relationship between origin and history, or between eternity and time, that separates it
from the secular view.[34] Despite being fiercely opposed to the latter, he never
flattened it into the canonical perspective of the Catholic tradition, to which
he nevertheless continued to subscribe. The remarkable theoretical originality of a book like *The Problem of Atheism* is not so much its rejection of the
secularization theorem as an interpretative criterion of modernity, so much
as the viewpoint from which his argument is conducted, which is itself modern. By this, I do not mean to say he did it along the lines that Hans Blumenberg followed during the same years, challenging Karl Löwith's theses
in defense of the paradigmatic autonomy of modernity. Rather, Del Noce

33. See the following works, all by Giacomo Marramao: *Potere e secolarizzazione: Le
categorie del tempo* (Rome: Riuniti, 1983; repr., Turin: Boringhieri, 2005); *Cielo e terra: Genealogia della secolarizzazione* (Rome-Bari: Laterza, 1994); as well as *Dopo il Leviatano: Indi-
viduo e comunità* (Turin: Boringhieri, 2000); and *Passaggio a Occidente: Filosofia e globalizzazione* (Turin: Boringhieri, 2003).

34. See the collected essays by Augusto Del Noce in *L'epoca della secolarizzazione* (Milan: Giuffrè, 1970).

makes secularization an interpretive thesis inside the same modern horizon that he should have interpreted and that, precisely for this reason, was left unexamined by the paradigm. Thus, instead of taking up a position between Löwith's continuist hypothesis and Blumenberg's discontinuist one—made more similar than they appear by the shared reduction of modernity as a whole to a single axis of development—Del Noce opened up a different hermeneutic perspective based on the assumption of an inhomogeneity, and even a fundamental discordance, between the great modern philosophies regarding the problem of atheism. In his view, at stake in the clash between the two schools—both generated by Descartes' thought—passing in one case from Leibniz to Marx and, in the other, from Pascal to Rosmini, through Vico, is an issue crucial not only to modern philosophy but also to the meaning and fate of actuality. He expresses this view in a lexicon that is remarkably consonant with the one we have used: the question of atheism, he writes, is the most important locus "of contemporary politics itself: the point of intersection, in our time, between philosophy and life. Reflecting today on historical actuality is not at all tantamount to substituting a study of the eternal with a study of the ephemeral. Rather, it corresponds precisely to a frequently repeated dictum that the task left to the philosopher today is the deciphering of a crisis."[35]

The problematic picture that thus emerges is anything but homogeneous—and, indeed, from the outset is pulled (if not torn) between two logically conflicting requirements: on the one hand, to restore the relationship between theology and philosophy that modernity—or more precisely, that its prevailing interpretation—had severed; and on the other, to set it out in historically useful terms. Certainly, contrary to the conception interpreted most masterfully by Hegel (taken up again in different ways by the various theorists of secularization), according to which the divine is fully realized in historical becoming, for Del Noce the history of humankind is not capable of accounting for itself. Its truth is external, and presupposed, to a process marked by the sinful pretense of historicizing it. The clash that began at the onset of the modern era between the two camps we have just described focused specifically on the acceptance, or rejection, of the idea of sin, and therefore of grace, as the only means of redemption from a fallen natural state. So far, in its essentials, Del Noce's

35. Augusto Del Noce, *Il problema dell'ateismo*, ed. Nicola Matteucci (Bologna: Il Mulino, 1964), p. 11.

position remains faithful to the regular Catholic tradition. But with a series of increasingly important distinctions that, taken together, orient it in a different and more complex direction. To begin with, this is because the opposition to the rationalist argument, as we have seen, is rooted not only in the Modern, but in the same thought that founds it philosophically, which is Cartesian.[36] This identification of difference in the birthplace of modern philosophy suffices to exclude Del Noce's perspective from being placed, as it has been, alongside those of antimodern, or premodern, critics of modernity. According to Del Noce, there are two reasons why the efforts of both these schools are destined to fail: first, due to the slavish acceptance of their opponent's theory on the undifferentiated character of the Modern; and second, their refusal to fight using the most effective weapons, namely, the use of the historical response as a testimony to the correctness of their point of view. The moment history is absolutized as the only reality, clearly it possesses the only legitimate claim to the final judgment on the philosophies that profess to define its meaning.

This is exactly the strategic shift Del Noce makes compared to the classic neo-Thomist tradition. Rather than enduring the hostile pressure while remaining in his own camp, he moves the battle over to his opponent's field, apparently accepting their premise, only to then refute it in a way that cannot be contested, because it derives from their own presupposition. If the logical conclusion of modern rationalism—as it appears on the one hand in Marxism and on the other in nihilism—is that there is no criterion of truth external to the success or failure of its historical bearers, the most effective method for countering it is not to falsify its premises, but rather, its results—leaving to history the role of ultimately verifying their validity or lack thereof. From this point of view, for Del Noce the disastrous collapse of communism was the negative confirmation of his basic thesis: namely, the inability of philosophical atheism, even when cast in eschatological terms, to create a historical product that endures over time. In the very century when thought made itself directly political, both on the right and on the left, a failure of this sort could only signal that a conception ruling out all other founts of legitimacy except for victory had been condemned without appeal. What has been defined as a "transpolitical" conception of contemporary history (to use an expression coined by Renzo

36. See Augusto Del Noce, *Riforma cattolica e filosofia moderna*, vol. 1, *Cartesio* (Bologna: Il Mulino, 1965).

De Felice and taken up by Ernst Nolte),[37] furnished Del Noce with an interpretive key endowed with extreme analytic flexibility, in that it assumed and reversed the adversary's perspective at the same time. If it is true, as Marx asserted, that philosophy must become world, this means that ideas and not economic forms are the driving force of history; hence, it is to them we must turn in order to understand the profound meaning of the twentieth century. On these lines, the author can maintain that without Gentile we would be unable to understand fascism, just as without Gramsci we would not have been given that peculiar historical phenomenon that is Italian communism.[38] But—this is the precipitating point of the entire discourse—if contemporary history acquires its most highly charged significance only in the force of opposing ideologies, this means that it, like every other history in the final analysis, is essentially political. It is no coincidence that its outcome was determined first by a hot war and then by a cold war.

This is one more element that distances it from traditional ontologism—both in the classic version of Étienne Gilson and in the more sophisticated one of Jacques Maritain. We have just seen why history alone, in the succession of its events, can serve as the ultimate criterion for judging the rightness of the philosophies, or ideologies that are realized in it over time. Of course, the truth remains external to history, preceding it and determining it in its very possibility. But, to be known, or at least knowable by human beings, the truth must pass through the narrow gate of a verification expressed in historical terms. This means that if the constitutive nucleus of philosophy is theological in nature—relating to the acceptance or rejection of God—its form is inevitably political; and, more precisely, theological-political, in a sense that is quite different from the one embraced by the neo-idealists. Not in the sense of neutralization, in other words, but in that of conflict. The "philosophical essences" themselves (as Del Noce defines systems of ideas), appear on the historical stage as forces fighting for dominance and willing to use every means to obtain it. Situated on a battlefield that admits of no escape, only victories or defeats, they are made recognizable, even to themselves, only by the antagonistic profile of their adversary, challenged until one or the other capitulates.

37. See Augusto Del Noce, *L'interpretazione transpolitica della storia contemporanea* (Naples: Guida, 1982).

38. See also by Del Noce, *Giovanni Gentile: Per un'interpretazione filosofica della storia contemporanea* (Bologna: Il Mulino, 1990).

Not by chance, these ideas reproduce themselves in increasingly extremist forms until reaching the apex of their aggressive thrust: thus, from moderate Cartesian rationalism is engendered Hegelian rationalism; and from that Marxist materialism; which is brought to completion and reversed, in its turn, by Nietzschean nihilism. Affirming its own point of view counts for less in this process than refuting—putting it at odds with itself—that of the enemy, in a no-holds-barred battle whose only possible outcome is self-destruction or destruction of the other.

What is striking in Del Noce's account—since it constitutes both its strength and its fragility, in a sort of internecine battle against itself—is its continual making itself equal to the opposing paradigm, to the point of endorsing it, although without ever totally identifying with it. Not surprisingly, the fierce polemic against modern rationalism seems to push him, perhaps more than he intended, toward a result that is more decisionistic than traditionally ontological. Even the initial choice of the various philosophies—for or against God—is reduced by Del Noce to an option that cannot be rationally deduced. Certainly, compared to the atheistic hypothesis, the Christian one has on its side the originary evidence of being, and the finitude of human life. But it stems from a decision that, like Pascal's wager, arises again at every turn of history, but which cannot be logically deduced from anything but its own internal cogency. Not only is the vocabulary of Del Noce's philosophy political, so is its content. If the theological error of Descartes was its subtle inclination toward Molinism, its real point of weakness, with respect to its libertine opponent, and even more, to the Machiavellian political culture, is its impolitical aspect, the inability to stand up to a comparison with either of them on the political-philosophical plane. This same political deficiency, albeit in a different, more solid theological framework, characterizes both the thought of Pascal and that of Malebranche, extending into different forms in Kierkegaard as well, and then, even more pronouncedly, in the dialectical theology of Karl Barth. Never as in this case has the absolute affirmation of God been matched by an equally stark autonomy of the world. This is the line—through Bultmann and Gogarten—that will lead to the theorem of secularization being adopted as part of the same theological lexicon. The necessary absence of God from a world that is declared—by Dietrich Bonhoeffer—to have become adult is, for Del Noce, the bridgehead of atheistic penetration into faith, subsequently brought to its extreme irreligious conclusions in the "death of God" theology by Harvey Cox, Paul Van Buren, Thomas J. J. Altizer, and others of their ilk.

At their foundation, prior even to a theological uncertainty, lies an absence of that intraworldly commitment that is instead constitutive of Catholic political theology. No wonder, from this point of view, that the beginning of the revolt, both for the external attack coming from the Protestant side and for the internal one starting with libertinism, is to be traced to the Italian tradition leading from Vico to Rosmini. It was Vico, before anyone else, who stood up against the impolitical and ahistorical philosophy of Descartes—not along the atheistic path carved out by Machiavelli, but in the forms of the civil theology that made him the champion of the Catholic Reformation. In assuming human actions as occasions for the manifestation of divine will—according to an occasionalism nudged in a historical-political direction—for Del Noce, Vico is the first philosopher to practice a genealogy of modernity that is radically different from what will later take the name of secularization.[39] The decisive mistake that led Croce's philosophy to its postwar decline, in spite of having rediscovered Vico's thought, was to not have lent it greater value, and to have even turned it on its head in an immanentistic key. Laid open on the side of transcendence, the liberal conception thus lost the battle with Marxism, which Gentile tried to go beyond, only to end up being surpassed on the left, however, by Gramsci. The final victory, moreover, would not go to Marxism—itself overwhelmed by history, even before being defeated by philosophy—but to the nihilism of the affluent society which, prophesied by Nietzsche, has today become Christianity's most formidable opponent. It is here that Del Noce's perspective, in a way victorious over communism, suffers a clear historical defeat and, therefore, according to his own principles, a philosophical one as well. Unlike communism, which was fought and ultimately beaten by liberalism, nihilism defeats Christianity not by confronting it in the open field but by neutralizing it from inside. Rather than excluding Christianity, nihilism includes it, eventually ending up declaring itself to be its inheritor, or even going so far as to identify with it.

2. This is exactly the position that Gianni Vattimo began working on the 1990s, developed in a form that has been widely accepted and discussed

39. See Del Noce, *Il problema dell'ateismo*, especially pp. 479 ff.

by contemporary philosophical culture. Without excluding other, perhaps more intrinsic, approaches to reconstructing the body of his work, a significant segment of it can be represented in an interpretation of secularization that is diametrically opposed to the one provided by Del Noce. Moreover, Vattimo himself has on many occasions used Del Noce's perspective as a polemical sparring partner, likening it to the position of someone who, like Blumenberg, despite having opposite assumptions and intentions, has defined modernity in terms of de-Christianization. Discovering that "the West, indeed, is a synonym for consumerism, hedonism, a Babel-like pluralism of cultures, loss of center, and obliviousness to any reference to 'natural' law," argues Vattimo, "paradoxically, although not particularly so, Catholic neo-fundamentalism finds itself in agreement with the secularist claim that modernity is radically autonomous from the Christian tradition."[40] What serves to link together such diverse argumentative strategies as those of Catholic critics and lay apologists of modernity, according to Vattimo, is the shared rejection of a more complex viewpoint that he identifies specifically in the "secularization theorem" initially formulated by Hegel and then developed differently by Max Weber, Ernst Troeltsch, and Karl Löwith. According to this theory, modern culture is anything but opposed to Christianity; on the contrary, it has fulfilled Christianity by realizing its fundamental inspiration. From this angle, secularization is neither a betrayal of the Christian view, as the antimoderns would have it, nor a completely new beginning, as the neo-Enlightenment thinkers maintain. Rather, secularization is an altered, distorted expression of the theological roots. In accordance with a hermeneutic approach rooted in the Italian philosophical tradition, Vattimo does not intend genealogy as the identification of an origin that is certain; but rather, as a movement backward toward a source that is always preceded, and affected, by a previous transmission.

But to grasp how he differs from Del Noce, in terms of the real theoretical stakes in play, we need to start from the shared horizon on which both are located—which is the one defined by the concept of tradition, as what links origin and history in a single continuous line. This is what rules out the thesis, maintained in particular by Blumenberg, of the self-

---

40. Gianni Vattimo, *Dopo la cristianità: Per un cristianesimo non religioso* (Milan: Garzanti, 2002); English version: *After Christianity* (New York: Columbia University Press, 2002), p. 70.

affirmation of the Modern as the radical liberation from that which precedes it. If this were true—if modernity were measured by the distance of the rift it creates from its own past—it would be disconnected from that destinal provenance without which it would not even be able to define its own novelty. Of course, this defense of the *traditum*, which engages both Vattimo and Del Noce against the thesis of the autonomy of the Modern, does not cancel out the fundamental differences that situate them on opposite sides of the same line. Although they both look at the relationship between origin and history, Del Noce does so from the angle opened up by the origin, while Vattimo examines it from the historical perspective. Thus, while the former remains in the contradiction we discussed—of hanging the historical process on an unhistorical truth that generates it—the latter dissolves this contradiction, but on condition of resolving the origin in history. What is lost, in this case, is the idea of Permanence: projected into the movement of its transmission, it is thus annulled as such. The same identification marks the relationship between tradition and revelation, superimposed on each other by Vattimo in a form that makes tradition not only the container but also the content of revelation; with the consequent nullification of both the revealed object and the revealing subject. More than a revealed truth, tradition thus transmits nothing but its selfsame translatability, along a path that in the final analysis coincides with the message it conveys. This means that preservation is one with dissolution; in the sense that what is being preserved is not the being, but its trace, destined to always be rewritten, and thus erased, by a subsequent trace. The nihilistic slant that Vattimo gives to his hermeneutics, at least in the mature phase of his production, must be understood in this dissolutive sense.

In this respect as well, the contrastive parallel with Del Noce is reaffirmed. While for Del Noce nihilism is the result of an unnecessary detour—and even of a subjective choice—cutting in to break off the classical transmission of the revealed truth, and clashing with a different, opposite facet of modern culture; for Vattimo nihilism is its unique and necessary expression. Not only that, rather than being external and opposed to metaphysics, nihilism appears as its secret driving force, inasmuch as it is an expression of the original absence of foundation that has characterized metaphysics from the very beginning. Therefore, it is not valid to contrast it—as does Enlightenment rationalism on the one hand, and Catholic traditionalism on the other—with the promise of a new refoundation, whether epistemological or normative. Moreover, the typically modern idea of "sur-passing" or "going beyond" nihilism would only intensify its dynamics, digging out an even deeper void in the underbelly of our civilization. If this breaching is experienced at an early phase as a negation of the Presupposed, from a certain point on it should be understood as the affirmative possi-bility for emancipation from the values that bind people to a prescriptive and exclusionary system. In this way, all the attitudes commonly associ-ated with nihilism, even by Del Noce—like consumerism, relativism, tech-nics—are reversed by Vattimo in a positive direction, as aspects of a truth that has always been inscribed in the history of the West, but which also coincides in its deep structure with the Christian message itself.

This is furthest point Vattimo's reflection arrives at, making it one of the most radical voices of contemporary thought: nihilism is not the ulti-mate product of atheism, as Del Noce would have it; on the contrary, it is both the outcome and the original premise of Christianity itself. Contrary to what is generally affirmed, the Nietzschean proclamation of the "death of God"—in other words, the definitive deconstruction of metaphysics—marks the end, not of Christianity, but precisely of atheism: "the end of metaphysics and death of the moral God have liquidated the philosophical basis of atheism."[41] From here—starting from the consciously antinomic idea that the true legacy of Christianity does not lie in the surviving Cath-olic tradition, but precisely in the anti-Christian philosophy of Nietzsche and Heidegger—came the overturning of the judgment on the process of secularization, now accepted, and even radicalized, for the same rea-sons Del Noce had rejected it, because of its inevitable nihilistic drift. Far from coinciding with a single path of secularization, it is divided into two distinct, although not opposing, phases: the first one, essentially modern, aimed at dissolving the sacred, transcendental core in an immanent dimen-sion; and the second, postmodern one, following on it, aimed at transfer-ring the universal values of the Gospel message into the same immanence, that is, into the earthly experience. Once again, like in a perfect game of mirrors, Vattimo reproduces and accentuates, in his own way, the same worldly, social, and even political choice as Del Noce's Catholicism. But of course with its premises reversed, and emptied of its dogmatic contents. Like Del Noce, Vattimo, too, initiates an explicit polemic against the dia-

41. Ibid., p. 17.

lectical theology of Barth because of its impolitical bias, destined to widen the gap between a God shut up inside His own absoluteness and a human history left to itself. Similarly, he takes his distance from the metahistorical or even messianic positions of thinkers who are in other respects close to him, such as Lévinas and Derrida, precisely insofar as they defer the advent of the Messiah to infinity, and with it the possibility of human salvation. A secularization that not only arises out of Christianity, but constitutes "its very essence,"[42] as Vattimo sustains, cannot act solely in a confrontational, and thus dialectical, mode against the false gods. It must realize the divine in the world—witnessing every day the salvific event of the Incarnation. Adult Christianity, to say it with Bonhoeffer, the faith of those who "live without God in the sight of God," no longer needs a religion of the Father, but must turn to the Son, and, even more, to the Spirit, as announced by Joachim of Flora,[43] to whom Vattimo refers more and more frequently in his recent texts. For those who read Joachim with the eyes of today, his privileging of the third age (that of the Spirit) over the first and second ages allows Christianity and history, drastically separated by Franz Overbeck, to be reunited into a single node. The idea that God is history must, in short, be understood in the literal sense that, on the one hand, salvation has already begun; and on the other, that it will never end, thus coinciding with the inexhaustible opening of becoming.

The Heideggerian motif of the difference between Being and being, intensified and transposed, shines through this idea of a God who is not being but becoming, of His absent presence which is both deferred and withdrawn. However, now it is shifted to the experience of the subject—human as well as divine—both of whom are exposed to a fate of necessary dispossession. Even the anti-Christian "death of God" can be interpreted as the transcription of the figure of kenosis—meaning the creation as a contraction of God for the sake of the world, and especially the Incarnation as a sharing of mortal finitude. In this way, in the message of the Gospel Vattimo was able to discover the same process of weakening that his philosophical journey had arrived at taking a different route. In these terms, history takes on a meaning as a whole only on condition that what we see in it is not the realization of an idea, but on the contrary, a pro-

42. Gianni Vattimo, *Credere di credere* (Milan: Garzanti, 1996); English version: *Belief*, trans. Luca D'Isanto and David Webb (Stanford, CA: Stanford University Press, 1999), p. 57.

43. Vattimo, *After Christianity*, chap. 2, "The Teachings of Joachim of Fiore."

cess of derealization expressive of that nothingness that cuts through and surrounds our creaturely experience. The weakening of Being,[44] from this point of view, is the secularized manifestation of the meaning of Christianity: namely, according to René Girard's interpretation, the critical revealing of the sacred violence that since the beginning of time has riveted human beings to the archaic but perpetually renewed need for sacrificial victimage. Christ was not crucified because he declared himself to be God, but because for the first time he tore away the bloody veil that had always enveloped us. Only a philosophical culture, and a politics, that takes on the task of implementing this message of revelation, thereby fulfilling it, can adequately respond to the salvific potential of the Cross.

Precisely from the political standpoint of the critique of the present, however, the thought of Vattimo has met up with a constitutive difficulty—one that is not only historical but also theoretical in character. We have seen how he rejects any messianic project that shifts the advent of justice to the end of time and, more generally, any traumatic rupture in the destinal continuity of tradition. Even an experience that is believed to be entirely new in reality can only be a reworking of the historical and linguistic material inherited from the past, based on the different, successive origins that conduct the material to the experience. Hence, every principle intended to interrupt the flow of time is excluded from the order of the possible. Neither the origin nor the end extend outside the process that is underway. They are the origin and the end of *that* process—so internal to it that they lose any excess in its regard. From this point of view—of the drastic expulsion of the exception and the decision—it has been repeatedly observed that Vattimo, notwithstanding his rejection of dialectics, remains fundamentally within the Hegelian horizon. The secularization that he examines has no other effect than to secularize, in turn, the historicization of the divine diagnosed by Hegel. It is certainly true that for

44. See Gianni Vattimo and P. A. Rovatti, eds., *Il pensiero debole* (Milan: Feltrinelli, 1983); the collection of essays is now available as *Weak Thought*, trans. Peter Carravetta (Albany: State University of New York Press, 2012); Vattimo's essay appeared as "Dialectic, Difference, Weak Thought," trans. Thomas Harrison, New School of Social Research, *Graduate Faculty Philosophy Journal* 10 (1984): 151–64. It should be noted, however, that since then Rovatti has moved into an independent theoretical perspective that can be characterized as more "French" than "German" compared to Vattimo's, as he recently recalled in "Foucault Docet," in *Italian Difference*, pp. 25–29.

him the historical process has the character of an emptying rather than a fulfillment—more of a loss than an acquisition; more of an opening than a closure. In fact, Vattimo has always claimed a greater affinity with the thought of Schelling, in accordance with the never forgotten lesson of his teacher Luigi Pareyson. Like for Schelling, and unlike Hegel, the theological core—of thought and of reality—is transmitted through the construction of symbolic universes expressed more in the imaginative language of myth than in the language of reason. Contrary to the Enlightenment perspective—but also to the demythologization reintroduced in theological terms by Rudolf Bultmann—for Vattimo, Christianity not only cannot give up its mythical tales, which, according to the author, includes the miracle of the Incarnation, it must welcome into its heart the myths coming from other sources as well, by reinterpreting them, of course. This is partly because the vocabulary of myth is the only one to express the nonoriginary character, continually removed and reconstructed, of Genesis. From this angle, too, even beyond his stated intentions, Vattimo seems to return to Vico, just like his inseparable "opponent" Del Noce, providing further proof of the connection that has never been broken between contemporary Italian philosophy and its classical roots. But, in this case, too, it is a very different Vico—not the metaphysical theorist of the divine mind and the originary mystery that it imprints in history, but the romantic mythologist of its secular dissolution in human time. Precisely in this choice of the secular side of Viconian thought—rather than the segment cut from the irremediable chasm between sacred history and profane history—we see glimpses of the minimizing, compliant, and, in some ways, yielding character of Vattimo's thought. Always careful to adhere to all the folds of interpreted reality, it is as if he were incapable of friction, and resistance, in its regard. Even the semantic transfer from theology to philosophy, and thence to politics, unfolds in a linear and smooth progression, as, indeed, befits a wholly affirmative conception of secularization. At the bottom of this tonality there is a complete historicization of the origin which, while rescuing Vattimo's perspective from the antinomy that affects Del Noce's thought, at the same time deprives it of tension vis-à-vis the effective modality that history has assumed thus far. If history is simultaneously sacred and profane—and indeed, if it is sacred *because* it is profane—then along with its unhistorical core, it will also inevitably wind up destroying the possibility for any sort of transformation.

3. The interpretations of the secularization paradigm offered by Del Noce and Vattimo do not completely cover the panoply of Italian thought on the topic. As we have seen, rather than being located on opposite ends of the field of investigation, they refer to each other like the two sides of a single page—from which Giorgio Agamben's reading in his recent book *The Kingdom and Glory* is clearly removed. Without reconstructing the entire structure of his argument (obviously tied to the complex of his work and more specifically to the research he began with the publication of *Homo sacer* to which this latest book adds another open-ended ramification),[45] the distance that it signals from other approaches to the paradigm is evident. The basic difference does not regard how the process of secularization is judged—positively or negatively—since this issue, as such, is alien to the interests of the author. Nor does it relate to the definition of secularization. The difference, rather, lies in its possible use in studying the present and the past—and the relationship between the two. This has nothing to do with the alleged primacy of the theological point of view over the philosophical and political ones, let alone with the dispute between atheism and religion, both of which are ways, expressed theologically, of understanding the role (active or passive) of the signifier "God." This is because, as it can always be argued even from the Christian quarter, "theology can resolve itself into atheism and providentialism into democracy, because *God has made the world just as if it was without God, and governs it as though it governed itself.*"[46] Similarly, many of the dichotomies or bipolarities around which our political lexicon was organized, such as those between monarchy and democracy, legality and legitimacy, or power and authority, are nothing but the two, largely complementary sides of the same theologically derived dispositif whose depths we have yet to fully sound.

The cause for this was a poor understanding of the secularization theorem; but even prior to that, to a linear, or on the contrary, a disjointed

45. Giorgio Agamben, *Homo sacer: Il potere sovrano e la nuda vita* (Turin: Einaudi, 1995); *Homo Sacer: Sovereign Power and Bare Life*, trans. Daniel Heller-Roazen (Stanford, CA: Stanford University Press, 1998).

46. Giorgio Agamben, *Il Regno e la Gloria: Per una genealogia teologica dell'economia e del governo* (Vicenza: Neri Pozza, 2007); English version: *The Kingdom and the Glory: For a Theological Genealogy of Economy and Government*, trans. Lorenzo Chiesa with Matteo Mandarini (Stanford, CA: Stanford University Press, 2011), p. 286. Italics appear in the text by Agamben.

way of structuring the relation between origin and actuality, which is the same relation at stake, not only in this specific segment of discourse, but in the entire framework of Italian thought. When Agamben departs from both Löwith's and Blumenberg's theses, his intention is not only to give a different answer to the problem they posed, but to frame it in a completely different form. At its center there is no vertical relationship between present and past, in terms of contiguity or heterogeneity. If anything, what we have is their differential overlap, or in other words, the antinomic presence of one inside the other. In this case, rather than being closed in on itself or dissolved in the process that derives from it, the origin is the secret point of resistance—like an archaic shard lodged inside contemporariness, destined to complicate it and, at the same time, to explain it in its most recondite meaning. But the relation needs to be understood in the reverse direction as well, from the present to the past; in the sense that the present becomes perfectly understandable only if examined from the perspective of a later age. Just as contemporariness is revealed by the heterogeneous presence of one or more originary fragments inside it, similarly, the origin is recognizable in its constant removal from itself—which is to say, in its different effects of meaning—only starting from a contemporary gaze: "It is something along these lines that Michel Foucault probably had in mind when he wrote that his historical investigations of the past are only the shadow cast by his theoretical interrogation of the present. Similarly, Walter Benjamin writes that the historical index contained in the images of the past indicates that these images may achieve legibility only in a determined moment of their history."[47] Secularization, on these lines, can be defined as the topological transfer of the origin into the present, or of the present into the origin, designed to disrupt the one and the other by giving them a different configuration.

It is understandable at this point why the closest explanatory model to Agamben's analytical strategy is the one put into action by Schmitt: not to pronounce a judgment of legitimacy, or illegitimacy, on the modern epoch compared to the one coming before it; but to provide a more insightful key to understanding both, which is constituted precisely at

47. Giorgio Agamben, *Qu'est-ce que le contemporain?* (Paris: Rivages, 2008), p. 40; English version: "What Is the Contemporary?" in *What Is Apparatus? and Other Essays*, trans. David Kishik and Stefan Pedatella (Stanford, CA: Stanford University Press, 2009), pp. 53–54.

the intersection between the lexicons of theology and politics. But in this instance, too, far from taking on this theoretical construct as a block, he opens it like a fan, extending its scope even to the sphere that Schmitt neglected: the economy, by which he means the government of people and things. To grasp the meaning of this difference—and in particular the meaning given here to the term *government*, distinct as such from the more specifically political term—Schmitt's perspective must be sifted through the one subsequently introduced by Foucault. At the same time, the later thinker's view must be corrected from the perspective of the earlier. Just as the Schmittian paradigm needs to be expanded, horizontally, toward the economic lexicon, similarly, Foucault's investigation into governmentality needs to be taken backward, on the vertical plane, much farther than the French philosopher did in reference to the pastorate, going back to the early Christian treatises of the first centuries on the double mystery of the Trinity and Providence. Agamben's thesis, certainly an innovative one, is that these treatises contain the key to the modern concept of government to a far greater degree than the medieval political treatises *de regimine* that generally receive scholarly attention. This fact alone testifies to how, in an archeological survey like the one undertaken by Agamben, the genesis of a given phenomenon or concept can be discovered in a discipline different from the one to which it is later ascribed. Not only that, but what is thus discovered is always something other than what was sought. This something, which destabilizes the previous hermeneutic apparatuses, including the theological-political one used by Schmitt, is the structure of the *oikonomia*: that is to say, of an administrative order governing domestic relations, such as parental or menial ones, in a managerial form not bound by a normative system.

This means that, just as the paradigmatic structure of modern politics is to be sought in its theological roots, the latter also presents itself, in its turn, marked by economic terms—proving that the analysis can only proceed by going backward from one origin to another which is even more originary than the one preceding it. But perhaps the most surprising fact to emerge from the sources is that for a long period the Christian texts absorbed that "alien"—or at minimum, heterogeneous—vocabulary without molding it into a meaning different from the one it originally possessed. For example, in Paul, the divine *oikonomia* does not exhibit a redemptive value; instead, it retains the meaning of an assignment or task of a managerial type. Of course, starting at a later time, the language of *oikonomia* tended to become more specialized, taking on a more technically theological form; just as, already in the Hellenistic period, economic and political vocabulary began to enter into a zone of mutual indistinguishability, in which they appear to overlap each other, without ever stifling the first meaning, however. This means that, unlike what is generally assumed, the analogical extension of denotation into other lexical areas left the original semantic imprint unchanged. This is precisely the course that the "signature" took,[48] whose paradigmatic process of secularization Agamben traces out, rigorously delimiting its scope: this is not a protocol of metaphorical translation; nor is it an axis of metonymic slippage. Rather, it is a strategic operator which marks and simultaneously exceeds the political concepts, referring them back to their theological origin. This does not mean that in this passage, or excess, no transformation occurs. However, rather than deriving from semantic mutation, it comes from its opposite, namely, from the repercussion caused by retaining the same meaning in different contexts. Variance, in this instance, instead of being located at the opposite end of invariance, must be thought of as its contradictory effect. What matters is the outcome, or the use, of such an exchange, constituted by the management of an otherwise unresolvable contradiction in the first language. This is what happened when the economic variation of the Trinitarian mystery allowed Christian theology to combine divine unity and plurality without issuing into pantheism.

Of course this decision in favor of contamination did not play out without a cost—which was to introduce the division that had been avoided on the external plane into God instead, understood at the same time, but distinctly, as being and as practice, as primary cause and as subject of government. This is where the dualism originates—between kingdom and government, politics and economy, authority and power—destined to shape the order of the entire Western civilization by cutting it in two different planes that are continually articulated further, according to a single bipolar mechanism which the author calls the "governmental machine." All dichotomies, historical and categorial, by which our experience is both shaped and captured, from this standpoint, are nothing but the direct, or

---

48. See Giorgio Agamben, *Signatura rerum* (Turin: Boringhieri, 2008); English version: *The Signature of All Things: On Method*, trans. Luca D'Isanto with Kevin Attell (New York: Zone Books, 2009), pp. 33 ff.

oblique, effect of that original splitting, one we must trace back to if we want to grasp the thread to which our existence is still tied. What matters is not to lose sight of the antinomic process that binds the different languages precisely through their mutual alteration. So, for example, to grasp the real stakes of a political institution we must trace its theological presupposition; and similarly, to know this, we must identify the economic meaning that ultimately underlies both. The most complex, and therefore least recognizable, element in all this lies in the fact that in the relationship between economics and politics, or between government and kingdom, the first term is simultaneously one of the poles and the one from which both derive their motion. It is thus true that the governmental machine has determinate political effects, but also that these effects, to be thoroughly understood, must be brought back to their initial economic mold. Both the democratic form, in its unresolved duality between popular sovereignty and government, legislative and executive power, identity and representation; and, perhaps to an even greater extent, the liberal form, with its providentialistic reference to the "invisible hand," go back to the same theo-economic roots, without ever being able to adequately conceptualize them. This is why when liberal democracies claim that they are operationally autonomous, far from marking an impermeable boundary against invasion from the theological paradigm, all they do is fulfill its immanent side, which has been present from the outset and is complementary to the transcendent side, as already theorized by Boussuet, when he derived human freedom from the will of God.

From this angle, the dispute over secularization that for forty years pitted Schmitt and Peterson against each other over the possibility, asserted by the former and denied by the latter, of a political theology that is Christian, which is to say, Trinitarian, gets resolved, for Agamben, in the defeat of both: if it is true, against Peterson, that modern political concepts retain a Christian theological signature, it is also true, against Schmitt, that this is a theology of an economic nature. What eluded them both, however, was an obscure truth from which both remained blinded: that is, the relationship between government and glory. Peterson, in denying the possibility of a political theology with a Trinitarian character, and even more strongly, that of a Trinitarian-type economy, identified the intrinsically political nature of Christian liturgy in other texts almost without grasping its importance. For his part, albeit instrumentally, Schmitt theorized the decisive importance of the rite of acclamation already codified by Roman public law within the plebiscitary democracies. What neither of them grasped, however, is that the glory—beyond the use that ancient and modern power made of it and continues to make of it for lawful purposes—is precisely the point of articulation between the two regimes of the kingdom and the government, authority and power, sovereignty and biopolitics. It is the threshold of indeterminacy, at once hidden and entirely obvious, across which the different discourses of theology, politics and economics, although never deposing their original profile, continuously bleed their colors into one another. Only in the insignia and rituals of glory are they refracted into a single mirror, in which origin and modernity turn out to be each other's shadow. It is then, from the greatest possible distance, that the Berlin of the 1930s can replicate the glorious ritual of Byzantium. But the final result that Agamben's genealogy arrives at is that this point is empty, like the throne depicted on the apses of Byzantine basilicas. Just as the kingdom begins to shine when the figure of the government gets tarnished, and vice versa; the locus where they are articulated by dividing, or divided by articulating, is constituted by a black light whose ultimate meaning continues to escape us, precisely because it is split continuously between what it reveals and what it leaves veiled.

On the one hand, it alludes to divine and even human idleness—which makes up the inactive ground of action—to the "decreation" which alone, with its retreat, allows each creation to occur. Under discussion here is that nothing, or that nondoing action, that we have already encountered on the outer fringes of the impolitical—the impotence, residing at the heart of potency, intended to keep it as it is, to prevent its transposition into action. On the other hand, however, rather than being an unveiling, this allusion has the sense of a capture and an inversion. Its purpose is not to liberate the idleness implicit in every work but to inscribe it as its secret motor, in the ganglia of that governmental machine by which we continue to be directed. Glory is the nourishment of power—both in its political and economic versions, both in the sovereign kingship and in the administrative task, both of which are welded together by their shared theological joining. In this way, in response to eternal life, it constitutes the derisive form, the one that is eternally separate from itself. After all, never before as in Western democracies has the glory, now reduced to pure media acclaim, played its constituent role of a power increasingly flattened into bare economic

management. The attempt to reactivate the political logic of modernity—
to which our current logic is the natural, designated heir—seems futile
in the face of this unstoppable current. But the reverse attempt, sketched
out by Agamben, to limit oneself to deactivating it in a messianic perspective, is also highly problematic. Not so much because of its impracticability—which is precisely what it seeks to the extent that it blocks the passage
from potency to act—but because of its adherence to the same theological
paradigm that it aims to defuse. Even the idea of profanation—meaning
the return of what has been consecrated to common use—which, at least
for now, Agamben seems to point to as "the political task of the coming
generation,"[49] still remains, albeit negatively, a tributary of the theological
lexicon. Understandably, instead of calling into question the paradigm of
secularization, he limits himself to joining it to the latter, as its antinomic
variant: "Both are political operations: the first guarantees the exercise of
power by carrying it back to a sacred model; the second deactivates the apparatuses of power and returns to common use the spaces that power had
seized."[50] Once the category of secularization has been assumed—regardless of how much it is deconstructed in all its irreflexive assumptions and
pushed to the point of maximum hermeneutical productivity—even when
going beyond it, we still remain in its shadow. Just as atheism is the form of
theology that cancels out God, desecration—or profanation—is the reverse
and symmetrical path of consecration.

The Mundanization of the Subject

1. Since the category of secularization—in all its possible variations—has proven incapable of going beyond the inevitably theological
lexicon in which it remains caught, it is no wonder that contemporary
Italian thought has sought another way out of political theology through
a paradigm we have already encountered a number of times: immunization.[51] Before delving into its internal logic, what needs to be immediately

---

49. Giorgio Agamben, *Profanazioni* (Rome: Nottetempo, 2005); English version: *Prof-
anations*, trans. Jeff Fort (New York: Zone Books, 2007), p. 92.
50. Ibid., p. 77.
51. See my book *Immunitas: Protezione e negazione della vita* (Turin: Einaudi, 2002);
English version: *Immunitas: The Protection and Negation of Life*, trans. Zakiya Hanafi

brought to the fore is the lexical shift it causes not only to the categories of secularization and legitimation that we have just discussed, but also to the philosophical dispositif that dates much further back, namely, the pre-supposition as a form of institution of subjectivity. The reference here is both to the subject's antecedence—established by modern philosophy—with respect to the world of experience, defined from that time onward as object; as well as to the same constitutive process of the *subiectum suppositum*: posited in support, or foundation, of itself. According to a now classic formulation, the subject is that entity which, being posited on itself, becomes present to itself, thus making possible all other representations. Compared to this logical construct, formulated variously in the modern tradition running from Descartes to Hegel—but which, expanded into the figure of intersubjectivity, returned to a large part of the twentieth-century philosophical culture—the theme of the community, as it has recently been elaborated upon in Italy, marks a sharp reversal. Naturally, in order to grasp its most theoretically conspicuous feature, it has to be distinguished—with respect to its formulation and its outcomes—from both the organicism of twentieth-century German sociology and American neocomunitarianism, both of which, once transferred from the plane of the individual to that of the collective, became conceptually related to the semantics of subjectivity. What Italian thought on *communitas* should instead be brought close to, as one of its initial sources of inspiration, is the French reflection that stretches from Bataille to Blanchot, up to Nancy, intersecting with the *Mit-sein* (Being-with) of Heidegger with an explicitly critical attitude toward all substantialist metaphysics.[52] What these thinkers take as their theme, instead of a substance or property, is

(Cambridge: Polity, 2011); see also my *Termini della politica: Comunità, immunità, biopolitica*, with an excellent introduction by Timothy Campbell (Milan: Mimesis Edizioni, 2008; English version: *Terms of the Political: Community, Immunity, Biopolitics*, trans. Rhiannon Noel Welch (New York: Fordham University Press, 2012); and *Diacritics* 36, no. 2 (Summer 2006), entirely devoted to the categories of *Bios, Immunity, Life: The Thought of Roberto Esposito*, also edited by Timothy Campbell.

52. An important book on the theme entitled *La comunità come fondamento: Fichte, Husserl, Sartre*, by Aldo Masullo, appeared back in 1965. Bruno Moroncini's works on the concept of community are also significant, including "La comunità impossibile," in *L'ineguale umanità: Comunità, esperienza, differenza sessuale*, ed. B. Moroncini, F. C. Papparo, and G. Borrello (Naples: Liguori, 1991), pp. 9–77; and *La comunità e l'invenzione* (Naples: Liguori, 2001).

the pure relationship and nothing else, which is always both singular and plural, and therefore, irreducible to a presupposed unity. However, in this form, too, the paradigm of community turns out to be more useful in deconstructing the traditional model than in introducing a truly new perspective. As Derrida also observed, all the formulas (even the attractive ones) that have succeeded one another along this line of thought—from the "unavowable" or the "unworking" community to the community "of those who have no community"—take up a reverse position to what they are attempting to challenge, giving the feeling at a certain point of going around in circles.[53]

A different perspective was opened up by focusing on a more originary term—the Latin *munus*, understood as the law of reciprocal giving or donation—from which the concept of *communitas* derives by extension and intensification.[54] This approach allows a precise meaning to be given to the empty spot around which community takes form, like a "nothing in common," calling into question the subjective logic of the presupposition: rather than being presupposed, the subjects in common are exposed to that which deprives them of their status as such. Moreover, when considered starting from its opposite, the term opens up a crucial path toward the category of immunization—to be understood deprivatively as an exemption, or waiver, from the common *munus*—that we talked about earlier. Before reconstructing its genesis and effects, we need to clear up a possible misconception that tends to multiply itself, thus obscuring the more densely theoretical kernel. Community and immunity should not be thought of in the form of a simple opposition: as two blocks of meaning facing each other, or alternating, over time, within a force field defined from one time to the next by the prevalence of one over the other. If this were the case, if community were opposed to immunity from the outside, it would be a "thing," a public *res* that was historically and ontologically identifiable with itself, or with the undivided whole of its members, rather

53. See Jacques Derrida, *Politiques de l'amitié* (Paris: Galilée, 1994); English version: *The Politics of Friendship*, trans. George Collins (London: Verso, 1997).

54. See Roberto Esposito, *Communitas: Origine e destino della comunità* (Turin: Einaudi, 1998, 2006); English version: *Communitas: The Origin and Destiny of Community*, trans. Timothy Campbell (Stanford, CA: Stanford University Press, 2010). The next issue of *Minnesota Review*, ed. Federico Luisetti, is dedicated to the relationship, proximity, and distance between my perspective and that of Jean-Luc Nancy.

than a nonentity that acquires meaning precisely from its *not* being an individual or collective subject.[55] The theorization of the society/community dichotomy, a classification defined by Ferdinand Tönnies, came into being as a method of critical self-interpretation within the same society—the only one that turned out to be historically feasible and was effectively realized. In modernity, nothing can exist except society, variously shaped in its different expressions—certainly not any sort of form of community that is alternative to it. Community as such, in the originally expropriative meaning of the *munus*, has never really been seen, in the ancient or premodern eras. It is nothing but an epistemological threshold; or, in other words, a critical measure (positive or negative depending on your point of view) of the transformation experienced by modern society. Or even, in a sense that is in no way chronological, it is its origin, which is always resurgent but never intentionally realizable—one that vanishes the moment one seeks to pinpoint it. This is something Vico had already intuited in his own way, representing it in mythic terms in the semantic implosion of the Nemean forest.

The same relation of differential overlap exists between what has been defined as "community" and the mechanism of its immunization[56]—coinciding, ultimately, with the institution of society, perpetually repeated and always incomplete. In this case, too, what we're able to perceive is never the community as such, since it is unrepresentable in its original form, but rather, always and only its immunitary conversion.[57] Community, from this point of view, is nothing but the object, or the point of friction, of the immunization procedures that affect it. In the same way that the category of immunity takes on meaning only from that of community, it is only in the interruption of immunity that community becomes recognizable to us. Not only in the sense that all communities proclaiming themselves to be such—from those coinciding with entire populations to those of a smaller size—have so far always proved

55. On the philosophical question of "nothingness"—strikingly interpreted in a tragic key—see Sergio Givone, *Storia del nulla* (Rome: Sagittari Laterza, 1995).

56. On the theoretically unresolvable dialectics between community and immunization, see the timely observations by Massimo Donà, in *Sulla negazione* (Milan: Bompiani, 2004), pp. 245–68.

57. On this point, see also Alain Brossat, *La démocratie immunitaire* (Paris: La Dispute, 2003); and Frédéric Neyrat, *Biopolitique des catastrophes* (Paris: MF, 2008).

to be immunized in their conformation and their attitudes. But also in the sense that the concept of subject, far from being posited prior to the constitution of the experience, must itself be construed as being derived from the immunitary logic.[58] Not unlike the main categories of political modernity—such as sovereignty and property—the paradigm of the subject is also, in fact, a logical mode of preventive protection against the self-dissolutive risk of "being in common."[59] Separated from the world of objects and master of itself, the subject closes itself off inside a circle, one that is exclusive and exclusionary, which safeguards it against a potentially hostile outside world. At the origin of this path, in different forms but with convergent effects, stand Descartes, Hobbes, and Locke. Descartes seeks, and finds, the certainty of the objective world in the subject's presence to itself; Hobbes ensures the subject by abolishing the community-based relationship in favor of the vertical exchange between protection and obedience; while Locke makes its property certain through the acquisitive projection of the body onto the goods it has labored upon. The threat represented by the common is directly countered by an act of individual confinement in order to satisfy the need for immunitary protection. Immunity, which gradually extends throughout the world of human relations, constitutes a sort of state of exception to the burdensome law of the *munus*. Of course, to legitimize this process, the origin—the original community—must be depicted by modern philosophy so negatively, as primeval chaos or a state of nature, that there is no question about the need to bar it. Compared to the "natural" immune system that protected the ancient and premodern societies, the one set up in modernity acquires the characteristics of a knowingly induced, artificial apparatus: instead of being limited to protecting people from the risks involved in living together, it rhetorically amplifies their power in order to bolster the mechanism for neutralizing them.

58. For a genealogy of the modern subject, see Rossella Bonito Oliva, *Soggettività* (Naples: Guida, 2003); but also, on the immunitary strategies used to reassure the subject, see Elena Pulcini, *La cura del mondo: Paura e responsabilità nell'età globale* (Turin: Boringhieri, 2009). Finally, on the relation between the subject and its body, see Adriana Cavarero, *Corpo in figure* (Milan: Feltrinelli, 1995).

59. We owe a precious reworking of the immune paradigm in psychoanalytical terms to Massimo Recalcati. See for example his most recent book *L'uomo senza inconscio: Figure della nuova clinica psicoanalitica* (Milan: Cortina, 2010).

Thus far, however, we've only arrived at an initial stage in the modern process of immunization. During the first phases it was primarily aimed at ensuring order against the conflict of the originary community; later, however, the moment the legal lexicon intersects with the biomedical one, its function sharply escalates. The increasing importance afforded to public health, demographic, and urban policies from the end of the eighteenth century onward marks a significant growth of this dynamic. From then on, the stakes of all politically decisive conflicts would be human life— the body of individuals and populations. What mattered above all was to keep it protected from every type of infection that could threaten the body's biological identity and ability to function. At that point not only did medicine take on an increasingly political role, politics itself eventually expressed itself in medical or even surgical terms. The separate, crisscrossing steps in this lexical process need to be kept distinct. Until the turn of the nineteenth century, the paradigm of immunity—coined in ancient Rome to establish the rights and privileges of classes or towns not subject to taxes—preserved a purely legal significance. However, with the birth of biological science and the first resounding successes of antiviral therapies, first achieved by Jenner against smallpox and later by Pasteur and Koch, the immune paradigm penetrated deep into the territory of biomedicine. As the battle continued to be waged against the epidemics and pandemics that propagated across the Western world in successive waves, often originating in developing countries, what had an even greater effect was the use of a military-derived jargon in the medical protocols. Based on this specialized language, the concept of the human body introduced by the practice of immunology acquired the features of a battlefield, where the forces hostile to life clashed in deadly conflict with its defenses, whether natural or induced. Never before, it might be said, had politics, technics, and biology entered into a gradual zone of indistinguishability as they did around the immunitary dispositif. The primary law of self-defense, theorized by modern philosophy, was transferred from outside to inside the human body. This had a reciprocal, doubly naturalizing effect: on the one hand, what was considered a natural right from the point of view of political knowledge was transposed inside the living body as a biological law; on the other hand, this biologization of the natural had a retroactive effect in the world of politics, legitimizing practices aimed at defensive, or preemptive, strikes against real and imaginary enemies. This is how the transfer of immunity from nature to politics, and vice versa, made biology into a matter of law, and law into a matter of biology.[60]

One can say that, as a whole, Italian philosophy has remained outside this vicious circle—and indeed, in some way, has contributed to deconstructing its neutralizing effects. Not that Italian thinkers fail to grasp the risks implicit to the origin, or to the development, of community—which is to say, the potentially dissolutive character of the expropriative logic of the *munus*. On the contrary, its major interpreters have clearly apprehended the possible nexus between community and death. Both for Machiavelli and Vico the origin is characterized by violence and lethal conflict. The unsustainable nature of the originary community, represented by the impenetrable darkness of the *ingens sylva*, is captured no less dramatically by Vico than it is by Hobbes's state of nature. For him, too, the preservation of humankind depends on the institution of authoritarian apparatuses—from divine lightning to esoteric law to the sovereign regime—capable of curbing the self-destructive impulse of a life lived in common without limits and boundaries. In other ways and with different intentions, this also applies to Leopardi—who seeks protection from the dissolutive fury of nothingness in the dual immunitary apparatus of illusion and poetic imagination. Even Croce, in a different horizon from both of theirs, counters the vitality unleashed by the Origin with the shield of the ethical-political bond. And yet none of them imagines ending the contest by definitively bridling the telluric powers of life. None of them believes that the originary community can be completely immunized. Indeed, what they all see in a pretense of this sort is a danger even more insidious than the one feared—namely, the drying up of the vital wellsprings of individual and collective experience. Whether this prospect takes on the Machiavellian face of corruption, the Viconian barbarization of the advanced age, or the Leopardian image of bloodless intellectualism, the result remains the same. Even the dramatic retreat of Italian history lamented by Cuoco and foreshadowed by de Sanctis alludes to an abrupt halt of the vital flow that binds time to its bodily roots. Once the umbilical cord connected to a past charged with symbolic energy has been cut, it threatens to reemerge in ghostly form. The common can never be entirely exorcized, just as his-

---

60. For more on this dynamic—analyzed earlier in *Immunitas*, pp. 145–77—see the book now out by Ed Cohen, *A Body Worth Defending: Immunity, Biopolitics and the Apotheosis of the Modern Body* (Durham, NC: Duke University Press, 2009).

tory cannot fully reclaim the unhistoric stratum from which it is generated without the risk of being swallowed back into it. This awareness that jars so stridently with the legitimizing aims of modern ideology derives from a representation of the origin that is different, and more complex, than the merely negative image developed by the moderns. The beginning is now captured in its dissolutive side, but along with its vitally energetic and constitutive aspect as well. Which explains why we can never rid ourselves of it once and for all. This dual vision of the origin—the identification of its ambivalence—is a distinguishing feature of all Italian thought, both modern and contemporary. The critical distance it takes from the secularization paradigm, understood as the completed historical fulfillment of the originary genetic nucleus, is thus understandable. But also, for the same reason, the distance it takes from the idea of self-legitimation, of a radical rupture to what comes before. This also explains the increasingly problematic assumption of the immune paradigm—the perception of its constitutive antinomy. On the one hand, its inevitability is acknowledged; but on the other hand, so is its equally necessary coimplication with community. Just as a community devoid of any immunitary system is destined to explode, similarly, when pushed beyond a certain threshold, the system is likely to lead to implosion. The premise of great Italian thought is that the reproduction, and enhancement, of life can only be permitted by the balance—or more precisely, by the perennial tension—between *communitas* and *immunitas*. When they diverge, or exceed one another, the consequences can be catastrophic.

But this isn't all. Once the immune paradigm has been brought into focus, its internal rotation needs to be worked on: in other words, it has to be shifted from a defense barrier against the outside to a process of differential transformation of the very subjects it identifies. To facilitate this semantic transfer, the first step is to untangle the deadly knot that ensued, starting from late modernity, from the intertwining of the biological lexicon with military jargon. Once the paradigm has been removed from the aggressive metaphors, or tropes, which characterized its early representations, the immune system of our bodies is revealed in all its internal complexity. Far from constituting an impenetrable armor set in place to protect our identity, it proves instead to be its epicenter of continuous modification, as well as a filter for contact and communication with the surrounding environment. The very possibility of organ transplants—to say nothing of the original implantation of one body inside another during pregnancy—is the most vivid testimony of this function. What in technical language is referred to as "immune tolerance" should not be understood as a sort of suspension, or silencing, of the body's immunity, but, on the contrary, as its reversed effect, turned inside out. From this angle we begin to get a glimpse of the "common"—in other words, the positively contaminating—side of what is also intended as immune. One could say that just as *communitas*, in all communities, is always immunized, at least to a certain extent, when viewed in the depths of its reproductive mechanism, *immunitas*, in its turn, also reveals an element of community. The hermeneutic passage from one perspective to the other is created by deconstructing the individualistic character that modernity has attributed to the modern subject. We have seen how this is posited on the prior separation of the subject from a world—also made up of other subjects—that is reduced to an object of its own knowledge and initiative. This point, or line—from Bruno to Gentile—is exactly where Italian philosophy, despite all its internal differences and contradictions, takes another direction: on the one hand, by picturing the individual subject as the constitutive locus of a community that is never stuck inside the identity of its internal constituents; and on the other hand, by deeply rooting it in the productive rhythm of infinite life. What lies at the heart of Italian philosophy is not the individual but the world in common, with all its vital and inexhaustible potency.[61] The last step in a thought on community that seeks to assimilate itself to such a tradition would be to expand the protective function of the immune system from the restricted sphere of the individual to the unlimited space of the entire world—itself conceived as a massive living body. Only in this way can the origin coincide with the present, and immunity with community.

2. As we know, this substitution of the semantics of subjectivity with the semantics of life—as far as they concern the dynamics of power—is what took the name of biopolitics, starting from the research conducted by Michel Foucault. It would be superfluous to dwell further on the general

61. For more on the "transindividual," in addition to Paolo Virno, *Grammatica della moltitudine* (Rome: DeriveApprodi, 2002); and Sandro Mezzadra, *Diritto di fuga: Migrazioni, cittadinanza, globalizzazione* (Verona: Ombre Corte, 2006), see the journals *Forme di Vita* and *Quaderni Materialisti*.

processes and methods of this development, since its genesis and effects of meaning have been widely understood and discussed.[62] What counts most for our inquiry is to recognize the singular role that Italian philosophy has played in defining it. Some interpretations in particular have set off international echoes with even greater resonance than those created by the Foucauldian "discovery." Despite even significant differences in approach and method, one peculiar aspect that assimilates these Italian voices to Foucault's discourse, but especially to studies initiated in other contexts, is their markedly philosophical tone. Unlike a number of empirical studies, mostly conducted from a historical or sociological perspective, both initially and subsequently, the development of Italian biopolitics has maintained a pronounced theoretical inflection. But what is even more important, also for explaining its dissemination in nonspecialist venues, is that this philosophical inclination did not come about in opposition to, but rather as reflection of, a strong commitment to militant activism. This acute mixture of philosophical rigor and critical tension has had the effect of placing Italian reflection about biopolitics on a different plane from other political philosophies, one that is transversal to them, making it perhaps a new political philosophy or, more accurately, a different philosophical practice. Rather than a method of contemporary knowledge, it has presented itself, or been received, as a dispositif of thought—and even as thought in action—designed, even beyond its intentions, to produce definite consequences external to it.[63]

We would not be unjustified in viewing this particular performative attitude as a long-standing feature of the Italian tradition as well. This is the same extroversion into the world that, from Machiavelli to Gentile and Gramsci, qualifies Italian thought in various ways, in a style that exceeds

---

62. Roberto Esposito, *Bíos: Biopolitica e filosofia* (Turin: Einaudi, 2004); English version: *Bíos: Biopolitics and Philosophy*, trans. Timothy Campbell (Minneapolis: University of Minnesota Press, 2008).

63. See the dossier dedicated to biopolitics in *Filosofia Politica* 20, no. 1 (2006), with essays by Roberto Esposito, Michele Cammelli, Gaetano Rametta, Laura Bazzicalupo, and Simona Forti and G. Guaraldo; Antonella Cutro, ed., *Biopolitica* (Verona: Ombre Corte, 2005); Adriano Vinale, ed., *Biopolitica e democrazia* (Milan: Mimesis, 2007); Ottavio Marzocca, *Perché il governo* (Rome: Manifestolibri, 2007); Aniello Amendola, Laura Bazzicalupo, Federico Chicchi, and Antonio Tucci, eds., *Biopolitica, bioeconomia e processi di soggettivazione* (Macerata: Quodlibet, 2008).

the disciplinary status of philosophical scholarship, constituting, rather, a sort of practical deconstruction of philosophy. This description cannot but bring to mind the school of critical thought, located as it happens in Italy, that has defined itself as philosophy of praxis. But with something more and different compared to its original Marxist mold, involving the lexical transfer from the sphere of history to that of biological life. Not in the sense of a simple substitution, but rather, in the sense of their articulation structured in such as way as to make one the rotational pivot of the other. In this effect of reciprocal modification we catch a glimpse of the second typical feature of Italian reflection on biopolitics. This is a sort of mobilization, and contamination, between the vocabularies that it connects at different times with an aggregative force rarely to be matched. This explains the unprecedented proliferation of theories, or disciplines, that within a few years have grown around the same semantic center of gravity. Biopolitical studies in the narrow sense have been flanked first by biolaw,[64] then by bioeconomics,[65] and finally by bioaesthetics[66]—not to mention bioethics and the various biotechnologies. The inevitable hulling of the theoretical statute and the sometimes occasional approach that results from this proliferation are balanced by a broadening of the investigative scope, attesting to the extraordinary fecundity of the heuristic paradigm in question. But there is more going on here. At play in this semantic expansion is not only a convergence of the various discourses, but also a mutation affecting them internally. This has led to the unearthing of the underlying mechanism that controlled the constitution of the various human sciences in a form that, between the late eighteenth and early nineteenth centuries, seems to have made one discipline issue out of the other, or at least linked them together in a metonymic chain. We know how the birth of biological science influenced political theory through a process of naturalization crossed between legal assumptions and biomedical protocols. But this development, which had so many consequences for the biopolitical paradigm,

64. See Eligio Resta, *Diritto vivente* (Rome-Bari: Laterza, 2008); Luigi Garofalo, *Biopolitica e diritto romano* (Naples: Jovene, 2009), with an introduction by Umberto Vincenti.

65. See Laura Bazzicalupo, *Il governo delle vite. Biopolitica ed economia* (Rome-Bari: Laterza, 2006), in which the author introduces an original interpretive approach to the relationship between life and economy.

66. On the relationship between biopolitics and totalitarianism see Pietro Montani, *Bioestetica: Senso comune, tecnica e arte nell'età della globalizzazione* (Rome: Carocci, 2007).

did not run its course in a direct path. In other words, in order for this to take place, it had to involve—and in its turn transform—other human sciences like anthropology, linguistics, sociology, even skirting along zoology and botany. Without going into the details of these events, which have been reconstructed from a closer distance elsewhere, what matters is to point out the transformation that the life sciences gave rise to in other disciplines of knowledge; and their mutual encroachments on each other in a way that, from time to time or even simultaneously, changed their respective rules. As we have seen regarding the genealogical relationship between theology and economics, we are left with the impression that no language can progress beyond a certain threshold, resolving otherwise insoluble problems, unless it proceeds through the opening caused by the grafting of another lexicon. This explains the concatenation of disciplinary plexuses around a single signifier—that of biological life in all its possible resonances—that constitutes both their object of analysis and the semiotic commutator. The continued proliferation in Italian theory of new disciplines marked by a reference to *bios* has brought to light, by elucidating its method, the dispositif that has governed the human sciences from the beginning: according to a movement that perpetually constitutes the sciences by depriving them of their original value and then reconstituting them, but from a different slant.

But this horizontal mobility between different languages intersects in the Italian interpretation of biopolitics with another, even more problematic relationship of a vertical type, which is perhaps its most distinctive hallmark: the relationship between past and present, or between origin and history, referred to repeatedly in this book. Critics have noted that Foucault left this issue largely undecided, or rather open to different and even conflicting solutions. At its heart there lied the complex relationship between sovereign order and biopolitical regime. How one was supposed to have sprung from the other, completely replacing it, or on the contrary, retaining a latent remainder of it, was never thoroughly explained, and was even obfuscated by a series of statements leading in diverging directions. The relationship between biopolitics and totalitarianism was also affirmed and denied at the same time according to an ambivalent modality that gave rise to the equally ambiguous notion of thanatopolitics, understood as both the negative reverse of biopower and its ultimate fate.[67] The

67. See Simona Forti, ed., *La filosofia di fronte all'estremo: Totalitarismo e riflessione filosofica* (Turin: Einaudi, 2004).

preliminary focus of Italian reflection on biopolitics, even if not always explicitly stated, hovers precisely around this set of questions—providing different answers to them, of course. Even the titles of some of the texts it has produced—from *Homo sacer* to *Bios*, to *Empire*, passing through *Immunitas*—all refer to an epoch-making alterity, situated between classical Greece and ancient Rome, indicative at minimum of the problem. It cannot be by accident that books devoted to the biopolitical configuration of the contemporary world have all sought their exegetical keys in ancient or even archaic semantics—almost as if the actuality of today could only be penetrated through its opposite, retracing its meaning by way of its most remote stratum. In fact, a recurring question, generally aimed at delegitimizing the paradigm of biopolitics, concerns whether this coimplication between politics and life necessarily has a modern character. While Foucault, in the midst of unresolved uncertainties and vacillations, tended to narrow it down to the late modern period, these authors date its origins back to the remotest of times.[68] How, they ask, are the agrarian politics of the ancient empires to be described, or the direct ownership of the body of slaves—a practice found in all premodern regimes—if not in biopolitical terms? And why not attribute the eugenic precepts contained in the political writings of Plato—not surprisingly, used and abused as apologetics for Nazi racial propaganda—to some form of biopower?

This question—upon which the very utterability of a biopolitics depends—has received a variety of responses, addressing the impossibility in general of assimilating practices and attitudes that are too heterogeneous to come under the same hermeneutic model. It is clear, for example, that Plato's ideas were aimed at eliminating everything that escaped the community sphere of the *polis*, and thus did not go in the immunitary direction of disciplinary control. Similarly, in other ways, the politicization of certain health and hygiene procedures cannot be made to fit with modern processes involved in the biologization of politics. The truth is that to grasp the connection between actuality and origin[69]—but also, to some extent, between biopolitics and sovereignty—we must go beyond the stark alter-

68. For a careful discussion of the matter, see Francesco M. de Sanctis, *Vita, diritto, proprietà: Una contrapposizione tra antico e moderno* (Naples: Università degli Studi Suor Orsola Benincasa, 2009).

69. See the intelligent observations in Emanuele Stolfi, *La genealogia, il potere, l'oblio: L'inattuale e l'antico; A proposito di alcune recenti pubblicazioni* (Siena, 2008).

native between continuity and discontinuity assumed by the theorems of secularization and legitimation, so as to open a crosswise view that seeks the point of refraction of one in the depths of the other. Contrary to what one might imagine, it is not contiguity, but precisely an epochal gap that triggers the reoccurrence of an originary phenomenon within a different horizon of meaning. What we need to conceive in order to capture this dynamic is not a continuous or discontinuous sequence of segments along the same line of flow, so much as the relationship of two superimposed planes resting on top of each other but also, to some extent, lodged inside each other: the one above, historical in nature, and the other below, indescribable in historical terms. Whether or not the latter can be identified with nature, life, or the originary community depends, of course, on the viewpoint of those who, from one time to the next, either create or are subjected to the effects of this splitting, which is simultaneously both ideological and real. What matters to the paradigm of biopolitics, in any case, is the peculiar and apparently inescapable mode of its internal movement—the way the lower level comes to the surface whenever an opening or a fracture appears in the upper level. In modernity, the tearing of the fabric of history and, thus, the resurgence of the unhistorical, is produced by the same acceleration of time that, the farther it rushes forward, the more it tears itself from its provenance, thereby opening up a hiatus between past and present. It is inside this gap, the same way a water jet or a flow that has been stopped up for a long time, returns by gushing upward, that the origin—if not as such, at least a splinter of it—pierces the flesh of the present, replenishing it with new blood or leeching it dry depending on the circumstances.

The diversity of this effect, whether it is affirmative or negative, energetic or entropic, or even one inside the other (as Vico saw clearly in the figure of the *ricorso*), depends on the relationship that the actuality establishes with its own originary provenance. In the first case, when recognized as a vital potency, the origin shows its positive side; in the second, when rejected as such, it returns in a phantasmal form, as it did a number of times in history when it was torn from its roots in a more sudden and violent manner. This is when its ghost returns to knock on the door of the present until it smashes it down. Something of the sort occurred in the old European world in the early decades of the twentieth century, with a destructive charge difficult to equal. Never as in those times—in a full-blown biopolitical regime, in other words—did the old sovereign right to put to death reappear in all its ghoulish force. But this happens, in different forms and degrees, each time history imagines that it can release itself from its debt with the common origin—rejecting the *munus* that the common origin bears within. What returns in these circumstances is never the past as such—but its masked or inverted double. This is the case as far as the sovereign principle is concerned: it returns to the biopolitical horizon no longer as the order that creates the law, as it did during its classic modern appearance, but on the contrary, as what shuts the law down, inaugurating a state of exception that is legally entitled to suspend the law.[70] This reversal has been seen at its greatest intensity in all the most recent international conflicts—and is increasingly seen in the difficulty of restoring conditions of legitimacy in militarily occupied territories, especially in the attempt (at least according to the publicly stated intentions) to reestablish a new legal order. But the same flipping mechanism, overturning the original modern function, is to be found in the new political use of religion: in the genuine politics of theology that, in this case, too—in the West as in the East— overturns the old dispositif of political theology, reflecting the fact that in an entirely secularized world the theological can only come back into play in a spectral form of its original mandate. The same distortion can be recognized in the return, now throughout the world, of the local within the global—no longer in defense of an area perceived as originary, but rather as an offensive stance against everything outside that can only be confronted by a preemptive strike. The basic difficulty, in all these cases of negative biopolitics (if not full-blown thanatopolitics), arises from the transfer into the horizon of life of models, categories, and methods which came into being in other historical contexts, and which can therefore not be used again in the new one without paying the price of intolerable distortion.

From this point of view, to say that biopolitics is the outcome of an epochal turning point that only came to maturity with modern history, as some do, or that it is the paradigmatic form of all Western politics, as others

70. See Judith Butler, *Precarious Life: The Powers of Mourning and Violence* (London: Verso, 2004), esp. "Infinite Detention," pp. 50–100. Judith Butler's analysis of the category of "vulnerability" has been picked up and developed in the Italian philosophical context by Adriana Cavarero, in *Orrorismo or violence sull'inerme* (Milan: Feltrinelli, 2007). On the total transformation of the war in the global age and on the dissolution of the modern political spaces see the books by Carlo Galli, *Politici e guerra. L'età moderna e l'età globale* (Bologna: Il Mulino, 2001), and *La guerra globale* (Rome-Bari: Laterza, 2002).

do, does not shift the essential question, which is identifiable precisely in the line of tangency, and tension, between ontology and history. Our life does not lend itself to an absolute naturalization or to an absolute historicization, since, as Foucault understood in his time, it is placed "at the same time outside history, in its biological environment, and inside human historicity, penetrated by the latter's techniques of knowledge and power."[71] It may well be said that all the early symptoms of negative biopolitics are historically consequent to one or the other of these two absolutizations: to the violent dissolution of human life either from the world of history in a project for total naturalization, or from the depths of nature in the illusion of its definitive historicization. In each of these cases, what is missing is a living relationship with our common origin, in its dual aspects of donation and risk, exposure and alteration. From this point of view we can even accept that the "material" of all politics has always been biopolitics—but with the addendum that its qualitative intensification, and also its thanatopolitical drift, only began with the immunitary "turn": first, of the modern political categories, and then, of the management of life itself. Biopolitics, in a certain sense, is nothing but the immunitary closure of the void from which all politics derives, or upon which it rests. This occurred when modernity, having identified its expropriative side—one that therefore threatens identity—imagined it could break the constitutive link with the origin—and move life into an area protected from its dangers and resources. Without imagining that we can retrace this route backward in a form that would inevitably duplicate its aporias, it is a matter of examining it with a critical eye, one that is capable of looking at the origin from the perspective of innovation, not preservation. Only in this way—one not unfamiliar to Italian thought—will the inseparable unity of nature and history, *zoe* and *bios*, *communitas* and *immunitas* be able to reveal itself once again.

3. The obvious difficulties of articulating something like an affirmative biopolitics—recognized by Italian philosophy as one of the most urgent tasks of contemporary thought—are not solely contingent in nature. True, they also relate to the continuous change in the relationship between power and life that, for some time now, has been caused by the dizzying

71. Michel Foucault, *La volonté de savoir* (Paris: Gallimard, 1976); English version: *The Will to Knowledge: History of Sexuality, Vol. 1*, trans. Robert Hurley (London: Penguin Books, 1998), p. 143.

development of technology;[72] or to the economic, social, and environmental differences that cut the global world into blocks that are increasingly difficult to reduce to the unity of a single living organism. Moreover, to translate paradigms with a philosophical provenance into concrete options and operational initiatives has never been easy—if only because of the heterogeneity of principle that distinguishes the analytical sphere from the normative one. But there is something further, or prior, to this difficulty that concerns the very conceptual grammar we use, and in which we remain caught. To begin with, it must be said that it would be futile, and indeed mistaken, to seek a positive outcome in the simple opposite of what is being negated—in other words, to imagine that the keys to an affirmative biopolitics can be found in the diametrical opposite of the thanatopolitical dispositifs. This does not mean that identifying them is pointless for a constitutive type of thought. The practical and theoretical digging into the Nazi factory of death begun recently by Italian thought was a necessary step in this direction. But not a sufficient one, in itself, because when focusing on a single phenomenon—no matter how decisively important because of its unique, exemplary character—there is the risk of losing sight of the whole: the logical construct that organizes the entire philosophical, economical, and political discourse starting from something that precedes it and obscurely determines it. To trace back to this underlying element is extremely difficult, not only due to its inherently elusive character, giving it the tendency to retreat farther and farther, but also because the conceptual and linguistic tools that we have at our disposal for dismantling it are largely conditioned by it. This difficulty, inherent in every deconstructive process (identified differently, in their time, by Heidegger and Wittgenstein even before Derrida's contribution), can only be confronted by recognizing it as such. That is to say, by taking it as a foregone conclusion that the original matrix can never be reached, that it can only be approached through the often distorted or ambivalent signs that it projects onto the mirror of the contemporary world. Whence a splitting of intersecting planes with which the genealogist is by now familiar, based on which what happens today is conditioned by what comes before it, often from quite a distance, while what comes before it takes on importance only on the screen of what we now have in front of our eyes.

---

72. For more on this topic, see Aldo Schiavone, *Storia e destino* (Turin: Einaudi, 2007).

A similar anachronistic paradox also affects the category that we examined earlier of the subject, in its elusive relationship with the figural notion that anticipates it and at the same time follows it: namely, that of the "person." As we know, starting in the 1930s and then in successive waves and with increasing intensity, the idea of personhood has gradually established itself as the most adequate way to universally represent the human being as such, to the point of undermining the primacy of the close, but evidently more restricted concept of the "individual." The "subject of law" paradigm seems to have been rejuvenated by the paradigm of person, which has given concrete substance to a status which has always tended toward abstraction.[73] What has been lost sight of in the process is the clear antecedence of the conceptual construct that appears to come after the one that is in reality much more recent—that of the subject—understood in its modern sense, as it was developed along the theoretical segment leading from Descartes to Leibniz.[74] That the term *subject* had until then had a meaning very close to what we now assign to the concept of "object" is symptomatic of its inherent oscillation. But the element that refers more intrinsically to a more originary categorial block, certainly one that is a great deal earlier than the "invention of the subject," is the dialectic internal to the latter—which especially drew Foucault's attention—between subjectification and subjection.[75] The fact that each increment of subjectivity causes or is the result of a possible subjection—to the extent that the same term may indicate, depending on the case, but also at the same time, being "subjects of" or "subjects to" something—agrees with the logical

73. A revival of the personalist tradition has been proposed, in a different way and with different meanings, by Stefano Rodotà, in *La vita e le regole: Tra diritto e non diritto* (Milan: Feltrinelli, 2006); and by Roberta De Monticelli, in *La novità di ognuno: Persona e libertà* (Milan: Garzanti, 2009).

74. Franco Rella, whose important works stand at the crossroads between philosophy and literature, has taken up the issue of subjectivity again today, in a critically aware manner, in *La responsabilità del pensiero: Il nichilismo e i soggetti* (Milan: Garzanti, 2009).

75. Pier Aldo Rovatti has for years provided a philosophically important contribution on the aporetic structure of subjectivity. Of his many books I suggest for example his *Trasformazioni del soggetto* (Padua: Poligrafo, 1992), and *Il paiolo bucato: La nostra condizione paradossale* (Milan: Cortina, 1998). The work of Rosi Braidotti is significant on the feminist horizon, also for her attention to the biopolitical deconstruction of the category of subject. Of her books, see, for instance, *In metamorfosi: Verso una teoria materialistica del divenire* (Milan: Feltrinelli, 2003), and *Trasposizioni: Sull'etica nomade* (Rome: Sossella, 2008).

mechanism that we came across earlier in the figure of the presupposition as a founding structure of subjectivity: to be such, the subject must presuppose itself—to rest on itself and, at the same time, be the support on which it rests. As is evident, this means that, in its logical makeup, it is the result of a unification—between it and itself—in turn based on a prior division. Only starting from this can the subject exist, as we have said, by unifying itself with itself. It is true, in fact, that it has the form of a unification, but also that this logically presupposes a separation, without which it could not come into being. This is implicit, for that matter, in the very structure of the presupposition, in which the position is always preceded, in its presenting of itself, by something which precedes it, thus making it possible. It is precisely this splitting, or doubling, of what is nevertheless united that is the prime mover of the dialectic between subjectification and subjection that subjects the subject, before others, to itself, submitting it to, or superimposing it onto, its selfsame subjective substance.

The thesis I presented in a recent book is that this gap cannot be closed up by the category of person, although personhood is also used for this purpose;[76] on the contrary, it is what causes this breach, in a way that is hard to recognize because the category is fractured internally by a series of turns and bends that preclude its full visibility. At its origin, there is the paradigm, or more precisely, the dispositif, both Roman and Christian, that, in different ways and with different effects, has marked the entire development of the theological, philosophical, and political categories of the West. Without being able to reconstruct the internal scansions, analyzed elsewhere, we can say that it goes back to that peculiar logic that separates an entity of a spiritual or artificial type, defined as personal, from the human as a natural being. Thus, by isolating a site of legal imputation—or processing of consciousness—within the bodily substrate in which it is housed, the dispositif of the person presupposes the separation from itself,

---

76. See Roberto Esposito, *Terza persona: Politica della vita e filosofia dell'impersonale* (Turin: Einaudi, 2007); English version: *Third Person: Politics of life and philosophy of the impersonal*, trans. Zakiya Hanafi (Cambridge: Polity, 2012). Remo Bodei has for some time now engaged his philosophical energy in probing the crisis of personal identity and the need to overturn the humanistic view that goes from people to things, by investigating their secret life. See especially Remo Bodei, *Destini personali: L'età della colonizzazione delle coscienze* (Milan: Feltrinelli, 2002); and also by Bodei, *La vita delle cose* (Rome-Bari: Laterza, 2009).

as opposed to the unity of the living being. Furthermore, anticipating the dialectic between subjection and subjectification discussed above, it subordinates the role of one part to the mastery of the other. On the basis of the paradigm of person—understood as that which, inside the body, is more than the body—having rights, for anyone, really means being the subject of one's own objectification. Whether the entire human race or a single individual is involved, when the bodily sphere is thrust into the realm of animality, it is submitted to the dominance of the rational and voluntary sphere. Authentic persons—unlike human beings who have only partial or no claim to this title—are those who have full control over their animal part. Of course, in the transition from Christian dogma, or even from the Roman codification to modern thought, this *dispositif* undergoes a series of extremely profound transformations, mostly related to the structural difference between an objectivist logic, like the Roman one, and another with a subjectivist tone, like the modern. What remains constant, inside and despite this categorial gap, is precisely this continuously shifting and oscillating distinction between a type of human being who is completely human, and another bordering on the regime of things. The fact that the return of this exclusionary device, in more or less dramatic forms, occurs in a discontinuous fashion, at different times and under different circumstances, is further evidence of what we were saying about the antinomic but unavoidable relationship between origin and contemporariness. It is a relationship that is completely incomprehensible to linear hermeneutic models because it expresses an irregular topology that weaves together different times, but also continuously reverses their chronological progression. What matters is to not lose sight of the paradigmatic grid that subterraneanly connects highly heterogeneous lexical expressions—so as to perceive, under the cracks in the surface, the underlying geological strata in which they open up.

In this topological framework that obliquely connects the archaic and the present-day,[77] the special role played by Roman law, and the history of ancient Rome in general, is difficult to overlook. Of course, something like this goes for all the great civilizations of the past—for ancient Greece above all, so present and influential in modern philosophical culture, which has repeatedly declared itself to be its inheritor. Yet, especially as regards the constitution of the political, there continues to arrive from

77. On the relationship between the archaic and the present-day, see Mariapaola Fimiani, *L'arcaico e l'attuale: Lévy-Bruhl, Mauss, Foucault* (Turin: Boringhieri, 2000).

ancient Rome—via sudden changes or unexpected drifts rather than direct lines—something different and more penetrating as far as contemporary history is concerned.[78] The category of person (no less than those of empire and dictatorship, sanctity and immunity) provides a remarkably important example that did not escape Simone Weil: with a brilliant twist, in just such an anachronistic form, she connected the politics of Nazism to those of ancient Rome.[79] More than bringing to light any given analogous contents—like the methodical deception, the generalized slavery, the extermination of the defeated—what she grasped by superimposing one on the other was a kind of obsessive repetition that ties human history into a tight metaphysical knot around the primacy of Force. In the heart of the contemporary world, the most terrible sovereign dispositif for the reduction of human beings that history has ever known resurfaces from its depths, threatening to suck the life out of the gash in its mortal opposite. The most disturbing element in this dynamic, for Weil, is that it is based on the same legal body that hinged on the *ius personarum*, which for two millennia regulated relationships between people through their relation—of difference

78. An exceptionally fascinating depiction of the Roman legal paradigm can be found in Aldo Schiavone, *Ius: L'invenzione del diritto in Occidente* (Turin: Einaudi, 2005). On the juridical dispositif of the person, see Alessandro Corbino, Michel Humbert, Giovanni Negri, eds., *Homo, caput, persona. La costruzione giuridica dell'identità nell'esperienza romana* (Pavia: IUSS, 2010), which includes my essay "Il dispositivo della persona," pp. 49–63. The English version, "The *Dispositif* of the Person," appeared in the journal *Law, Culture, and the Humanities* 8, no. 1 (2012): 17–30, in an issue entitled *Symposium: On the Work of Robert Esposito*, followed by a wide-ranging debate on the topic by American legal theorists and philosophers.

79. I am alluding in particular to Simone Weil, *Sulla Germania totalitaria* (Milan: Adelphi, 1990), as well as to her "La personne et le sacré," in *Écrits de Londres et dernières lettres* (Paris: Gallimard, 1957); English version: "Human Personality," trans. Sian Miles, in *Simone Weil: An Anthology* (New York: Grove Press, 1986), pp. 49–78. On Simone Weil, see a book by one of the most intelligent Italian philosophers, who passed away prematurely: Angela Putino, *Simone Weil: Un'intima estraneità* (Troina: Città Aperta, 2006). With great clarity, Putino identified an exit point for feminist thought on difference, in order to escape its internal contradictions, precisely in the category of the "impersonal." Or, perhaps more precisely, as a critical point for assuming them as such. See Angela Putino, "Impersonale della politica," in *Per Angela*, ed. V. Dini (Fisciano, 2008), pp. 59–62. On the need to launch a thought of the Third, or of the Neuter/Neutral, beyond the aporias of thought based on the Two—in which female difference remains—see also, from another perspective, Fabrizia De Stefano in an important book, *Il corpo senza qualità: Arcipelago queer* (Naples: Cronopio, 2010).

or identification—with things. The pivot of this *dispositif*, in the name of the person, is the translation of the logical mechanism of the presupposition into the onto-political one that subordinates some human beings under the command of others who are placed above them. It is striking that almost identical expressions are used, during the same years, by an author who is not only philosophically remote to Weil, but also in her opposing camp, so to speak, in ideological terms: namely, Martin Heidegger. It was he who argued that "since the time of the Imperium, the Greek word 'political' has meant something Roman. What is Greek about it now is only its sound," concluding: "To be superior is part and parcel of domination. And to be superior is only possible through constantly remaining in the higher position by way of a constant surmounting of others. Here we have the genuine *actus* of imperial action. . . . For the Romans, the essence of deceiving, of leading into error, of dissembling, and thus of *pseudos*, is determined by *fallere*, by felling. The erroneous becomes *falsum*."[80]

Without wishing to establish any direct relationship between arguments and perspectives that are in no way comparable, it is useful to recall that the reference to Roman history constitutes one of the most frequently recurring traits throughout all Italian philosophy. Far from seeking a mere filter for comparing types of governments, Machiavelli searches Roman history to locate the keystones for penetrating the black box of human governance; while Vico sees in it the most meaningful arena where the dialectic between *communitas* and *immunitas* is played out, and in which the history of humankind finds its essential gait. In each case, and at different levels, ancient Rome constitutes the protrusion of the archaic into the actual, or of the actual into the origin; like in a sort of hermeneutic surplus, it makes possible, on the one hand, the foundation of the political, and on the other, the foundation of history. But what must be brought to attention is that this exemplary reference does not, in any case, pass through the narrow gate of the person and its exclusionary devices. I would say rather that history and politics are constituted, throughout Italian thought, in a polarity that is broader and more diverse even than the modern one of subjectivity, and which belongs, rather, to the category of life. It is certainly no coincidence that Bruno recognizes this category, in its limitless potency, through his un-

---

80. Martin Heidegger, *Parmenides*, in *Gesamtausgabe*, vol. 54 (Frankfurt am Main: Klostermann, 1982); English version: *Parmenides*, trans. André Schuwer and Richard Rojcewicz (Bloomington: Indiana University Press, 1992), p. 45.

equivocal and explicit rejection of the concept of person—both in the transcendental version of the divine Person as well as in the secularized one of an immaterial subject superior to its own body. In the horizon that he lays open, just as the divine person cannot be posited prior to the world through the idea of creation, similarly, the secular one cannot be understood outside the cosmic/natural process of which it is an internal and temporary element. Bruno's conception of the human creature, formed of an inseparable compound of body and soul, as only a part (and not necessarily a privileged one) of the same infinite substance—a simple link in the chain of beings through which the life of the universe unwinds—was the first sharp rap on the dispositif of the person, which was based, as we have said, on determining thresholds, and shifting functions, between not only different species of living beings but also within the human race itself. Everything in Italian thought that goes in the same direction—from the metaphysical primacy of the body in Vico to the value Leopardi attaches to the animal world—springs from that source of meaning that even Gentile situated at the origin of the "method of immanence."[81] Beyond the distortions that the philosopher himself disseminated, an immanent life is one that germinates from itself, not posited after or subordinated to some subjective figure—of any shape or form—that is posited before its development.

Considering the fundamental line of Italian philosophy, it is hard to miss a natural inclination toward the thought of the impersonal. Of course, in the late twentieth century, this came to the surface in several areas of contemporary culture: from Freudian psychoanalysis to literature, and in avant-garde art in general, to a segment of the French thought that goes from Merleau-Ponty to Foucault to Deleuze.[82] What was lacking in all these, however, is a clear articulation with the critique of the dispositif of the person, something that is to be found in Italian philosophy starting from its fifteenth-century roots—and without which, the choice

81. For a wide-ranging genealogy of the category of immanence, see Roberto Ciccarelli, *Immanenza: Filosofia, diritto e politica della vita dal XIX al XX secolo* (Bologna: Il Mulino, 2008).

82. An original reinterpretation of contemporary French philosophy has been put forward by Enrica Lisciani Petrini, in "Fuori della persona: L'impersonale' in Merleau-Ponty, Bergson, Deleuze," *Filosofia Politica* 3 (2007): 393–409, entirely dedicated to the category of "person." By the same author see also "Per una 'filosofia dell'impersonale,'" in *Impersonale*, ed. Laura Bazzicalupo (Milan, 2008), pp. 39–55.

in favor of the impersonal may seem unconsidered or even arbitrary. But there is something else, perhaps even more disqualifying, to take into consideration. It regards the differential character (anything but undifferentiated, in other words) indicated by the thought of the impersonal that was sparked by the deconstruction of the metaphysics of the person. As we have said, from the beginning of the Italian tradition, the impersonal has referred to a category of life that is not separate from—and, indeed, is always joined differently with—those of history and politics. It is precisely this rootedness in a historical-political horizon—sometimes antinomic but always active—that drives the critique of the person in Italy, formulated and developed, then as now, in a sphere of meaning marked by difference and by conflict. How else could it be, for that matter, in a tradition originating in the thought of Machiavelli? Contrary to philosophies of life that took shape in different ways and in different contexts—such as the one in the twentieth century, first in Germany and then in France—Italian thought, from Bruno to Gramsci, never opposed life to forms. It has always thought about the form (and the forms) of life, understood as modes—impersonal and singular—to escape from the prescriptive and exclusionary dialectic between subjectification and subjection. If life should not be posited after the subjects that embody it from one time to the next, it should not be presupposed before them, either. Rather, it should be thought of as the living substance of their infinite singularity.[83] If life is essentially substance or mode—and not simply an attribute, or, worse, a property of those who are its bearers, or of anyone else who claims it, this means that it cannot be conceived independently from them, whether in theological or scientific terms. Life is in any case, and only, a single life, no matter how many times it is reproduced, always as it is and always different, in each of us. This impersonality and this irreducible specificity are what living thought addresses—a thought that is itself inseparable from the spiritual and animal life from which it originates and toward which it continues to move.

83. Along these lines, see Davide Tarizzo, *La vita: Un'invenzione recente* (Rome-Bari: Laterza, 2010).

Cultural Memory | *in the Present*

Gyanendra Pandey, *Routine Violence: Nations, Fragments, Histories*

James Siegel, *Naming the Witch*

J. M. Bernstein, *Against Voluptuous Bodies: Late Modernism and the Meaning of Painting*

Theodore W. Jennings, Jr., *Reading Derrida / Thinking Paul: On Justice*

Richard Rorty and Eduardo Mendieta, *Take Care of Freedom and Truth Will Take Care of Itself: Interviews with Richard Rorty*

Jacques Derrida, *Paper Machine*

Renaud Barbaras, *Desire and Distance: Introduction to a Phenomenology of Perception*

Jill Bennett, *Empathic Vision: Affect, Trauma, and Contemporary Art*

Ban Wang, *Illuminations from the Past: Trauma, Memory, and History in Modern China*

James Phillips, *Heidegger's* Volk: *Between National Socialism and Poetry*

Frank Ankersmit, *Sublime Historical Experience*

István Rév, *Retroactive Justice: Prehistory of Post-Communism*

Paola Marrati, *Genesis and Trace: Derrida Reading Husserl and Heidegger*

Krzysztof Ziarek, *The Force of Art*

Marie-José Mondzain, *Image, Icon, Economy: The Byzantine Origins of the Contemporary Imaginary*

Cecilia Sjöholm, *The Antigone Complex: Ethics and the Invention of Feminine Desire*

Jacques Derrida and Elisabeth Roudinesco, *For What Tomorrow . . . : A Dialogue*

Elisabeth Weber, *Questioning Judaism: Interviews by Elisabeth Weber*

Jacques Derrida and Catherine Malabou, *Counterpath: Traveling with Jacques Derrida*

Martin Seel, *Aesthetics of Appearing*

Nanette Salomon, *Shifting Priorities: Gender and Genre in Seventeenth-Century Dutch Painting*

Jacob Taubes, *The Political Theology of Paul*

Jean-Luc Marion, *The Crossing of the Visible*

Eric Michaud, *The Cult of Art in Nazi Germany*

Anne Freadman, *The Machinery of Talk: Charles Peirce and the Sign Hypothesis*

Stanley Cavell, *Emerson's Transcendental Etudes*

Stuart McLean, *The Event and Its Terrors: Ireland, Famine, Modernity*

Hent de Vries and Samuel Weber, eds., *Religion and Media*

Niklas Luhmann, *Theories of Distinction: Re-Describing the Descriptions of Modernity*, ed. and introd. William Rasch

Johannes Fabian, *Anthropology with an Attitude: Critical Essays*

Michel Henry, *I Am the Truth: Toward a Philosophy of Christianity*

Gil Anidjar, *"Our Place in Al-Andalus": Kabbalah, Philosophy, Literature in Arab-Jewish Letters*

Hélène Cixous and Jacques Derrida, *Veils*

F. R. Ankersmit, *Historical Representation*

F. R. Ankersmit, *Political Representation*

Elissa Marder, *Dead Time: Temporal Disorders in the Wake of Modernity (Baudelaire and Flaubert)*

Reinhart Koselleck, *The Practice of Conceptual History: Timing History, Spacing Concepts*

Niklas Luhmann, *The Reality of the Mass Media*

Hubert Damisch, *A Theory of /Cloud/: Toward a History of Painting*

Jean-Luc Nancy, *The Speculative Remark: (One of Hegel's bon mots)*

Jean-François Lyotard, *Soundproof Room: Malraux's Anti-Aesthetics*

Jan Patočka, *Plato and Europe*

Hubert Damisch, *Skyline: The Narcissistic City*

Isabel Hoving, *In Praise of New Travelers: Reading Caribbean Migrant Women Writers*

Richard Rand, ed., *Futures: Of Jacques Derrida*

William Rasch, *Niklas Luhmann's Modernity: The Paradoxes of Differentiation*

Jacques Derrida and Anne Dufourmantelle, *Of Hospitality*

Jean-François Lyotard, *The Confession of Augustine*

Kaja Silverman, *World Spectators*

Samuel Weber, *Institution and Interpretation: Expanded Edition*

Jeffrey S. Librett, *The Rhetoric of Cultural Dialogue: Jews and Germans in the Epoch of Emancipation*

Ulrich Baer, *Remnants of Song: Trauma and the Experience of Modernity in Charles Baudelaire and Paul Celan*

Samuel C. Wheeler III, *Deconstruction as Analytic Philosophy*

David S. Ferris, *Silent Urns: Romanticism, Hellenism, Modernity*

Rodolphe Gasché, *Of Minimal Things: Studies on the Notion of Relation*

Sarah Winter, *Freud and the Institution of Psychoanalytic Knowledge*

Samuel Weber, *The Legend of Freud: Expanded Edition*

Aris Fioretos, ed., *The Solid Letter: Readings of Friedrich Hölderlin*

J. Hillis Miller / Manuel Asensi, *Black Holes / J. Hillis Miller; or, Boustrophedonic Reading*

Miryam Sas, *Fault Lines: Cultural Memory and Japanese Surrealism*

Peter Schwenger, *Fantasm and Fiction: On Textual Envisioning*

Didier Maleuvre, *Museum Memories: History, Technology, Art*

Jacques Derrida, *Monolingualism of the Other; or, The Prosthesis of Origin*

Andrew Baruch Wachtel, *Making a Nation, Breaking a Nation: Literature and Cultural Politics in Yugoslavia*

Niklas Luhmann, *Love as Passion: The Codification of Intimacy*

Mieke Bal, ed., *The Practice of Cultural Analysis: Exposing Interdisciplinary Interpretation*

Jacques Derrida and Gianni Vattimo, eds., *Religion*